THE ABSENCE OF GRACE

Contents

Preface   ix

Introduction   1

Part 1. Falling from Grace: Sprezzatura, Suspicion, and the
Perils of Mastication

  1. Sprezzatura and the Absence of Grace   9

  2. Count Ricciardo's Tiny Defect   26

  3. *Galateo* and the Civilizing Process: A Short History
of Table Manners   34

Part 2. Losing Control: The Woman Question in *The Book of
the Courtier*

  4. A Perfect Gentleman: Performing Gynephobia in Urbino   63

  5. A Perfect Lady: Pygmalion and His "Creatura"   87

Part 3. Missing Hercules: Unreliable Narrators in *The Book of
the Courtier* and *Galateo*

  6. Internal Distance: At Home and Abroad with
Castiglione's Author   119

  7. Narratorial Sour Grapes: Reading *Galateo*   179

Notes   231
Bibliography   255
Index   263

This is a study of male fantasy, representation anxiety, and narratorial authority in a particular period and cultural context. The time and place are early modern Europe, the context is the interaction between changes of elite culture and the changing construction of masculine identity. To be more specific, it is a study of the ways in which two sixteenth-century Italian books of manners, Baldassare Castiglione's *Il libro del Cortegiano* (1528) and Giovanni della Casa's *Galateo* (1558), cope with and represent this interaction. In both texts, questions concerning male fantasy and masculine identity are inseparable from questions about the authority and reliability of narrators, and are focused on narratorial attitudes toward three interlocking forms of status: socioeconomic rank or class, political power, and gender. Because the two texts differ in narrative structure, the focus is sharper in *Galateo* and more diffuse in *The Book of the Courtier*. *Galateo* has a single narrator identified not as della Casa but as a fictive persona, an old man delivering a monologue to a young tutee. The *Courtier* has an author who identifies himself as Castiglione and who frequently employs direct discourse to ventriloquate the discussions of interlocutors represented, like the author, as real historical figures. Questions about attitudes toward status thus extend to the *Courtier*'s interlocutors.

The relation of gender to rank and power is more centrally featured in the *Courtier* than in *Galateo*. For example, after Castiglione's interlocutors have spent two books collaborating on the construction of the ideal courtier, they designate one speaker to carry out the Pygmalion-like project of imagining and describing that courtier's female counterpart, *la donna di palazzo*. While so engaged he graciously represents himself as a Friend of the Ladies and tries to unpack a profeminist perspective, which he defends against traditional misogynist arguments. This performance has been taken to task by several feminist scholars. They maintain that although the speaker may clearly intend to praise woman and redress the repressive sexism of patriarchal discourse, the text betrays the traces of misogyny and gynephobia that proclaim his continuing subjection to (and even his endorsement of) that discourse. But does the text merely *betray* those traces or does it *display* them? Does the *Courtier* unwittingly participate in the antifeminism some of its interlocutors take exception to and thus prove that even an apparently enlightened Dead White Male author is too deeply inscribed by his culture to produce texts that succeed in escaping or critiquing the dominant androcentric biases? Or does it display and perform the inability to overcome the antifeminism that hollows out the profeminist project? Does it manage some degree of internal distance from the failure it represents and thus attain to a more limited oppositional stance? These are the questions that occupy Part Two (Chapters 4 and 5) of the present study.

The sequencing and relative length of the preceding questions pretty clearly indicate where I stand on the issue of participation vs. critique. In the interpretations that follow it will be equally clear not only that the stand I take relies on sustained, dogged, at times claustrophobic close reading but also that the stand and the method of reading may be more intimately linked. As to the method, it presupposes a willingness to let oneself fall headlong through the interpretive rabbit hole from the sign/referent surface of discourse into the textual underground where, within the sign, signifiers and signifieds continuously uncouple, recouple, and proliferate as the reader shrinks into a tiny figure and the textual underbrush expands to a monstrous tangle of rhizomes. The more slowly our lectorial Lilliputian creeps and crawls and circles about in the subterranean jungle, the more fully the meaning conveyed by Book 3 of the *Courtier* changes: the initial impression that the author's discourse unwittingly participates in the antifeminism he claims to oppose is transformed into an impression that the text knowingly performs the failure to oppose it.

This is only a hypothesis, and I'm not sure I believe it. Someone may come along and challenge my close reading with another that more persuasively shows how the antifeminism discernible in the text is unwittingly betrayed rather than knowingly displayed. But that hasn't happened yet, and one reason for writing this book is to enable it to happen. Practitioners of cultural critique and proponents of cultural studies are too often content to be easy readers speeding about the discursive landscape and unwilling to settle in one place long enough to drop down into the textual underground. (In the action-oriented 1960s, "Let's not get hung up over words" was a politically correct sentiment.) My aim in this book is partly to show that Dead

White Males needn't be "cultural dopes" who can only transmit or celebrate the shackles of prejudice we enlightened latter-day liberals have finally
thrown off, and partly to demonstrate an interpretive method productive of
readings that can't be dismissed out of hand but are substantial enough to be
meaningfully resisted or disconfirmed by critics of another persuasion. Thus
I conceive of this study as an experimental probe into the possibility of in-
tegrating a practice I have called reconstructed old New Criticism with the
currently influential practice of cultural critique. In that respect it may be
called a politico-formalist approach.

The approach is not organized as a sequential reading of the two texts.
Part One begins with a discussion of a pair of key terms in the *Courtier*, *sprezzatura* and *grazia*. Castiglione's interlocutors initially use the word "grazia" in
a manner that conflates grace as natural or supernatural endowment with
graceful behavior. "Sprezzatura," which for the moment I shall leave untranslated, designates a learned behavioral skill rather than an inborn gift.
The difference between the two states the terms denote is one familiar in
anthropological discourse. Grazia derives from an "ascribed status," one that
is "assigned to individuals without reference to their . . . abilities" and that
"can be predicted and trained for from the moment of birth."[1]

Traditionally, for example, nobility and gender were characterized as ascribed statuses. Over against ascribed statuses are "achieved statuses" that
"are not assigned to individuals from birth but are left open to be filled
through competition and individual effort," and that depend on performance.[2] "Merchant" is one such achieved status, dependent on the acquisition of commercial skill. "Courtier" is another, and it depends on mastery of
the skill of sprezzatura, by which the performer may simulate the possession
of grazia.

The binary opposition between these terms and its impact on the discourse of manners structures my argument during the remaining chapters.
Chapter 2 explores this impact on the little drama of table manners that occupies the titular episode of *Galateo* and that sharply illustrates the difficulties and strategies characteristic of a culture of sprezzatura. From there the
discussion broadens in Chapter 3 to an account of the way Norbert Elias
reads medieval and early modern texts dealing with table manners as indicators of social change. My account of Elias benefits from critiques of his approach that enable me to graft elements of his history of manners onto a
somewhat different view of structural change centered on the problematic
substitution of sprezzatura for grazia. Chapters 4 and 5 return to Castiglione
to show how Book 3 of the *Courtier* depicts the effect of this substitution

on the gender debate that swirls around the discussion of the ideal *donna di palazzo*. In the battle between putative pro- and antifeminists, it becomes clear that assertions of masculine identity, misogyny, and gynephobia betray the uncertainty introduced into social discourse by the performative requirements of sprezzatura, clear also that the same uncertainty jeopardizes narratorial (or interlocutorial) authority. Part Three, comprising the final two chapters, examines this impact. They are by far the longest chapters because they explore in minute detail the representation of the narrator in the *Courtier* and *Galateo* respectively.

It's a great pleasure to name the friends and colleagues who contributed to the completion of this study. At various times, Professors Deanna Shemek, Giulia Centineo, and Patricia Reilly helped me translate and understand difficult passages in the Italian texts, and saved me from some bizarre guesses. I'm grateful to them not only for the assistance and encouragement they gave an old non-Italianist but also for their skepticism. They knew what I was hoping they would find in certain texts but opted for the truth. My interpretation of *Galateo* began to take shape several years ago while I was teaching it to an undergraduate class. The seeds were planted by two students in that class: Richard Gabri and Erik Ehrke collaborated on a remarkably perceptive essay, a genuinely new reading of della Casa's text, which I gladly raided. I hope they recognize their ideas in the present version. I know Kristen Brookes will recognize her contribution because it is acknowledged in Chapters 2 and 7 below. Her essay, written for a graduate seminar in 1996, taught me how to handle the problem of the narrator, and also how to interrogate the question of gender *Galateo* raises. I also learned a lot from discussing *Galateo* with the other students in the seminar: Robin Baldridge, Scott Davis, Valerie Foreman, Robin Gaura, Catherine Newman.

My greatest debt is a double one. What started me off on this topic in the early 1980s and made me seriously consider writing about the *Courtier* was Wayne Rebhorn's remarkable study *Courtly Performances*. This book was a model for me because it exemplified the kind of critical practice I had always aspired to but never adequately mastered: the practice of a historically informed and theoretically reconstructed version of the old New Criticism. *Absence* began as a student's *imitatio* of *Courtly Performances* and soon succumbed to the predictable fate or law of mimetic activity; it turned into an *aemulatio* and a critique. But throughout the years of revision, my reading of the *Courtier* developed primarily as a dialogue with Rebhorn's book, to which it remains no less deeply indebted for my departures from than for my repetitions of its insights.

Having provided the first inspiration for *Absence*, Rebhorn returned as the reader of the manuscript for Stanford University Press. The manuscript itself was submitted in something less than final form because there were problems of organization I hadn't solved, and I went looking for help from the press reader. I got just what I wanted. With unparalleled generosity and in an exemplary act of colleagueship, Rebhorn provided a detailed critique and list of suggested revisions that substantially solved my problems for me. I incorporated all his suggestions in the final draft, and they led to what I think is a much more coherently and tightly organized study than the version he read. I hope he's satisfied with the result, since he, after all, is mainly responsible for it.

During the later stages of my work on *Galateo* I had the privilege and good fortune to discuss parts of Chapters 1 and 7 with the members of a Folger Institute Colloquium that took place the evening of April 15, 1998. It gives me pleasure once again to thank my friends Kathleen Lynch and Carol Brobeck of the Folger Institute for arranging so congenial and—for me, at least—so productive an occasion. And I thank my dear Washington family, Susan Zimmerman, Leeds Barroll, and Lena Orlin, for friendship and kindness that extends well beyond the Beltway. My fellow colloquialists were responsive, articulate, probing, and skeptical in the best tradition of collegial friendship and criticism—the Folger tradition. I'm grateful to them for taking my work seriously enough to want me to make it better—and for helping, by their discerning comments, to make it better. Their suggestions traveled with me to Amsterdam the following summer and were massaged into the final draft of the book.

It also gives me pleasure once again to thank the friends at the Santa Cruz campus who have always gone out of their way for me, supporting my work with their expertise, compensating for my technophobia and the computer idiocy it breeds, and, on certain occasions, shoring up my morale with their care and kindness. They often interrupted other tasks to help me meet deadlines, prepare manuscripts for publication, and guide me through the dark tangle of bells and whistles sometimes (inaccurately) designated as the culture of the copy. For their good offices and good will my warmest thanks go to Marianna Alves and Lisa Leslie of the Cowell College Steno Pool and to Cheryl Van De Veer and Zoe Sodja of the Document Publishing and Editing Center. Also, for the third time in three years, I'm happy to acknowledge the help and support I have received from the Committee on Research of the University of California at Santa Cruz.

This project would never have gotten off the ground had it not been for the encouragement and good auspices of Helen Tartar. Helen's patience, openness to new ideas, critical sensibility, and willingness to Just Say No have for several years kept me from both writing too much and not writing at all. And after *Absence of Grace* did get off the ground and stumbled toward the copy-editing desk, it had the very good luck to meet up with Barbara Salazar, who immediately suggested that my preface was really my introduction and my introduction my preface. She was dead right about that, and each has now replaced the other. Ms. Salazar was also right about a lot of other things, even when she resisted my occasional tendency to indulge in such puffy hangovers from the 1980s as "diegetic." I'm deeply appreciative of the care, intelligence, good will, and good humor with which she went over the manuscript, purging it of the effects of bad grammatical habits, making it read more smoothly (and I hope she gets to fix this sentence up before it goes to the printer). My thanks also go to Anna Eberhard Friedlander for her good offices in seeing the book through the press, and to Kasey Hicks, who once again produced an index that made even me want to read the book again.

While I was writing *Absence*, I had great times with my grandson, Ezra Berger, whose height and checkers capability increased rapidly between the first and second drafts, and who read more books than I did in that period. I thank him and Cindy for that, and Dylan, whom he occasionally chases, and Caroline, who lets him. The final draft of the *Galateo* chapters was completed in Amsterdam in June and July of 1998. I thank Sarah Whittier for her support and companionship during that period and the following two years.

H. B.

THE ABSENCE OF GRACE

Introduction

The Absence of Grace derives from my *Fictions of the Pose* and extends its method of close reading combined with cultural analysis from visual to verbal artifacts—more specifically, from portraits to courtesy books. The outlines of the present study were sketched out in the third and sixth chapters of *Fictions*: Chapter 3 briefly discusses *sprezzatura*, self-representation, and performance anxiety in Baldassare Castiglione's *Book of the Courtier*; Chapter 6 undertakes to critique and revise the account Norbert Elias gives, in *The History of Manners*, of pressures exerted by sociopolitical change on the interiorization of behavioral norms, pressures that problematize the practice of exemplary self-representation. Because both discussions are fundamental to the views of the *Courtier* and Giovanni della Casa's *Galateo* unpacked in *The Absence of Grace*, I have decided that it would be easier for the reader to have direct access to them rather than be forced to track them down in references. Therefore several pages in both Chapters 1 and 3 of *Absence* consist of direct quotation from Chapters 3 and 6, respectively, of *Fictions*.

Absence follows *Fictions* in exploring a phenomenon that has received a lot of attention during the past four or five decades: the representation of what has come to be called "inwardness" in the various media of Renaissance and early modern culture. I made very little express use of that term while writing *Fictions*, though the concept it designates is treated there at some length. The term itself came to my attention only recently, in the specific context of Katharine Maus's *Inwardness and Theater in the English Renaissance*. This wonderfully smart book centers on a problematic similar to the one explored in *Fictions*: how to read inwardness from the surfaces that obliquely, inadequately, and deceptively convey or conceal it. In the religious culture of the English Reformation, Maus argues, human inwardness is conceived of "as at once privileged and elusive, an absent presence 'interpreted' to observers by ambiguous inklings and tokens" (11):

For the English Renaissance, it is a commonplace that spectacle depends upon, sometimes betrays, but never fully manifests a truth that remains shrouded, indiscernible, or ambiguous. The period's social and religious upheavals arguably provoke a keen, apparently nearly universal suspicion of "appearances." Whatever the origins of this distrust, it produces a distinctive way of thinking about human subjectivity that emphasizes the disparity between what a person is and what he or she seems to be to other people. (210)

My own concern in the present study is not primarily the perception and interpretation of inwardness *by others*. Nevertheless, Maus's sharply focused isolation of that topic helped me define and better understand the specific boundaries of the different notion of inwardness informing the argument of *Absence*. She made it possible for me not so much to disagree with her account of inwardness as to find it inapplicable and thus to be forced to narrow, isolate, and articulate my sense of the term.

Maus trenchantly develops the thesis that "in a culture in which truth is imagined to be inward and invisible," theatrical attempts to represent inwardness involve "crises of authenticity" because an inwardness that is theatrically displayed is "an inwardness . . . that has already ceased to exist" (32).[1] During her account of *Measure for Measure*, she makes the following observations:

The complexities of monitoring sexual conduct in an increasingly unmanageable urban environment become the subject of . . . *Measure for Measure*. . . . Shakespeare acknowledges the furtiveness and diversity of sexual conduct, and the apparently inextricable relationship between secrecy and arousal, all of which create difficulties for "legislating morality." . . . The play's denouement imposes a secular judicial solution upon sexual dilemmas even while suggesting the inevitable limitations of such solutions.

Inwardness as we have seen it elaborated in legal situations can be either a privilege or a burden. The guilty, the obstinate, and the unjustly persecuted can expediently conceal truths about themselves. (211)

From whom do they conceal these truths? From others, and especially from the authorities. Maus's argument doesn't require her to ask whether they conceal things from themselves. She imagines relations among characters on the model of relations among bodies onstage or in courtrooms, and she discusses inwardness in terms of characters' relations, observability, and communicativeness to others (or lack of it). *Inwardness and Theater* contains discussions of heresy, treason, and witchcraft trials as "rituals of discovery" (117), and in one chapter Maus develops a persuasive analogy between theater and the jury trial in respect of the problems that beset the search for inward truth. Because her basic model is that of a theatrical performance or legal trial, she limits her inquiry to phenomena of objective self-representation, that is, to what speakers reveal or don't reveal to others. Insofar as her notion of inwardness is constrained by that model, it is dominated by the spatial metonymics of container and contained, outward and inward, body and soul or mind, and this metonymics is in turn spatially situated: a theater or courtroom, a hall, a space filled with embodied agents who interpret each other's visible and vocal expressions as indexes—conveyors or concealers—of inward intentions.

This is a legitimate and indeed powerfully generative model, as Maus puts it into play. But it is only one of several possible models of inwardness, and it is more appropriate for the venues and events she discusses—theaters, plays, jury trials—than it is for others. There is, for example, a psychological model of inwardness that is used to analyze the ways subjects represent themselves primarily to themselves rather than to others. And there is a discursive model of inwardness predicated on the duplicity of the relation between language and its speakers. Speakers get characterized by their language at two levels, as the subjects of their speech and the objects of their language. On the first level, their language represents what they mean to say or do with their words as they speak to each other and to themselves. On the second level, their language represents what goes on within speech rather than between speakers; it shows us what it—their language—does with (or to, or for) its speakers regardless of what they seem to say, mean, and hear. The first level correlates to some extent with the psychological model. The second level is oriented toward a structural model of inwardness that needn't be associated with unconscious desire or thought as an agency of the psyche. It can, however, be identified with the Lacanian notion of the unconscious as a discourse network possessed of its own sites of agency, sites any speaker, any language user, may occupy and activate whether or not he or she is aware of doing so. I have explored the textual representations of both models of inwardness in my studies of Shakespeare's dramatic language, and I continue this practice in *Absence*, especially in the final two chapters, which examine at length and in detail the portrayal of the narrator position in the *Courtier* and in *Galateo*.[2]

Maus discusses inwardness in the context of theater and the English Reformation, whereas I discuss it here as a property of literary texts in Renaissance and Counter-Reformation Italy. Both of us associate "the very wide-spread circulation of what might be called the 'inwardness topos'" with skepticism and suspicion, but Maus seeks a specific explanation for this phenomenon "in the far-reaching political, religious, and economic realignments that constitute the English Reformation." She observes, for example, that "Protestants typically describe themselves as cultivating internal truths while accusing Catholics of attending only to outward 'shows'" (15). Note that "describe themselves" is roughly synonymous with "represent themselves"; Protestants representing inwardness are already in a theater of self-representation. The same comment can be made about the terms in which Maus phrases the objective of her study: to "explore various quite specific ways in which the difference between socially observable externals and 'that within' (whatever it might be) is established, elaborated upon, exploited, exaggerated, pointedly ignored, or violently erased in early modern England" (14). The series of predicates picks out modes of representing inwardness to oneself or others. It thus presupposes the establishment, elaboration, and exploitation of such representational venues and media as writing, theater, conduct literature, anatomy and medicine, legal trials, and new forms of confessional discourse (e.g., diaries). This suggests to me that defining the problem of inwardness in terms of developments specific to the English Renaissance and Reformation may involve a category mistake. That is, the most relevant category is not the history of England and its religious, theatrical, and legal institutions but the history of technologies of representation in general, and of early modern technologies in particular. The suspicion about inwardness Maus explores is akin to the suspicion I describe in *Fictions* under the rubric of performance anxiety (or representation anxiety) and examine in a Catholic as well as Reformation context—in Renaissance Italy as well as in the Dutch Republic. *Absence* pursues the traces of this suspicion, this anxiety, through texts that depict sprezzatura not only as a representational technology but also as a normative demand: a demand for the performance of exemplary inwardness that's assumed to be inauthentic by the performers no less than by their audiences. The *Courtier* and *Galateo* focus on the skepticism the demand produces, but their approach to it is itself skeptical. They aren't content merely to reflect or portray, much less to celebrate, an emergent culture of sprezzatura. Rather, they demonstrate how the long shadow of suspicion cast by so expressly performative a culture reaches (to vary Robert Frost's phrase) both far out and in deep. Many of their modern interpreters have faulted Castiglione and della Casa for embracing that culture's moral values. My argument is that in the process of representing and defining the culture of sprezzatura, and under the *appearance* of embracing its values, the *Courtier* and *Galateo* distance themselves from what they represent. In their markedly different ways, the two texts undertake a critique that anticipates the very criticisms subsequent interpreters will aim at them.

One FALLING FROM GRACE

Sprezzatura,
Suspicion, and
the Perils
of Mastication

1.   Sprezzatura and the Absence of Grace

The interlocutors in *The Book of the Courtier* spend much of their time elaborating a technology of behavioral performance founded on what Castiglione calls *sprezzatura*. "Sprezzatura" is introduced in Book 1, Chapter 26, as "una nova parola," "a new word," by the speaker assigned to supervise the "game" of constructing the ideal courtier, Count Ludovico da Canossa.[1] What he describes under that term is an art that hides art, the cultivated ability to display artful artlessness, to perform any act or gesture with an insouciant or careless mastery that delivers either or both of two messages: "Look how artfully I appear to be natural"; "Look how naturally I appear to be artful." Killjoys might be inclined to dismiss this art as a culturally legitimated practice of hypocrisy or bad faith, but others would appreciate the suppleness of the high-wire act of definitional balance performed by the count and his interlocutors. For the sake of simplicity, I shall call this the sprezzatura of nonchalance even though that name is misleading, since what is involved is not merely nonchalance, *disinvoltura*, insouiance, the ability to conceal effort. Rather it is the ability to show that one is not showing all the effort one obviously put into learning how to show that one is not showing effort.

This, however, touches only on the instrumental or purely aesthetic aspect of sprezzatura. What is it for? A second definitional aspect is beamed up by the count in 1.28, and I give it in Wayne Rebhorn's paraphrase: sprezzatura is "an art of suggestion, in which the courtier's audience will be induced by the images it confronts to imagine a greater reality existing behind them," and this enables the courtier "to make himself into a much more enticing and compelling figure than he might otherwise be."[2] Since, as Frank Whigham concisely renders it, "modesty arouses inference in excess of the facts,"[3] we may think of it as a sprezzatura of conspicuously false modesty. Furthermore, the term's relation to the verb *sprezzare* (to scorn, despise, disdain) and

9

the adjective *sprezzata*, which appears several times in Books 1 and 2, suggests to Rebhorn that sprezzatura designates "an attitude of slightly superior disdain" by which the performer indicates his easy mastery of whatever he is doing, his "scorn for the potential difficulty or restriction involved" and "for normal, human limitations" (34–35). Eduardo Saccone and Daniel Javitch associate the "disdain, misprision, or depreciation" implied by the etymology with a strategy for maintaining class boundaries; they argue for a sprezzatura of elite enclosure founded on the complicity of a coded performance in which the actor and his peers reaffirm their superiority to those incapable of deciphering the code.[4]

Javitch gives sprezzatura a different look by moving it into the political arena and treating it as a strategic response to "the constraints of despotism" in the courtly context of "fierce competition for favors":

> The ruler's desire to keep his subordinates in check, as well as the court's standards of polite refinement, compel its members to subdue or at least mask their aggressive and competitive drives. That is why such qualities as reticence, detachment, and understatement are so valued at court. . . . The courtier . . . inhabits a world where graceful deceit is valued not only for its intrinsic delight but because the despot who governs that world makes it imperative. (23, 26)

This indeed suggests a fourth definitional aspect of sprezzatura as a form of defensive irony: the ability to disguise what one really desires, feels, thinks, and means or intends behind a mask of "apparent reticence and nonchalance" (Javitch, *"Cortegiano,"* 24). I hesitate to call this the sprezzatura of deceit because, as I'm about to suggest, it involves not deceit *tout court* but rather the menace of deceit, the display of the ability to deceive. I shall therefore, in the interests of vapid generalization and alliteration, refer to it as the sprezzatura of suspicion.[5]

These formulations don't quite catch a reflexive nuance that hovers cloudily about them. Most of them focus on a skill of performative negation, the ability continuously to display that something is being conspicuously withheld; the ability, for example, to present oneself as someone who may have and can keep secrets, who has power in reserve, who does indeed possess the "aggressive and competitive drives" he is masking, who knows how to conceal unpleasant truths under "salutary deception" ("inganno salutifero," 4.10). Deceit is among the "tropes of personal promotion" Whigham discusses in his fine chapter on that topic. He cites George Puttenham's assertion that the "profession of a very Courtier . . . is . . . cunningly to be able to dissemble," and he offers the following comment on the statement by Federico in 2.40 that this "is rather an ornament . . . than deceit": "Deceit is both denied and admitted, redefined and excused; . . . it becomes . . . a sauce or manner" (S, 100–101).

The push in all these observations is toward more than the ability to deceive; it is toward the ability to represent the ability to deceive, toward the courtier's ability *to show that* he has the art and, if called upon, is capable of deceiving. Disinvoltura is both the behavioral sign of this capability and the medium through which it will if necessary be actualized. It is also both a competitive act in itself and a sign that its possessor is willing to compete for favors in court; a guarantee that the ambition and aggressiveness the courtier pretends to mask is really there, and available for his prince's use (see 2.18–25, 32).[6] To modify Puttenham's "profession of a very Courtier" in a manner that brings out the pun in "profession" and "very," the true courtier professes himself capable of falsehood; among the accomplishments by which he prefers himself to princes is his ability to show that he is cunningly able to dissemble. Strictly speaking, then, the "trope of personal promotion" is not "deceit"—the ability to dissemble—per se. The courtier promotes himself and tries to win the prince's confidence by displaying his mastery of the behavioral rhetoric, the choreography, that signifies the ability and willingness to deceive.

The performance of sprezzatura is thus a figuration of power. But it is also a figuration of anxiety. The *Cortegiano*'s interlocutors show themselves sensitive to their precarious status in the Italian court culture of their time, a culture dominated by princes who were likely to be despotic and who more often than not were themselves perilously besieged as clients of the militarily superior nation-states. The threat or actuality of disempowerment is a concern not only noted by the book's critics but also expressed by its speakers, and it is against the background of this anxiety that the effortless if not lazy elegance of sprezzatura is depicted as a source and sign of manly inner strength rather than of effeminacy. In other words, sprezzatura is to be worn as a velvet glove that exhibits the contours of the handiness it conceals. But of course the glove could be filled with wet clay. Perhaps this signifier of virile manhood only "camouflages vulnerability," as Whigham phrases it in describing the trope he calls "cosmesis," "the use of cosmetic aids to conceal or repair defects."[7]

The idea of cosmetic sprezzatura puts a mordant and defensive spin on the second of the definitional aspects mentioned above, the "art of suggestion" or conspicuously false modesty picked out by Rebhorn as enabling the courtier "to make himself into a much more enticing and compelling figure than he might otherwise be."[8] Presumably this is an art the courtier would cherish and practice with pride, and presumably also, since the discussions about the perfect courtier and his female counterpart are prescriptive, those figures are ideals or models to be distinguished from both their inventors and their imitators. It may therefore be going beyond the purview of a study of sprezzatura in the *Cortegiano* to rewrite Rebhorn's phrase in a manner that highlights cognitive states—"more . . . than he might think himself to be, or fear himself to be"—and to ask what it might mean for a performer to think or fear that he is worse than he appears. Worse not merely as a matter of security or vulnerability (Whigham's chief concern) but as a matter of conscience; an anxiety that is not merely practical but ethical. The *Cortegiano* is a book about self-representation. But self-representation has two dimensions, objective—representing oneself to others—and reflexive—representing oneself to oneself. The explicit theme of the book is learning how to represent oneself to others. Is it then gratuitous to ask how this project may affect and be affected by the questions of trust and self-esteem that come into play when one takes reflexive as well as objective self-representation into account? Do all those who are urged to represent themselves as better than they think they are form a community in which it becomes as difficult to authenticate one's own performances as it is to accredit those of others? Doesn't such a community cast about itself a permanent shadow of representation anxiety? Can it avoid being haunted by its construction and representation of the unrepresented?—by the specter of an unrepresented community of hidden and less worthy selves that its commitment to the culture of sprezzatura conjures up?

In its multifold character, then, sprezzatura creates within and around its performers a self-fulfilling culture of suspicion. An art of behaving as if always under surveillance, an art that aims to ward off danger by appearing dangerous and thus to elicit cautious respect no less than admiration, it motivates increased surveillance and anxiety on the part of the performer as well as the observer. It is within the framework of this hypothesis that I now turn to those passages in Books 1 and 2 that focus on the acquisition of sprezzatura, and that represent this acquisition as a compensatory response to pressures affecting the status of noble families. In part these pressures were caused by the increasing vigor of court-centered seigneurial (as opposed to republican) regimes backed by French or Spanish force. In part they were caused by emergent frictions within the merchant class between new money and old, the *nuovi ricchi* and the older patrician families. In the *Cortegiano*, as we'll see, these changes are mythologized as a fall from grace, a fall from the *grazia* of divinely bestowed (that is, inborn, inherited) superiority.

Under the nominal topic of what the ideal courtier needs to know and to be able to perform, the interlocutors spend much time in Book 1 going through the standard arguments about the value of mastering techniques of literary, musical, and visual production. But the objective emphasis on the acquisition of learning and art is to some extent a misdirection. From the closing paragraphs of Book 1 through the first twelve paragraphs of Book 2 it gradually becomes clear that the artistic production of objects models the artistic production of subjects. The ultimate aim of the acquisition is to convert painting and writing to living self-portraiture and self-textualization: *ut pictura habitus*.[9] The clichés about learning the arts are continually displaced from the production and evaluation of artifacts to the production and evaluation of courtly behavior as a performance of "nature," "una artificiosa imitazion di natura" (1.50). Does art imitate nature or does nature imitate art? Or is the formula "art imitates nature" itself no more than an artful gesture toward naturalizing the art that creates in its own image the nature it claims only to imitate? In this expressly duplicitous conception, the naturalness art pretends to imitate is an artifact. The passage that immediately precedes the introduction of the term "sprezzatura" glances at another duplicity. In the process of imitating models of comportment, the ideal courtier is urged to combine the selectivity of Zeuxis with the sweet predations of Plato's apian poets, and to do so in the manner of a thief: "even as in green meadows the bee flits about among grasses robbing [carpendo] the flowers, so our Courtier must steal [rubare] this grace from those who seem to him to have it, taking from each the part that seems most worthy of praise" (1.26; S, 42–43).[10]

At the beginning of Book 2, the emphasis is shifted from the sprezzatura of nonchalance to that of suspicion when Federico's reprise of the previous evening's discussion centers on the importance of constant self-surveillance: "our Courtier must be cautious in his every action and see to it that prudence attends whatever he says or does," and this "diligent watch" is necessary because "we are all naturally more ready to censure errors than to praise things well done" (2.6–7; S, 96–97). He directs his strictures against the folly of affectation because it betrays the actor's ambition to excel—betrays it and thereby frustrates it, which is to say that this ambition is a precious resource and that it must be concealed in order to be preserved and fulfilled. But not, as I suggested above, simply concealed; it must be represented as concealed. Federico's is a recipe for sustaining the competition of every courtier with every courtier for the prince's favors, and the succeeding conversation (through 2.41) makes it clear that service to princes may both corrupt and disempower the servant.

The discussion of sprezzatura in Book 2 thus opens onto a prospect of apprehensiveness, distrust of hidden motives, fear of exposure, and a general sense of the weakness of the courtier's position. Both as observer and as observed, the courtier focuses his anxiety on the hidden "reality" of the unrepresented self produced by—and haunting—the culture of sprezzatura, with its emphasis on self-misrepresentation. The problems that beset this culture are concentrated in the interpretive combat between performer and spectators / auditors, a field of play charged with the tension between aesthetic *jouissance* and suspicion. Since in order to represent themselves to others performers represent themselves to themselves, since they watch themselves being watched, the force of persuasion and the production of meaning are reversible, alienable, circular: they can originate either in the observer or in the performer. This makes courtly negotiation a struggle for control over the power to determine the self-representation the performer conveys not only to others but also to himself or herself (a disjunction that reminds us the determination may include gender). Courtly practice is fetishistic but ambiguously toned: the subordination of the conspicuously artless performance to the conspicuously artful achievement of it keeps the product, the self-representation, from transcending the etymological limits implied by the term "fetish," which derives from *facticere*—that is, the product remains factlike but factitious and fictitious because made by art. This achievement and the dialectic that enables it may be culture-specific but they are not culture-wide. They are still the privilege of social and political elites trying to protect the continuously changing boundaries of new aristocracies.

Eduardo Saccone has shown how the *Cortegiano*'s conception of courtly performance recognizes the need of boundary maintenance and contributes to it by requiring and producing a double audience: it divides the insiders who appreciate the art of sprezzatura from the outsiders who take it at face value.[11] Saccone cites Canossa's analogy of courtly sprezzatura to the art of ancient orators who concealed their knowledge of letters in order to make "their orations appear to be composed in the simplest manner and according to the dictates of nature and truth rather than of effort and art; which fact, had it been known, would have inspired in the minds of the people the fear that they could be duped by it" (1.26; S, 43–44). The analogy, as Saccone points out, is misleading because Canossa doesn't distinguish from the "populo" the orator's "fellow advocates," who will admire his art of deception "and in him recognize an excellent compeer" (61).

Saccone emphasizes the exclusivity and bonding of the mutual admiration society. But apart from the fact that compeers are also competitors, courtiers are not orators, princely courts are not popular assemblies, and duchies are not republics. Since courtly audiences are composed mainly of courtiers and princes, aren't the expectation and awareness of duplicity sources of apprehension as well as admiration? The danger, the risk, the *frisson* are part of the game, but so also is the institutionalized distrust that characterizes an apprehensive society—a society based on the desire to take and the fear of being taken. For the insiders in such a society, the value of the face as index of the mind, or of the body as index of the soul, must be imagined to have been problematized. Saccone's benign emphasis responds to the conspicuously reductive focus on the aesthetics of sprezzatura that dominates Book 1. The reductiveness is conspicuous because allusions to violence, duplicity, and the *lex talionis* of court life are scattered throughout the text.

To the extent that the representational techniques associated with sprezzatura rely on study, performance, and dissimulation, they subject physiognomic norms of authenticity and truth to the pressure of continuous mimicry. Such norms are initially associated by Count Ludovico with the gifts of nature when, in 1.14, he defends the proposition that the ideal courtier should be nobly born and introduces the term "grazia" into this discussion. "For noble birth is like a bright lamp that makes manifest and visible deeds both good and bad. . . . And . . . this lust of nobility does not shine forth in the deeds of the lowly born," rather "it almost always happens that, in the profession of arms as well as in other worthy pursuits, those who are most distinguished are men of noble birth, because nature has implanted in everything that hidden seed which gives a certain force and quality of its own essence to all that springs from it, making it like itself" (1.14; S, 28).

"Grazia" first appears in 1.14 about halfway through the chapter, and in the passages that follow I leave it untranslated. The count concedes that if aristocrats lack proper tendance they can go bad, and he also concedes that not every aristocrat is "born endowed with such grazie" as the illustrious don Ippolito da Este, cardinal of Ferrara. This appearance of "grazia" is followed shortly after by another: the cardinal "enjoyed such a happy birth that his person, his appearance, his words, and all his actions are . . . ruled by this grazia." But, he adds, "those who are not so perfectly endowed by nature" with "this excellent grazia . . . can, with care and effort, polish and in great part correct their natural defects. Therefore, besides his noble birth, I would wish the Courtier fortunate in this respect"—fortunate, that is, in having been corrected and polished so that he is "endowed by nature not only with talent and with beauty of countenance and person, but also with a certain grazia and, so to speak, an 'air' [sangue], which shall make him at first sight pleasing and lovable to all who see him; and let this be an adornment informing and attending all his actions, giving the promise outwardly that such a one is worthy of the company [commerzio] and the grazia of every great lord" (1.14; S, 29–30, slightly altered. See C, 69–70).

"Una certa grazia e, come si dice, un sangue" (C, 70). The formula the count uses three times in 1.14, "una certa forza (dolcezza, grazia)," conveys the sense of the *je ne sais quoi*, the mysterious force or sweetness or grace beyond the reach of art. "Sangue" is a physiognomic term connected with the sanguine complexion in humoral psychology, and it therefore suggests the organic and natural—or, to use the more disenchanted anthropological term, ascribed—basis of grazia. It's obvious that the count wishes to embed grazia securely among the qualities guaranteed by noble birth. Even when common sense forces him to concede that noble birth may require help from art, the prerequisite of noble birth remains standing until the very last clause in the chapter, where it is shaken by a small (but eventually serious) jolt: "tale esser degno del commerzio e grazia d'ogni gran signore" (C, 70). Here, as Charles Singleton's translation makes clear, grazia becomes "favor," and the gift together with the power of giving have been alienated from nature to princes. In addition, although Singleton tames "commerzio" by translating it as "company," the term's other—and etymologically salient—senses (commerce, intercourse, trade, negotiation) inject connotations that threaten the autonomy of the aristocrat's possession of grazia.

With the utterance of this phrase, the count betrays the pressure of contemporary reality on a deeply conservative fantasy in which noble birth as a gift of the fathers is conflated with grazia as (in its Christian context) a gift of the Father. Saccone, who notes that the very first occurrence of "grazia" in 1.1 refers to princely favor, demonstrates how the vertical father/son relationship is displaced in the *Cortegiano* to the prince and his courtier, where it is not merely a gratuitous gift but a reward for the latter's "good accomplishments."[12] When Gasparo Pallavicino protests that noble birth isn't essential to noble behavior (1.15), the count is forced into a further concession and another defensive maneuver: he grants Gasparo's point and argues that since, therefore, upward mobility is possible, the strategic importance of noble birth increases. First impressions are important, and in the competition between the lowborn and the nobly born the aristocrat gets a head start because public opinion sides with the one who "is known to be of gentle birth" (1.16; S, 31). Whether or not he *is* of noble birth, the point is that he exploits that "knowledge" (= rumor) to reinforce his performance of noble behavior.

Saccone notes the significance of a distinction made at 1.19 by Bernardo Bibbiena "between the 'beauty of [his] person', which he doubts, and 'the grace of countenance' . . . , which, as Canossa declares, 'you can truly be said to have.'"[13] This drives a wedge between the physiognomic signs of inherited quality and the (loosely speaking) pathognomic signs of its manifestation in grazia. At 1.24, however, Cesare Gonzaga reminds the count that since he has often described grazia as "a gift of nature and the heavens," it cannot be "in our power to acquire it [acquistarlo] of ourselves," though what we are given we can, if it isn't perfect, improve by *studio e fatica*. This is a crucial intervention: grazia is once again assimilated to noble birth as a gift of the fathers and the Father, not something that can be acquired. Cesare then pops the money question that will elicit from the count his recipe for sprezzatura: "for those who are less endowed by nature and are capable of acquiring grace [poter esser aggraziati] only if they put forth labor, industry, and care, I would wish to know by what art, by what discipline, by what method, they can gain [possono acqistar] this grace" (S, 41; C, 79).[14]

In Saccone's reading, Cesare's move places the emphasis of the remainder of the discussion on the "Aristotelian middle ground between two exceptional conditions," the "absolute perfection" of those who are "perfectly endowed by nature" and the imperfection of "the absolutely ungifted."[15] But I think it does something more complex and interesting. It relegates the ascriptive ideal of natural perfection to the background as a reality possessed by a lucky few, and leaves it standing *as* a real ideal to be imitated by the less fortunate majority, which may include not only klutzy patricians but also clever arrivistes. To reiterate that grazia is a grace beyond the reach of art just before the account of sprezzatura is to make deficiency in grazia the enabling condition of ideal courtiership. The ideal courtier is not the absolute courtier. The latter is a *rara avis*, though a real one; his *grazia* is fully embodied, "organic," and inalienable, the transcendent state of self-possession to which others may aspire but can never attain. The ideal courtier is being imagined by the interlocutors as a simulacrum necessitated by the failure of the ascriptive ideal, which is also a physiognomic and logocentric ideal. They portray a typified abstraction (a schema, an Idea) that may be copied and copiously replicated in rule-governed acts of reincorporation through which the actors transform faces and bodies into signs of the perfect mental and psychic grace denied them by nature. Sprezzatura is envisaged as the false lookalike that threatens to displace grazia.

It is possible to view the construction of this relation—the relation of the real presence of perfect grace in the absolute courtier to its representation by the ideal courtier—as a symptom of nostalgia. Carol Houlihan Flynn claims that conduct manuals "document nostalgic belief in a 'natural' self that 'ought' to be in harmony with its needs and desires," and they seek "a lost unity of body and soul . . . that could exist only in an Edenic imagination."[16] If she is right about the run of conduct books, the *Cortegiano* is an exception on two counts.

First, as a literary performance it dramatizes and criticizes the impulse to nostalgia: on the one hand it represents itself as the memoir of a better time, a lost golden moment (prefatory epistle and 1.2); on the other hand it knowingly criticizes such nostalgic evocations as manifestations of the bitterness of the aged who mourn their lost youth (2.1).

Second, the unattainability of the real presence of grazia provides what, in the contemporary parlance of the image industry, would be called a performance opportunity. But at the same time it guarantees performance anxiety. Not only because the courtier is always performing before an audience composed of performers like himself, and not only because he knows they are performing, and knows they know he is performing. There is also anxiety about the performer's own practice of dissimulation—about his need to keep the performance of naturalness from being spoiled by unwanted leakages of the less ideal nature he is expected to suppress/transcend. The by-product of the courtier's performance is that the achievement of sprezzatura may require him to deny or disparage his nature. In order to internalize the model and enhance himself by art, he may have to evacuate—repress or disown—whatever he finds within himself that doesn't fit the model. This complex set of relations places the new ideal in a revisionary rather than nostalgic relation to the genealogical norm introduced by the count at 1.14 as the traditional wisdom.

The count's is the opening gambit in a series of dialogical moves that conspicuously exclude the norm from consideration in order to open up the space for the performance that dissimulates it. The conspicuousness of the exclusion is important, as I noted, to keep the unattainable norm in play as a prediscursive reality—a real presence—that validates the discourse of courtiership dedicated to its representation. But equally conspicuous is the emphasis on the difference between the absolute and ideal courtiers, the original and the image. This is registered in 1.24 by Cesare's redundant triplets: "as for those who are less endowed by nature and are capable of being aggraziati only if they put forth labor, industry, and care [fatica, industria e studio], I would wish to know by what art, by what disciplines, by what method [con quale arte, con qual disciplina e con qual modo], they can gain this grace" (S, 41; C, 79). The first triplet marks the fall from grace by its focus on uncourtly labor and sweat, but the shift to terms of art in the second triplet marks the beginning of the fantasy of renovatio that will be completed by the disclosure that Cesare's art/discipline/method not only conceals labor/industry/care but also theatrically conceals—displays itself as concealing—itself. Part of the signifying activity of sprezzatura is thus to index a mode of behavioral production that selectively abstracts from, doesn't fully correspond with, what may actually have taken place. Its objective is to edge its performances with some form of indexical reference to the art and difficulty, the conspicuous mastery and transcendence of which gives the ideal its value.

It is, finally, the revelation of this double art, this graceful duplicity, that enables "a gentleman living at the court of princes [in corte de' principi] . . . to serve them in every reasonable thing, thereby winning favor from them [acquistandone da essi grazia] and praise from others" (1.1; S, 11; C, 55). In this, the thesis sentence of the *Cortegiano*, Castiglione draws attention to the challenge, the contingency, the jeopardy to which the art responds by juxtaposing the singular "gentleman" ("gentiluomo") to the plural "princes" ("principi"); "the court of princes" possibly denotes a particular court with a series of princes but more probably it denotes the court as an institution, the instability of which forces the courtier to move from one principality to another. Thus to the traditional validation supplied by the real presence of the absolute courtier's unattainable grace is added the validation of the ideal courtier's political art as a response to the real presence of princes.

Castiglione's speakers are pragmatic if guarded about "the political pressures of an autocratic order," and at times they seem to mention them as justifications for gratifying their delight in the art of dissimulation.[17] The performance of courtly fictions is part of the reality of court life. What makes it an edgy and exhilarating challenge is that princes also delight in the performance of fictions. Stephen Greenblatt has remarked on the tendency of princes in this era to demonstrate their power by their

> ability to enforce submission, manifested in those signs of secular worship—bowing, kneeling, kissing of rings—that European rulers increasingly

insisted upon. If these signs always have an air of fiction about them . . . so much the better, because . . . one of the highest achievements of power is to impose fictions upon the world and one of its supreme pleasures is to enforce the acceptance of fictions that are known to be fictions.

The more outrageous the fiction, the more impressive the manifestation of power. . . . The point is not that anyone is deceived by the charade, but that everyone is forced either to participate in it or to watch it silently.[18]

It is easy to imagine the edge of mockery, even self-mockery, that must accompany such performances and manifestations. But in Castiglione's Italy, the courtier's contribution to the charade may have been more gratuitously artful and responsive than in Sir Thomas Wyatt's Europe and Sir Thomas More's England, the subjects of Greenblatt's comments. The interplay between artfulness and anxiety was represented in a more positive light in a familiar episode in the history of mannerism to which I now briefly turn.

"Una artificiosa imitazion di natura": the paraphrase I gave above—courtly behavior as an artful performance of "nature"—was perhaps a little affected, a disingenuous attempt to rouse the phrase from its slumber as a cliché in art-historical discourse, where it is central to the story of Mannerism in which Castiglione's book plays a not insignificant part. John Shearman reminds us that in the sixteenth century

the word *artifizioso* was wholly complimentary, and to a great extent concomitant with *maniera*; books ought to be written, and pictures painted, with artifice. Benedetto Varchi (1548) defined the intention of artistic creation as "an artificial imitation of nature," which is the more interesting for being a widely held view rather than an original one.

The concept *maniera* was borrowed from the literature of manners, and had originally been a quality—a desirable quality—of human deportment. . . . [It] meant approximately savoir-faire, effortless accomplishment and sophistication; it was inimical to revealed passion, evident effort and rude naïveté. It was, above all, a courtly grace. This meaning survives, not only through its transference in Italy to the visual arts but also in its modern equivalent, "style." *Maniera*, then, is a term of long standing in the literature of a way of life so stylized and cultured that it was, in effect, a work of art itself; hence the easy translation to the visual arts.[19]

But the vector of translation doesn't go only in one direction. The discourses of visual art, verbal art, and human deportment run together and mutually influence each other, with familiar if interestingly ambiguous results, as illustrated by Shearman's comment on some of Michelangelo's *ignudi*,

> in which the qualities of grace, elegance and poise are so intense that the beauty of the work of art becomes more nearly its subject than ever before. . . . How easy and just was the transference of the word "maniera," a term for an ideal of behavior, to a work of art we can see if we look beyond the clearly appropriate idealization and polish of form to the deportment of such a youth. We recognize already an air of refined detachment, and . . . a formula for twisting the wrist and holding the fingers in an apparently easy and elegant tension, that will be endlessly repeated in Mannerist works to the end of the period. Was this how Castiglione's young courtiers relaxed, or did it take the imagination of a supreme master of the human body to invent a stylish deportment that is only too easily imitated in life? (53)

The phrase "supreme master" adds a touch of irony to the words with which Shearman describes contemporary reaction to the work of Raphael and Michelangelo, "the reaction that the artist was *divino*, in the sense that his material was god-like"; "the divine right of artists" was "the right to create . . . not in imitation of nature but on the basis of nature already conquered in works of art" (48).

In such a context, "una artificiosa imitazion di nature" means not simply an artificial imitation of nature but an artificial imitation of a grace beyond the reach of art. Yet from the standpoint of an ideology oriented toward the production of truth effects, the distinction doesn't matter. "Nature" may be equated with "a grace beyond the reach of art" insofar as both categories, the natural and the transcendent, are ascriptive displacements that belong to the ensemble of discursive strategies by which human production either validates itself or else represses, displaces, misrecognizes, and defictionalizes itself. To the extent that such discursive claims to prediscursive status become conventional moves associated with the technology of the representation of self or others, the claims themselves become subject to fictionalization, which could, depending on one's perspective, be a bad or a good thing. On the one hand, they could be dismissed as mere rhetoric. On the other hand, the rhetoricity of the claims could itself be a positive signifier of something better than mere nature. A scopic regime increasingly dominated by a variety of forms of graphic production and representation in both visual and verbal media sets in motion a cultural dialectic in which (1) behavioral, postural, physiognomic, and psychological norms are displaced from their comfortable home in custom to the more challenging domain of art, and (2) the domain of art gets treated as a second and better form of nature. This shift has social cachet and motivates an interestedly "disinterested" ideology of the aesthetic of which Mannerism is a hyperbolic and often parodic expression.

Among the changes that mark the particular transitionality of the centuries we call early modern is the development of relatively specialized and varied venues of secular schooling.[20] These arose as supplements or competitors to religious pedagogy and the more informal customary practices of domestic training that Pierre Bourdieu calls "implicit pedagogy":

> If all societies . . . that seek to produce a new man through a process of "deculturation" and "reculturation" set . . . store on the seemingly most insignificant details of *dress, bearing,* physical and verbal *manners,* the reason is that, treating the body as a memory, they entrust to it in abbreviated and practical, i.e. mnemonic, form the fundamental principles of the arbitrary content of the culture. The principles em-bodied in this way are placed beyond the grasp of consciousness, and hence cannot be touched by the voluntary, deliberate transformation, cannot even be made explicit; nothing seems more ineffable . . . than the values . . . *made* body by the transubstantiation achieved by the hidden persuasion of an implicit pedagogy, capable of instilling a whole cosmology, an ethic, a metaphysic, a political philosophy, through injunctions as insignificant as "stand up straight" or "don't hold your knife in your left hand."[21]

At first glance, this may seem applicable to the level of—as well as the motives for—behavioral training discussed in the *Cortegiano*. But that is misleading. The passage describes only the practices of primary socialization Bourdieu refers to collectively as "the habitus"; it can't apply to the programmatic formats and explicit pedagogy characteristic of the forms of secondary socialization.[22] Nor does Bourdieu explore the transgressive interactions and politically charged negotiations that go on between these two levels of pedagogy.[23] These interactions are central to the *Cortegiano*. As we've already seen, the premise that founds the discussion of sprezzatura is that a practice of "voluntary, deliberate transformation" guided by an explicit pedagogy should aim to represent, to impersonate, to dissimulate the behavioral product of involuntary, embodied principles of mimesis. Such an objective itself presupposes an educational system in which forms of explicit pedagogy have split off from the structures of primary socialization and become institutionalized in their own right. Courtesy books like the *Cortegiano* are the end result of a revolution in schooling about which so much has been written that I need only describe it in a few sentences.

Though the training of apprentices and novices for craft guilds and the religious orders was carried on at the level we call secondary socialization, it tended to be recoded in the linguistic and kinship categories of primary socialization that dominated domestic life in nuclear households and extended families.[24] The effect of this tendency was to endow the secondary identifications developed through explicit pedagogy in role-specific training with the affective force of primary identifications developed through the implicit pedagogy of early childhood; a procedure, in short, for alienating affection. But from the thirteenth century on different forms of (more explicitly) explicit pedagogy were instituted within the civic or national community: church schools declined; the master/apprentice system of workshop training persisted; merchant schooling (vernacular) and humanist pedagogy (Latin) emerged into prominence. Communal and independent schools provided alternatives to household tutors.[25] If these developments worked to sustain existing class differences, the diverse forms and curricula of explicit pedagogy have in common a structural emphasis, a way of directing attention, that would ultimately reinforce factors contributing to the erosion of inhibitions on mobility. Whether in republics, principalities, or the Venetian patriciate, oligarchs and aristocrats who expected to pursue careers in banking, commerce, and politics prepared for a competitive public life that presupposed some competence in the skills of self-representation (aka rhetoric). The sociopolitical subtext of whatever was taught—whether Latin or vernacular, Cicero or Ariosto, Euclid or the *abbaco*, composition for *orationes* or for *ricordi*—involved instruction in those performative skills—instruction, that is, in mastering the know-how needed to fashion the equivalent of what Aristotle in Book 2 of the *Rhetoric* called the ethos of the speaker. The ethos in this context would be the persona of speaker or writer as notary, merchant, magnate, statesman, father, clergyman, prince, or courtier.

Lurking under the discussion of sprezzatura and emerging fitfully but definitively throughout the *Cortegiano* are hints of a general cultural failure: the failure of ascriptive norms of blood and lineage to sustain their moral authority and sometimes their political efficacy; a crisis of the aristocracy not dissimilar in some respects to the one made famous by Lawrence Stone.[26] Two centuries of wars, social conflicts, economic crises, and epidemics had produced, as Randolph Starn and Loren Partridge put it in their wonderful study of the Camera Picta in Mantua, "a world of desperate remedies."[27] In the face of redistributions of power exploited or endured by self-made princely regimes and mercantile oligarchies, ascriptive norms remain necessary but are no longer sufficient. They have to be supplemented by skills of self-representation that respond to new legal, political, and ideological pressures on aristocratic status. For example, it has been shown that in Venice from the early fifteenth century patricians had to meet state-instituted requirements to prove their noble credentials; the confirmation of noble identity came to depend less on family history than on legal procedures and official documentation that redefined the patriciate as an "essentially political" entity. In Tuscany, "governmentally conferred *dignitas*" came to supersede "ancient . . . lineage" as the primary determinant of noble status.[28] Thomas Kuehn's study of arbitration in Florence—like Stephanie Jed's account of merchant writing—brings out the increasing importance of performative techniques in the reproduction of family status and solidarity.[29] In the lordships of Northern Italy, to return to Starn and Partridge's account, factitious "court genealogies" with their "masquerade of distinguished origins" were more openly presented and perceived as the rituals of performance that signified the rippling muscles of new power, "sheer political domination," just under the silky and transparent skin of traditional aristocratic authority (86–88).

The common theme uniting these examples is increasing emphasis on the need to *perform* status, the need to develop strategies of self-representation and class self-definition. One way to look at this change is to borrow C. B. Macpherson's models of customary and possessive market societies.[30] What you then begin to see is something like the irruption of elements of the possessive market society model exerting pressure on those who find it in their interest to preserve—and this comes to mean *to perform*—elements of the customary or status society. It is within this general context that I want to situate the questions I asked at the end of the first part of this chapter. Do all those who are urged to represent themselves as better than they think they are form a community in which it becomes as difficult to authenticate one's own performances as it is to accredit those of others? Doesn't such a community cast about itself a permanent shadow of representation anxiety?

Whether or not the text of the *Cortegiano* will respond to questions of this sort remains to be seen. My motive for returning to these questions is to gesture toward an interpretive framework that may make such a response as possible to us as I think it was to Giovanni della Casa writing in the Tridentine culture of the 1550s. Della Casa's *Galateo*, as I read it, performs an ironic critique of the culture of courtesy books, representing it as a paranoid system of pornographic surveillance and containment. It brings to the surface misanthropic undertones that are displaced and subordinated in *The Courtier*. I shall argue that although *Galateo* misreads the *Cortegiano*, the misreading is a productive one: della Casa's text deeply appreciates the problematic of manners in a culture of suspicion but misunderstands the extent to which the same appreciation/insight is inscribed in the text of the *Cortegiano*. *Galateo* is equally easy to misread, perhaps for the same reasons, and the final chapter of this study explores the means by which it represents and interrogates what I just referred to as a paranoid system. In the next two chapters I contextualize my interpretations of the *Cortegiano* and *Galateo* by using an analysis of the latter's titular episode as an entry into an account of the sociocultural changes that produced what Castiglione's speakers perceive as the absence of grace.

2.   Count Ricciardo's Tiny Defect

Galateo was published two years after its author's death in the 1558 *editio princeps* supervised by della Casa's secretary, Erasmo Gemini de Cesis. Introducing the treatise to the reader, this Erasmo Gemini divulges the inside story of its origin. He tells us that during a conversation between the author and Galeazzo Florimonte, bishop of Sessa, the bishop first suggested that there was need for a book of manners written in "nostra volgar favella," and then, after praising della Casa's superior "stile," offered to collaborate with him by sharing his knowledge of the fine manners he had observed in courts throughout the world and especially in the house of Bishop Giberti of Verona.[1]

Thus Erasmo Gemini. In the *Galateo* the two episcopal principals of this origin story appear in the fourth chapter under the following descriptions: The bishop of Verona, wise and "very learned in scripture, ... was also courteous and generous with the noble gentlemen who came and went about him, honoring them in his house with a magnificence which was not overdone, but moderate, as was fitting to a cleric."[2] The other figure is introduced not as a bishop but as a "discreto famigliare" residing with the bishop of Verona. "Famigliare" is a strategically elastic term. It denotes a member of the household who may be an intimate, a confidant, a servant, or some blend of the three. It is repeated in the next sentence: "il detto famigliare" was "a man of advanced age, very learned and unbelievably pleasant and well spoken and handsome, and in his time he had much frequented the courts of the great lords."[3] We are then told that he "was, and perhaps still is, called Messer Galateo [fu e forse ancora è chiamato messer Galateo]." This should make us sit up and take notice because it mentions the name of the treatise and because the "forse ancora è" coyly disclaims closer acquaintance, or at least more up-to-date information, and flatters the reader: "Something is being withheld; you and I, of course, know what it is," and the answer follows immediately: "It was at his bidding and on his advice that I first started to dictate this treatise [dettare questo presente trattato]"—presumably to Erasmo Gemini (D, 8; *Op.*, 373).

Thus, I was about to say, della Casa, but that would be jumping the gun. Thus, to be on the safe side, della Casa's narrator, about whom more later. But one question may at least be asked now: Did the dutiful Erasmo Gemini get his information as well as his dictation from della Casa's narrator or from della Casa? If from the narrator, and if the narrator's view of things is not della Casa's, and if Erasmo Gemini wasn't aware of this, what does it tell us about poor Erasmo's reliability as an authoritative source? Can we trust in the narrator's reliability?[4] For example, when della Casa describes Bishop Galeazzo Florimonte in a letter to Cardinal Contarini, his picture is slightly but significantly different in emphasis from the narrator's picture of the unbelievably polished Galateo. Galeazzo is "a man adorned not only with every genteel manner, but above all with a chaste and irreproachable manner of living, and . . . very fervent in his religious practices and piety." He is also, della Casa adds, "more shrewd and open than anyone else in noticing and reproving his friends' faults, and sometimes he is even a critic who is not quite restrained" (D, 65).[5] The addition implies that Galeazzo's preeminent virtue and piety are the sources of a not entirely "genteel" tendency toward captiousness.

As we'll see, that tendency is displaced from Galateo to the narrator, who represents himself as a counter-Galateo in his professed lack of gentility and whose discourse is a faultfinder's manifesto. He glorifies both the danger and the moral heroism of this discursive stance when, in the penultimate chapter, he mentions the fate Socrates suffered because he "used to go about pointing out everybody's faults" (D, 59). Finally, after he devotes the last chapter to still another inventorial tirade against unsightly behavioral tics and peccadilloes, the narrator breaks off abruptly and concludes with the acknowledgment that perhaps many will accuse him of having already dwelled excessively on the "innumerable stupid things [innumerabili sciocchezze]" people do (D, 61; *Op.*, 440).

In an unpublished essay to which I am much indebted, Kristen Brookes points out that the contrast provided by the letter to Contarini makes conspicuous the absence of any reference by the narrator to Messer Galateo's piety, virtue, and captiousness. These are irrelevant to the role he is assigned in Chapter 4, which calls only for the more superficial characteristics singled out by the narrator: "exceptional appearance, manners, and conversational skills."[6] Brookes's analysis suggests the following differential proportion:

Galateo : Galeazzo :: Narrator : della Casa. Because Erasmo Gemini's profile of Florimonte resembles Galateo more than Galeazzo, one is entitled to suspect that the source of his anecdotal embroidery may have been Chapter 4 of the *Galateo* rather than della Casa himself. Placing Erasmo Gemini under this suspicion reduces him to the scribe or double or dupe of della Casa's narrator, whom I have already, if tentatively, placed under suspicion and whose claim to be dictating and transmitting the true discourse of manners presented by the text of *Galateo* I shall do my best to discredit. What I designate as "the text of *Galateo*" is synonymous with "my interpretation of *Galateo*," and it is from this interpretation that I conjure up the specter of an authorial agent named della Casa to whom I transfer responsibility for "the text." I make no ontological claims for the existence of this della Casa. I suggest only that he is not the della Casa Erasmo Gemini was acquainted with, and that he is not the character my della Casa delightedly watched himself perform in the theater of dictation while his diligent secretary with lowered eyes scribbled down the words but missed the play. So, as we enter the theater, we bid farewell to Erasmo Gemini de Cesis, whose stenographic skills are no longer needed.

It was at Messer Galateo's "bidding and on his advice that I first started to dictate this treatise," and since the treatise bears his name, his brief appearance in the anecdote that constitutes Chapter 4 commands our attention. Is the *Galateo* so named only to celebrate his role as muse or instigator, or does it also celebrate his stature as a paragon, a living model, of good manners? If indeed we are encouraged to think of Galateo as a *figura di Galeazzo*, why is he demoted from his episcopal status to that of another bishop's "famigliare"? If his participation in the anecdote is exemplary, what is it exemplary of, and what does it suggest he would expect to find in a treatise on manners adorned with his name? The anecdote concerns a Count Ricciardo, who spent several days in Verona with Bishop Giberti and his household ("la famiglia di lui"), a household that consisted for the most part of "well-mannered and learned men" (D, 7). Because the count seemed to them to be a "gentilissimo cavaliere . . . e di bellissime maniere" (*Op.*, 373), "they commended and praised him highly, but he had one tiny fault in his deportment," which the bishop, "an attentive [intendente] man, noticed," and of which, "after consulting with some of his closer friends [più domestichi], he decided to make the count aware, without, however, causing him any distress" (D, 8, altered). Thereupon he instructed one of his gentlemen to accompany the count on his departure and to wait until he thought the time seemed right before telling him politely what the others had decided among themselves.

This delicate task was assigned to none other than Messer Galateo, who broaches the topic just before taking his leave of Count Ricciardo. He extends the bishop's thanks to the count for the honor of his visit, and adds that "as recompense for all the courtesy you have shown towards him he has commanded me to present you with a gift on his behalf." And this is the gift:

> "Having carefully observed your manners and having examined them in detail, he has found none that was not extremely pleasant and commendable except for an unseemly motion you make with your lips and mouth at the dinner table, when your chewing makes a strange sound that is most unpleasant to hear. The bishop sends you this message, begging you to try to refrain from doing it, and to accept as a precious gift his loving reprimand and remark, for he is certain no one else in the world would give you such a gift." The count, who had never before been aware of his fault, blushed slightly on being chastised for it; but, being a worthy man, he quickly recovered himself and said: "Please tell the bishop that if all the gifts they gave each other were such as this, men would be far richer than they are. And thank him profusely for all the courtesy and generosity he has shown towards me, assuring him that from now on I will diligently and carefully avoid this fault." (D, 8–9, altered)

To learn of the particular defect that the bishop and his friends observed, and to visualize them observing it, is to conjure up a wonderfully ridiculous dinner scene in which polite conversation and discreet mastication are periodically disrupted by the unseemly sight and sound of Count Ricciardo's mouth at its labors, and in which the count innocently chomps away unaware of the laserlike network of sidelong glances shooting toward him like orthogonals sucked in by their vanishing point. But the features that make this anecdote hilarious make it at the same time deeply unsettling.

First, Galateo describes the much ado about nothing of the bishop's mannerly microscopy in rhetoric that conveys a voyeuristic desire of surveillance and faultfinding: "avendo egli attentamente risguardato alle vostre maniere ed essaminatole partitamente [i.e., una ad una], niuna ne ha tra loro trovata che non sia sommamente piacevole e commendabile, fuori solamente un atto difforme che voi fate con le labbra e con la bocca masticando alla mensa con un nuovo strepito molto spiacevole ad udire . . ." (*Op.*, 374). The thrust of "attentamente risguardato" is weakly parried by the penultimate phrase in the count's response, "diligentemente mi guarderò."

Second, the bishop's inventorial precisianism at first appears softened by his concern for the count's feelings, but this concern only leads to an elaborate stratagem that sounds like more ado about nothing and thus magnifies the fault; it makes "picciolo" seem to be a polite and conspicuously understated way to describe the count's "difetto," a euphemism for "enorme" or "immenso." In the final chapter of the treatise, the narrator returns to the danger of such *piccioli difetti* when he warns that "out of many little mistakes one big error is made. . . . The smaller they are, the more others will make it their business to scrutinize them, for they are not easily seen and they sneak into our habits without our noticing them" (D, 61, altered).[7] Count Ricciardo's problem is a little different: the bad habit he hadn't noticed is all too obvious to others. But the narrator's general admonitory principle applies to it: "Just as continual small expenses quietly consume our wealth, so these small sins [peccati] stealthily undermine, with their multitude and number, our fine and good manners" (ibid.). The statement harks back to the caveat that concluded Chapter 3 and set the stage for Count Ricciardo's tiny defect in Chapter 4: one should not dismiss apparently trivial lapses in table manners as "of little importance, for even light blows can kill, if they are many" (D, 7).

Third, the targeted "difetto" may well signify the vice of gluttony, but the bishop and his friends show themselves concerned more with the sign than with the referent, and the implication is that one may enjoy and indulge one's vices so long as one politely conceals them.[8] Manners ("modi"), not virtues, are the object of their critical attention. This point, driven home throughout the treatise, is restated in the twenty-eighth chapter, just before the narrator recalls the example of Count Ricciardo. He reminds his tutee that although "it is most advisable for those who aspire to be well liked . . . to flee vices, especially the fouler ones such as lust, avarice, cruelty, and . . . gluttony," his teaching has a different objective:

> Since I undertook to show you men's errors and not their sins, my present
> care must be to deal not with the nature of vice and virtue, but only with
> the proper and improper manners we use toward each other. One of these
> improper manners was the one used by Count Ricciardo, of whom I told
> you above. It was so different from and discordant with his other beautiful
> and fitting manners that the worthy [valoroso] bishop immediately noticed
> it, as a good and well-trained singer notices wrong notes. (D, 54)

The associative effect of this reprise is to link the narrator's reaffirmation of his limited objective to the episode featuring Messer Galateo.

Fourth, Bishop Giberti's aggressive scrutiny and tact are followed by an equally aggressive deployment of the power of the gift to inflame the do-nee's humiliation with fresh wounds of gratitude and obligation. This partic-ular move exhibits both the sprezzatura of elite enclosure (mentioned in Chapter 1) and the art of generating representation anxiety. Its resonances ripple out far beyond the perimeter of the episode; they fill the space of so-cial interaction shaped by *Galateo*'s discourse of manners, and I shall consider them in the next chapter. For the present I note only the problematic en-tanglement of the discourse of the gift with two other cultural discourses, those of honor and gender.[9]

One can easily imagine the relief with which the poor count utters the formula of leave-taking that allows him to escape the diluvian force of the grazia flowing from the bishop and his messenger: "andatevi con Dio" (*Op.*, 374). But is Galateo only the messenger? Was his resorting to the discourse of the gift his idea or the bishop's? Or is the question itself idle, the sign of overattentive scrutiny? Even though the text provides no answers, the ques-tion is not idle because it leads us to appreciate the irrelevance of the dis-tinction it interrogates. The *Galateo* is named for and celebrates not Bishop Galeazzo Florimonte but a reductive shadow cast by his more superficial achievements as a man of manners, the shadow of a peregrine frequenter of courts, a professional courtier who is his current host's "famigliare," as much his servant as his confidant. Some of the terms of the mawkish self-depreca-tion T. S. Eliot puts in Prufrock's mouth perfectly describe Galateo: "not Prince Hamlet" but "an attendant lord"—"no doubt, an easy tool, / Defer-ential, glad to be of use, / Politic, cautious, and meticulous."[10] The anecdote presents Galateo as a perfect courtier; a figure straight out of the *Cortegiano* and thus a metonymic reflector of the values its speakers articulate; a facili-tator who can be trusted to follow orders and discharge delicate offices effi-ciently; a model of unquestioning—and uncritical—commitment to the code of manners, the set of values, the discursive practices that prevail among his betters.

The code, values, and practices exemplified by the anecdote and Galateo's role in it are precisely those articulated by the narrator in the first two chap-ters, when he argues that people who know how to be "grazioso e piace-vole" have "attained to the highest ranks and left far behind those endowed with the nobler and more illustrious" cardinal virtues of justice, fortitude, generosity, and magnanimity. The latter "require greater resources, lacking which they amount to little or nothing, while this [good manners] is rich and powerful without any such patrimony precisely because it consists solely of words and gestures."[11] Thus the narrator exhorts his tutee to devote all his energy to learning how to please others, especially those whose mastery of this knowledge and skill has helped them to positions of power and authority in civic life: "it will be to your advantage to temper and adapt your manners not according to your own choices but according to the pleasure of those with whom you are dealing and act accordingly" (D, 4). A few pages later, such an attitude materializes in the exemplary figure of Messer Galateo, who both inspired and embodies this conspicuously restricted discourse on manners.

The chapters that lead to the anecdote introducing Galateo lay out the general principles of the code (Chapters 1 and 2) and run through a general inventory of indecent acts to be avoided (Chapter 3). The inventory concludes with examples of bad table manners that anticipate the central theme of the anecdote. Table manners are the sole concern of no more than three of the treatise's thirty chapters (4, 5, and 29), but since the first of these involves the only appearance of the titular figure, one is tempted to attach importance to the theme and inquire into its contribution to the larger picture, that is, to the overall argument of the *Galateo* and to its position in the courtesy book tradition.

During the course of a compendious historical study of gluttony, William Ian Miller speaks both to Bishop Giberti's scruples and to Count Ricciardo's condition when he observe that

> there is something very dangerous about eating. It is hard not to offend God or your fellow man or woman when you do it. And God and humanity seem to be taking offense at roughly the same thing: the unseemliness of gratifying bodily urges. Eating is like other necessary bodily functions: dangerous in the extreme and best done out of sight. . . . [It] must be hemmed in with all kinds of rituals and rules precisely because the process is so likely to prompt disgust when viewed by others. Watch with a detached eye as someone, even a well-mannered someone, eats. It is not a thing of beauty. But if skilled we can at least make feeding ourselves relatively inoffensive when . . . we agree to put ourselves at mutual risk by eating together so as not to make ourselves so vulnerable to the gaze of a non-eating other.[12]

Eating, Miller argues, was made "even riskier than it already was" (106) by "the civilizing process" that "led to an increase in sensitivities of disgust and embarrassment and an internalization of norms of bodily decorum" (104). This process "shifted the emphasis in gluttony from a matter of excessive amounts to a matter of excessively concentrated sensation. And at the same time the advancing notion of refinement shifted the moral focus of gluttony from a disgust prompted by the perversion of proper spiritual values . . . to a disgust for bad manners, for looking vulgar as you ate" (106)—precisely the shift of focus from ethics to manners that the *Galateo* stages. Miller's obvious bow to Norbert Elias, for whom the *Galateo*, the *Cortegiano*, and Erasmus's *De civilitate morum puerilium* were major documents of—and contributors to—the civilizing process in early modern Europe, provides me with a cue to turn to the larger context via Elias's theory.

3.   *Galateo* and the Civilizing Process: A Short History of Table Manners

Norbert Elias's aim in *The Civilizing Process* is to characterize, track, and correlate the psychogenesis and sociogenesis of that process from the early modern period—in other words, to correlate historical changes "in the structure of behavior and psychical makeup" with the changes in sociopolitical structure that transformed decentralized feudal institutions into the centralized formations of the early modern state.[1] The thesis of the psychogenetic argument is that during this period there is a significant increase in the restraint of affect, the lowering of the threshold of shame, and the internalization of social norms. Elias models this argument on the theory of repression developed by Freud in *Civilization and Its Discontents*, and he carries out his analysis primarily through the examination of the changes in behavioral codes represented in conduct books. The thesis of the sociogenetic argument is that while "the monopolization and centralization of taxes and force over a large area"[2] diminish the dangers of physical violence, they generate new and subtler forms of nonphysical violence that, with their attendant anxieties, call for more stringent practices of self-restraint.

A major organizational weakness of Elias's account is that the sociogenetic argument is not fully elaborated until the second volume and the two arguments are spliced together only in the Synopsis that occupies the last third of that volume. As a result, except for occasional vague references to the emergence of a new aristocracy during the sixteenth and seventeenth centuries, the psychogenetic argument developed in *The History of Manners*, the first volume of *The Civilizing Process*, initially floats free of the sociogenetic explanation that integrates it with large-scale changes in political structure. The story of the civilizing process told in this volume is dominated by an emphasis on specific changes in the economy of affect: emotions in feudal societies "are expressed more violently and directly" with "fewer psychological nuances and complexities in the general stock of ideas.

There are friend and foe, desire and aversion, good and bad people" (*Manners*, 63). During the Renaissance these "simple oppositions" give way, and people begin to "see things with more differentiation, i.e., with a stronger restraint of their emotions" (71).

It is true that in *Manners* Elias pays much attention to the "increased tendency of people to observe themselves and others" and their tendency to "mold themselves and others more deliberately than in the Middle Ages" (79). These tendencies are connected with the anxieties of an arriviste class, "the new courtly aristocracy . . . coalescing from elements of diverse social origin" (100) in postfeudal conditions that demand increased vigilance in the sphere of everyday social behavior and that involve changing forms and standards of aggressiveness (191–205). The social and psychological "coercion exerted by people [in the upper classes] on one another increases, the demand for 'good behavior' is raised more emphatically" (79). During the course of the sixteenth and seventeenth centuries, after a period of increased social mobility,

> a more rigid social hierarchy begins to establish itself once more, and from elements of diverse social origins a new upper class, a new aristocracy forms. For this very reason the question of uniform good behavior becomes increasingly acute, particularly as the changed structure of the new upper class exposes each individual member to an unprecedented extent to the pressure of others and of social control. It is in this context that the writings on manners of Erasmus, Castiglione, Della Casa, and others are produced. (80)

Formulations of this sort recur throughout *Manners*, and we'll see that they can, when revised, provide a promising point of entry into the interpretation of the works Elias mentions—though it isn't a point of entry he avails himself of. In spite of their promise, however, the deferral of the sociogenetic component produces the misleading impression that the psychogenetic story unfolded in *Manners* is shaped by such self-sufficient and dubious developmental schemata as the passages from the simpler to the more complex and from less to greater repression. This has made Elias's account of the civilizing process vulnerable to the criticism that it is flawed by vulgar Freudianism and evolutionary gradualism.[3] But my concern here is with a related but different flaw, one connected to the *Galateo* episode I have just discussed: the isolated emphasis on changes in "affect economy" impoverishes Elias's treatment of the changing role of table manners in medieval and early modern courtesy books. In what follows I shall try to show that when this change is more fully irradiated by the context of the sociogenetic argument, it can throw light on problematic features of the civilizing process that not only impinge on the *Galateo* but indeed are critically represented by it.

Elias gets into the subject of table manners via a consideration of Erasmus's *De civilitate morum puerilium*, a work which, he claims, gave new meaning to the concept of *civilité*, and which he views as both a reflector of and a contributor to the shift toward increasingly performative—rhetoricized and theatricalized—codes of behavior. A brief introductory reference to *De civilitate*'s significance as an "instigator" of change (*Manners*, 54–55) precedes a synopsis of its contents (55–58), and the synopsis is followed by an extended genealogical backloop through medieval predecessors (60–70) intended to set up Elias's contrastive analysis of Erasmian innovations (70–74, 77–80). However, this analysis owes nothing to the synopsis because the latter was geared toward preparing the way for the backloop. That is, the synopsis has little or nothing to do with what is new in the treatise; it is almost entirely devoted to the one aspect in which the *De civilitate* most resembles medieval courtesy books: the attention to and proscription of disgusting behavior at table and elsewhere.[4] Why should this be?

The reason appears in the generalizing comments that conclude the synopsis. Elias there accentuates the modern perspective in terms of which our distance from Erasmus and his contemporaries increases while their attitude toward behavior is conflated with the less "civilized" sensibility of the Middle Ages:

> The unconcerned frankness with which Erasmus and his time could discuss all areas of human conduct is lost to us. Much of what he says oversteps our threshold of delicacy.
>
> But precisely this is one of the problems to be considered here. In . . . following back the concept of civilization to its ancestor *civilité*, one finds oneself suddenly on the track of the civilizing process itself. . . . That it is embarrassing for us to speak or even hear of much that Erasmus discusses is one of the symptoms of this civilizing process. The greater or lesser discomfort we feel toward people who discuss or mention their bodily functions more openly, who conceal and restrain these functions less than we do, is one of the dominant feelings expressed in the judgment "barbaric" or "uncivilized." Such then is the nature of "barbarism and its discontents."
> (58–59)[5]

This is the Freudian nub of the now famous or notorious thesis of Elias's history of manners.

In one of the more compelling critical revisions of the history, Anna Bryson begins by citing and taking issue with its account of medieval courtesy books. According to Elias, they differed from their Renaissance successors in being primarily concerned with table manners: "precepts on conduct while eating had a special importance" in the earlier manuals because "eating and drinking . . . occupied a far more central position in social life than today" (*Manners*, 60). It is important to note that the late medieval courtesy books surveyed by Elias and Bryson were, in her words, "directed at the child or gentleman-servitor in the noble or royal household" and not necessarily at his or her betters. For example, the recipients of prescriptions dominated by "stern warnings against plunging one's hands into dishes of food, fighting at table or blowing one's nose on the table-linen" are juniors and inferiors. The reader to whom these proscriptions are addressed "is told to salute his superiors and strangers respectfully, to wash before and after meals and to avoid loud belching and farting."[6] Presumably, those in power had more license to eat like slobs.

The burden of Bryson's critique falls on what Elias sees and doesn't see in this emphasis on table manners. He treats it as a response to dining practices that we today would find crude and unattractive because they corresponded to "a standard of human relationships and structure of feeling" marked by a high threshold of embarrassment and shame: since "conduct while eating . . . is a segment—a very characteristic one—of the totality of socially instilled forms of conduct," the crudeness of medieval table manners may be interpreted as "expressions of a society in which people gave way to drives and feelings incomparably more easily, quickly, spontaneously, and openly than today, in which the emotions were less restrained and, as a consequence, less evenly regulated and more liable to oscillate more violently between extremes" (*Manners*, 67, 68, 214).

For Bryson, this orientation toward the economy of affect exemplifies the limits of Elias's narrow concern with the "history of inhibition" and with the "rising level of sensitivity" to shame in early modern elites (Bryson, 139, 143). Elias ignores, for example, the fact that the proscribed crudeness of medieval eating habits may be historically less significant than the emphasis on proper table manners as a fundamental ritual of socialization. More important, he ignores the hierarchical focus of these proscriptions on the table manners of inferiors. As Bryson puts it, in medieval (fifteenth-century) courtesy books

attention is overwhelmingly directed to one sort of social occasion and to
the relationships which are to be expressed in the rituals of that occasion:
this is the main meal or banquet, the ever-renewed expression of the solidarity and hierarchy of the noble household and its relation to the outside
world in the obligation of hospitality. While "table manners" have continued
to this day to be an important theme in etiquette books, late medieval
courtesy literature was largely and sometimes exclusively devoted to this
area of sociability. . . . In the description of this ritual the stress is always on
the relations of lordship and service dramatized in the banquet procedures.
If the precepts about physical behavior often seem to us to indicate a remarkable crudity, they are embedded in complex rules about when, how
and to whom the courteous child or man must offer food, wine and water.
Moreover, even the rules forbidding messy eating are related less to an overt
bodily aesthetic than to the need to show due deference to the lord or host.
(140–41)[7]

Thus manners are for those who need to show deference, while crudity and
gluttonous or messy eating are the privileges of their betters—and privileges
by no means incompatible with the displays of hospitality and generosity
that express the prerogatives of lordship.[8]

This is not the case in the treatises of Erasmus and della Casa. Granted
that both are addressed to young men, the addressees are constructed as potential adult players in high society and politics. It is as prospective courtiers
and representative aristocrats that they must learn to rely more on their own
achievements in the various aspects of self-fashioning—moral, intellectual,
behavioral—than on the traditional combination of pedigree and superior
force encoded in the symbolism of heraldry. Although Erasmus reminds his
dedicatee, Henry of Burgundy, that he is "born into, and destined for, the
purple," he goes on to proclaim that "everyone who cultivates the mind in
liberal studies must be taken to be noble. Let others paint lions, eagles, bulls,
and leopards on their escutcheons; those who can display 'devices' of the intellect commensurate with their grasp of the liberal arts have a truer nobility."[9] In terms of this humanist program, good manners for boys are not only
for the boys as boys but also for the adults they are expected to become.
Thus if many of Erasmus's precepts are directed specifically to boys, many
others are equally applicable to the code of manners prescribed for their
elders, and are applicable in a nonhierarchic fashion—applicable, that is,
to anyone who wishes to master the skills of self-representation needed
to compete in the struggle for status and power.[10] More consistently than *De*

civilitate, the *Galateo* is directed through the young addressee to adults and their conduct, but it differs in restricting its teaching to good manners in isolation from moral and intellectual virtues.

Bryson's corrective expansion of Elias's approach to medieval table manners has the positive effect of situating his account of changes in the economy of affect firmly within the framework of the sociogenetic argument of *Power and Civility*, the second volume of *The Civilizing Process*. She thus helps to give that account the structural basis it needs in order to secure what is probably the most important and influential insight of *The Civilizing Process*: the insight that the new behavioral and pedagogical technologies driving the process from feudal through early modern times contribute to a long-term transformation in which more overt and direct modes of violence gradually yield pride of place to more covert and indirect modes. *Power* locates the structural ground of affective change in the process by which "an upper class of relatively independent warriors or knights [was] supplanted by a more or less pacified upper class of courtiers" in urban duchies and absolutist monarchies (196). As a result of the state's "monopolization of physical force and the growing stability of the central organs of society,"

> pacified social spaces are created which are normally free from acts of violence. The pressures acting on individual people within them are of a different kind than previously. Forms of non-physical violence that always existed, but hitherto had always been mingled or fused with physical force, are now separated from the latter. . . . [In this new situation] the individual is largely protected from sudden attack, the irruption of physical violence into his life. But at the same time he is himself forced to suppress in himself any passionate impulse urging him to attack another physically. . . . The closer the web of interdependence becomes . . . , the larger the social spaces over which this network extends . . . —the more threatened is the social existence of the individual who gives way to spontanous impulses and emotions, the greater is the social advantage of those able to moderate their affects, and the more strongly is each individual constrained from an early age to take account of the effects of his own or other people's actions on a whole series of links in the social chain. (235–36)

This level of analysis makes it easier to replace the first volume's emphasis on a changing economy of affect with an emphasis on a changing economy of representations.[11] Following Elias, and partly under his influence, there have been many accounts of the changes in representational economy by which the dominantly militaristic representations of feudal societies are transformed into the more diversified portfolios of displaced violence that characterize the graphic modalities of early modern representations. To cite one example, Jonathan Goldberg writes that Vives's Latin primer of 1538, describing (and prescribing) schoolboy life, "participates in what Elias calls the civilizing process, for these scenes of everyday life construct the everyday through grammatical and pedagogic proprieties."[12] Discussing a sentence in Claudius Desainliens's 1583 variation of Vives, *Campo di Fior*, Goldberg comments:

> "Venistis huc armati": "Have you brought your weapons? Have you brought your tooles?"... The "civilized" young men have been properly schooled, open violence restrained and resituated (the great shift charted by Elias ...), as when they recast colonizing as kingly "munificence," or when they recognize the proper tools necessary for the tasks of civilization—the writers' weapons of quill and quillcase (replacing arrows and sheaths).... The pen is mightier than the sword. (63)[13]

Elias had argued, in Roger Chartier's words, "that between the Middle Ages and the nineteenth century, . . . the necessary control of impulses was transferred from an exterior prohibition, imposed if need be by force, to a stable mechanism of self-restraint."[14] Chartier complicates the argument by crossing it with Louis Marin's studies of the politics of representation:

> Marin's work . . . permits us to understand how confrontations based on brute force or pure violence changed into symbolic struggles—that is, into struggles whose weapons and rewards were representations. The image has this power because it "effects a substitution of the external manifestation in which a force appears . . . with signs of force." . . . One might add, prolonging this encounter between Marin and Norbert Elias, that it was that same pacification (at least relative pacification) of the social sphere between the Middle Ages and the seventeenth century that transformed open and brutal social clashes into struggles between representations in which the stakes were the ordering of the social world, hence the recognition of the rank of each estate, each body, each individual. (95–96)

It goes without saying that feudal confrontations were no less representational than those in which violence was displaced to—for example—the rhetorical, theatrical, mercantile, and propagandistic registers of early modern discourses and practices.[15] The structural criterion of difference between earlier and later in this case is the relative distance of displacements from more transparent representations of force:

> A command on the one hand is always explicitly or implicitly comple-
> mented by an "or else" clause, a pointer to the command-giver's ability to
> use coercion in order to overcome recalcitrance or resistance on the part
> of the person receiving the command. On this account, there is a distinct
> (and sinister) factuality to commands, an implicit (and sometimes explicit)
> reminder that "we have ways to make you obey...."
>
> On the other hand, a command is a thoroughly intersubjective opera-
> tion: by means of it, one subject seeks to initiate and control another sub-
> ject's activity. It is also thoroughly symbolic in nature, and presupposes the
> other subject's ability to entertain and interpret the message....[16]

Because, as Gianfranco Poggi suggests, feudal institutions "were focused on the imperatives of military command" (35) and feudal negotiations were de-termined in the last instance by military threat, the sinister factuality was al-ways closer to the surface of representation. The "military aspects intrinsic to the political enterprise" were more conspicuous (39), and there was a closer "implication between war and political arrangements, and ... between political experience and violence," in feudal than in postfeudal representa-tions (35).

The "seigneurial" mode of production, as Georges Duby calls it, "was predicated on the firmly established power to exploit the land and the men who cultivated it"—a power that, in Jonathan Powis's words, "was made vis-ible in stone" and imposed its own localizing constraints: "Over the genera-tions, castles and land bound families to their locality."[17] The castle was itself a representation of defensive/aggressive power that materialized and charac-terized—and aggrandized—the social unit of the *domus*, which in "the high society of the twelfth century" in northern France consisted of

> the household or two-generation family.... The framework within which
> this group became aware of its cohesion was the house or *domus*.... The
> specific function of those who spoke of their noble status traditionally was
> and remained military.... This basic structure shaped an entire set of atti-
> tudes, especially those of respect and deference. So compelling was this
> structure that every metaphor that sought to express power relationships ...
> in some way made use of the image of the house. (Duby, 3–4)

More distinctly than either their forebears or their descendants, the knights of the twelfth century were basically inheritors. This process of taking root in an agrarian environment . . . served to ensconce the lay aristocracy more solidly than ever within the confines of the house (*domus*). It also explains why, ever since the second third of the eleventh century, the name of the house tended to become the common surname of all the offspring of the "race." Under these circumstances it is appropriate to view chivalric society as an assembly of juxtaposed houses. (9)

This context is necessary to supply the motivating factors not mentioned by Elias in his emphasis on the restricted scope of medieval conduct literature, the factors more explicitly indicated by Anna Bryson when she connects the learning of table manners to the general objectives of aristocratic pedagogy. The emphasis on table manners together with the orientation of that emphasis toward juniors and inferiors reflects the dominance of the scene of primary socialization—the noble household—as the site of pedagogy. Table manners are both the synecdochal representation of the existing hierarchic order and a central means of reproducing it:

Not only did great families inherit a power of command over others; the institution of the family itself provided a setting and an idiom in which command could be exercised. . . . The head of an aristocratic household enjoyed exceptional resources with which to assert both the distinction of his house and his own role as its leader. . . . Nothing better marked out the pre-eminence of a great lord than to dispense lavish entertainment for his kinsmen and followers. (Powis, 49)

Barbara Correll's more dialectical view of this privilege reveals it to be apotropaically inscribed with the shadow of the violence always lurking behind the representational surface: "Manners demonstrated ruling-class leadership, domination based on land, title, and physical force. One who offered hospitality in peace could offer hostility in war as well."[18] But the "manners" Correll refers to here are not table manners; rather they include the gestures and the expressions of the values mentioned in the following passage: "Loyalty was the chief value in peace and in war; hospitality, generosity, and politeness were gestures of peace in an environment otherwise structured by violence. . . . Such values came with historical contradictions. Loyalty, feudal order, hereditary power—all stood as ways of preventing conflict which preserved conflict" (40).

In the *Galateo's* value system, based on the distinction between manners and virtue, loyalty and generosity would be classified as virtues, politeness would be classified under manners, while hospitality might fall into either category.[19] Correll's point is that in the feudal context the mannerly virtues "were not practiced with an eye toward social competition or advancement," as they would be in such later contexts as the one featured by *Galateo*; "they served as the visible sign of a determined and legitimate place in a presumably unchallenged social order" (46), and as representations reinforcing the presumption, implicit in the term "unchallenged," of a monopoly of the means to violence, but violence held in reserve, a last resort, the iron fist of exploitation and brute force visible within the velvet glove of feudal hierarchy.

Reduced to its simplest and most general premise, the traditional account of the structural change involved in the passage from feudal to state society still provides a viable framework for the phenomena under discussion here. In this account, the political and economic orders are first embedded in and then differentiated from the social order:

> Previously, in the Christian West, the possession of political power had been embedded in other forms of social power; its practice had been the prerogative of privileged people *qua* privileged people, just another expression of their social superiority. By the same token, the loyalties which it sought to evoke were part and parcel of other people's general condition of social dependency. *Qua* organization, on the other hand, the state unifies and makes distinctive the political aspects of social life, sets them apart from other aspects, and entrusts them to a visible, specialized entity. (Poggi, 20)[20]

Correlatively, we may say that political and economic representations were first more fully embedded in and then gradually, partially differentiated from social representations that derive their authority from ascriptive and reascriptive indicators of status.[21] Among the factors serving to sustain embedded authority were the relatively underdeveloped infrastructures of transportation and communication that, by inhibiting long-distance negotiations, imposed a local or cellular character on feudal agrarianism and thus reinforced the personalistic, familistic, and domestic forms given to the representations of authority and deference.

It is precisely this cluster of forms—the forms in which what may be called the feudal body was invested—that was jeopardized by "improvements in the road systems in various parts of Europe, . . . the growth of literacy, . . . developments in the material and social technology of warfare, . . . [and] the increasing significance of economic processes mediated by money and centered on the towns" (Poggi, 40)—to which we may add the development of graphic media and methods of representation, a development including but much more comprehensive than the growth of literacy. The general consequence is that political, social, and economic power are not only alienated from the feudal body but also magnified, redistributed in an emergent network of institutions that give more scope to nonmilitary and nonagrarian forms of appropriation and competition. The specter of violence dissociated from physical force gradually gets disseminated throughout the social order, where it lurks as a specific, ever-present danger and anxiety within every nexus of symbolic exchange or negotiation: the danger of loss of control and the correlative anxiety Jacob Burckhardt pessimistically associated with individualism and Elias, more ironically, with the civilizing process.

Elias emphasizes the "increased tendency of people to observe themselves and others" and to "mold themselves and others more deliberately than in the Middle Ages" as

> the demand for "good behavior" is raised more emphatically. . . . Not
> abruptly but very gradually the code of behavior becomes stricter and the
> degree of consideration expected of others becomes greater. The sense of
> what to do and what not to do in order not to offend or shock others
> becomes subtler, and in conjunction with the new power relationships the
> social imperative not to offend others becomes more binding. (*Manners*,
> 79–80)

The new representational demands described by Elias have in recent decades been associated with the increasing theatricalization and rhetoricization of culture. For example, Bryson argues that although conduct books in the sixteenth and seventeenth centuries don't ignore the themes on which their medieval predecessors focus, they tend to emphasize the function "of presenting or 'representing' personality rather than simply acknowledging relationship." They "feature a vocabulary that continuously refers to manners as 'representations.'" Their express assumption that "the body was a text from which good and bad character could be read" led them to direct attention to rhetorical and theatrical techniques of body management (143–44). She notes in passing that while

all codes of manners involve the representation of idealized character traits,
. . . sixteenth- and seventeenth-century codifications of manners . . . show
a peculiarly intense interest in correct forms of behavior as modes of self-
presentation. . . . They were depicting an idealized personality as a model to
be imitated, but they were also recommending good manners as the means
of constantly producing the image of an idealized personality. (144–45)

This argument improves on Elias's approach by redirecting it toward
issues not merely of self-representation but of the quasi-theatrical production—that is, the performance, the presentation—of self-representation:
"Through his manners the gentleman was supposed to proclaim his 'natural'
virtue and title to authority, but such manners were self-evidently the product of education, effort and artifice" (153). The adversative construction of
this sentence quietly yet forcefully picks out the two major pressure points I
have been exploring in the present study. The first is the problematic of
sprezzatura. The second is the perception of self-division at once registered
and confused by the interdependence between the socially sanctioned "nature" one has to learn and is supposed to proclaim and the repressed "nature" everyone by the same token assumes is already there and must not
be proclaimed. Since these two natures and their difference are produced
simultaneously and are mutually implicative, the second is no less "the product of education, effort and artifice" than the first. The paradox hazily adumbrated by Elias but brought into sharper focus by more recent studies
such as Bryson's and Barbara Correll's is that the sense of an unrepresented,
perhaps unrepresentable, inner self is the specific product of relatively more
powerful regimes and technologies of representation—regimes that both encourage the expression of inwardness and limit the forms it can take.

In Correll's powerful revision of the trajectory elaborated by Elias, new
technologies and media of representation not only registered but also facili-
tated the gradual displacements and dissemination of the forms of power.
The result was that whereas in feudal conditions "aristocratic manners were
not practiced with an eye toward social competition or advancement," competitive anxiety was the prevalent motive in "sixteenth-century encounters"
between court and city. Aristocrats and bourgeoisie both sought

to encode competition through increased emphasis on consideration and
sensitivity to what in personal behavior might offend. Significantly, in this
point of transition, if the former court attempted to hold onto what it was,

the urban bourgeosie tried to codify and justify a less certain identity. In this respect, the modified precepts of the humanist and bourgeois etiquettes specifying what one does—and especially, what one does not do—expose what one is not yet and would like to become. . . . With a reflexive element not seen in chivalric culture, they negotiated uneasily between an ideal self-image and a phantasmal unknown with the capacity to loom horrifically. (45–46)

Foregrounding "anxieties and fears of . . . the unregulated" phantasm (46), bourgeois representations of conduct thus "produced an internalized punitive spectacle that was constitutive, rather than cathartic" (48). Among members of the socially—if not politically—more privileged classes and their clients (and *famigliari*, including, for example, the humanists who were secretaries and pedagogues) it was especially constitutive of a general lowering of the threshold of apprehensiveness in the micropolitics of everyday public life. Not only Burckhardt but also those he wrote about perceived that life as a system of relationships motivated primarily by apprehension, that is, by the prehensive desire to take and the apprehensive fear of being taken.

The increased insecurity Correll describes affects not only relations among peers but also those between peers and servants. One measure of the increase is provided by a comparison of references to hand-washing in *The Babees Book* and in *Galateo*. On the one hand, the eighteen references I counted in the former are all simple and straightforward injunctions that associate hand-washing with cleanliness and neat appearance alone, or with cleanliness and neatness as signs of piety and obedience, signs of the desire to make a good impression on one's elders or betters at table and elsewhere. One example will suffice:

Pare clene thy nailes, thyn handes wasshe also
To-fore mete, and whan thow dooest arise;
Sitte in that place thow art assigned to;
Prease nat to hye in no maner wise. . . .[22]

On the other hand, the three references to hand-washing in *Galateo* treat it as a sign that arouses not thoughts of cleanliness but fantasies of filth. In Chapter 3 the narrator warns that when "a well-mannered gentleman" returns "from nature's summons, he should not even wash his hands in front of decent company, because the reason for his washing implies something disgusting to their imaginations" (D, 5). In the final chapter, after this advice is repeated, the narrator qualifies it by urging gratuitous ablution that will re-assure one's fellow diners and palliate their febrile imaginings:

> One shouldn't . . . wash one's hands in public for . . . [this is something] to be done in one's bedroom and not in full sight of others. The exception to this is the washing of the hands which is done in full sight of others, even if you do not need to wash them at all, so that whoever dips into the same bowl as yours will be certain of your cleanliness. (D, 60, altered)

Servants are subject to the same distrust and must be as attentive to their masters' penchant for suspicion as to their gustatory demands:

> The servants who wait on gentlemen's tables must not . . . place their hands on any part of the body which is kept covered, nor even appear to do so. . . . They must rather keep their hands in sight and out of suspicion [sospetto], and keep them carefully washed and clean, with no sign of dirt anywhere upon them. (D, 9)

This proscription is then extended beyond the servants' hands to their fetid emissions and, later, to their manners:

> Those who serve the dishes of food and the drinks must diligently abstain during that entire time from spitting, coughing and, even more, from sneezing. Since in such actions suspicion [la sospezione] of misconduct is just as disturbing to the diners as the certainty of it, the servants must take care not to give their masters reason to suspect [sospicare] their actions, for in this case what may have taken place disturbs as much as what has taken place. (D, 10)

> The servant errs who makes a show of offering his services to his master, for the master will be offended, thinking that the servant intends to place in doubt his master's lordship over him, suggesting perhaps that he had no right to command and expect obedience. (D, 28)

Let's recall that the various texts collected in *The Babees Book* residually preserve and reflect the practices of aristocratic households under feudal conditions that preexisted the monopolization of force and the territorial pacification Elias attributes to strong central government. In those conditions—to revisit Bryson and Correll—"the relations of lordship and service dramatized

in the banquet procedures" continually reaffirmed "the solidarity and hierarchy of the noble household and its relation to the outside world in the obligation of hospitality" (Bryson, 140–41), but "hospitality, generosity, and politeness were gestures of peace in an environment otherwise structured by
violence" (Correll, 40). The table manners that emphasized cleanliness, deference, and propriety helped reproduce an encastellated oasis of order and
trust secure from the dangers lurking in the unpacified world outside the
domus. With the onset of pacification the protective boundary dissolves and
external perils infiltrating the household assume new forms. Hospitality and
politeness become gestures of competition rather than of peace, functions of
anxiety rather than of community, in the daily struggles of defensive self-
representation.

Thus it is that *Galateo* dramatizes a heightened "sensitivity to what . . .
might offend" and a consequent tightening of surveillance as *i signori* probe
for the slightest indications of all that might be going amiss beneath the surface. In their apprehensiveness they not only attune their sensors salaciously
to the warning signals of the poor body's potential and potent malfunctions.
They also sniff the surrounding air for the omnipresent signs of insult and
disrespect they may secretly acknowledge they deserve:

> one must not say or do anything that may give an indication that one holds
> the other person in little affection or harbors a low opinion of him. (D, 11)

> Everyone must dress well according to his status and age, because if he does
> otherwise it seems that he disdains other people. (D, 12)

> Men who wear rich and noble clothes that are . . . ill-made . . . make their
> companions suspect that they have a low opinion of them. . . . (D, 12–13)

> Arrogance is nothing else but a lack of respect for others, and . . . everybody
> wishes to be respected even if he does not deserve it. (D, 14)

The difference between this culture of suspicion and the more secure order of the domus is encapsulated by *Galateo's* anecdote of Count Ricciardo.
That an incident concerning table manners centers on a noble and powerful personage rather than on a youth or inferior is one index of the changes
discussed by Elias, Bryson, and Correll. Although Elias doesn't take this particular change into account, it reinforces his comment on the meaning of
the episode:

The precept not to smack the lips while eating is also found frequently in medieval instructions. But its occurrence at the beginning of *Galateo* shows clearly what has changed. It not only demonstrates how much importance is now attached to "good behavior." It shows, above all, how the pressure people now exert on one another in this direction has increased. It is immediately apparent that this polite, extremely gentle, and comparatively considerate way of correcting is, *particularly when exercised by a social superior,* much more compelling as a means of social control, much more effective in inculcating lasting habits, than insults, mockery, or any threat of outward physical violence. (*Manners*, 81–82; my italics)

Elias makes good use of this passage as an epitome of his argument, but a question is raised for me by the italicized phrase, which implies an invariable and positionally based criterion of social difference.[23] The phrasing suggests that the efficacy of the bishop's discreet reproach is increased by his preexisting social superiority to the count. It is interesting that in Edmund Jephcott's English version Elias's "Graf Richard" becomes "Duke Richard," as if *Graf* or *conte* and *Herzog* or *duca* were interchangeable. What criteria of social superiority determine the relative standing of those who hold the titles conte, duca, and vescovo? I assume that even though ducal investiture may have been more weighty and prestigious than that of count, access to all three titles would have been restricted to members of aristocratic or oligarchic families (the older lineages or the nuovi ricchi); that the *grado* of nobility is a necessary if not sufficient condition of their access to episcopal and comital office. The question I want to put to Elias's claim that the bishop is "gesellschaftlich Höherstehenden" concerns the grounds and stability of that putative "higher standing." But of course it is hardly a claim, only a casual characterization made in passing, and one that refers to a small detail of a single episode; it may therefore seem trivial to worry it. However, since Elias treats—and persuades me to treat—the episode as paradigmatic of a general change in social relations, the very casualness of the characterization is significant. Elias takes it for granted that the bishop is the count's social superior and, in so doing, he assumes what I think has to be questioned and will now proceed to question.

The form my question takes is this: In our anecdote, the most obvious difference between the bishop and the count results from a temporary and reversible contingency, namely, the count is a guest and the bishop his host; is the bishop's social superiority positional—a fixed superiority of rank—and thus one that preexists the contingency, or is it an effect of the contingency, and only a potential effect, relying for its actualization on his mastery of the micropolitics of manners? The latter possibility would obtain if the two were social equals regardless of their relative political or bureaucratic or titular status. Taken by itself, the anecdote in Chapter 4 sheds no light on the question. But much later in the *Galateo* we encounter a similar set of issues in a discussion that seems in fact to constitute a reprise recalling and elaborating on the tactical warfare waged by the bishop on the count.

After the anecdote has (as we saw) been briefly reintroduced in Chapter 28, Chapter 29 returns for the third and last time to the subject of table manners. Among the details of mensal misbehavior it describes, some are uncomfortably close to our poor hero's "picciolo difetto" and link it more explicitly with gluttony:

> We must . . . be careful not to gobble up our food and develop hiccups or some other unpleasant result, as happens with people who hurry and so gasp for air or breathe so heavily that they annoy their companions. . . . It is also unsuitable to sprawl over the table, or to fill both sides of the mouth with food until the cheeks puff out. Also, one should not perform [fare] any act that shows others [per lo quale altri mostri] how greatly one enjoys the food or the wine, for these are habits for the taverns and for drunkards. (D, 57, altered; *Op.*, 435)

If one wishes to gluttonize, one should do it decorously and tastefully, mindful that everyone is watching, and that every bite is perforce a performance. On the other side, discretion is enjoined of those in the audience whose solicitude might make the diner nervous and inhibit his intake:

> To encourage those who are at table by saying "Are you not eating, this morning?" or, "Is there nothing that you like?" or, "Taste some of this or that" does not seem to me to be praiseworthy. . . . Although in so doing they show concern for their guest, very often they are also the reason why he eats so sparingly, for it will seem to him that he is being carefully watched and will be embarrassed. (D, 57, altered)

The point, of course, is that he *is* being carefully watched; the observers are warned only to keep him unaware of their attention so as to let him continue unembarrassedly to embarrass them with his disgusting table manners. We have already encountered the mean between these extremes in the exemplary response of Bishop Giberti and his *famigliari*, including Messer Galateo, who deferred embarrassing the count until he had left the premises, and thus politely allowed him to go on making a spectacle of himself.

After the passages quoted above, the narrator turns to a topic the resonances of which evoke another aspect of the bishop's treatment of Count Ricciardo. He observes that it is acceptable for one person to offer food from his plate to another if the former is "of a much more exalted rank" (D, 58; "molto maggior di grado," *Op.*, 436), for then the latter will consider himself honored by the gift. But it is improper for the same offer to be made to a social equal because "between men of equal rank [tra gli uguali di condizione], it will seem that the person who is offering is somehow making himself the superior of the one to whom he is offering it, and sometimes what is given may not be to the other's taste.... But ... you must not refuse what is offered to you for it will seem that you either despise or rebuke the man who is offering it to you" (D, 58; *Op.*, 436).

This distinction may readily be extended to the general strategy of gift-giving, for it reflects the problematic of that discourse picked out by Marcel Mauss when he argued that to be the donor is to be *magister* while to be the recipient is to be *minister*.[24] Since the bishop and count had been reintroduced in the preceding chapter (D, 54), I'm tempted to ask what kind of light it throws on their respective roles as the donor and donee of constructive criticism, but the question can't even be entertained until we decide which of the two alternatives mentioned above better describes their status relations: are Bishop Giberti and Count Ricciardo socially "uguali di condizione" and "di grado" or is the bishop "molto maggior di grado"? It so happens that these very questions have been considered by a commentator whose opinions are valuable for many reasons, not the least of which is that they were formulated less than a century after the publication of *Galateo*.

The commentator is Thomas Hobbes, and he has this to say in *Leviathan* (1651):

> To have received from one, to whom we think ourselves equal, greater benefits than there is hope to requite, disposeth to counterfeit love; but really secret hatred.... For benefits oblige, and obligation is thraldom; and unrequitable obligation perpetual thraldom; which is to one's equal, hateful. But to have received benefits from one, whom we acknowledge for superior,

inclines to love; because the obligation is no new depression: and cheerful acceptation, which men call *gratitude*, is such an honor done to the obliger, as is taken generally for retribution.[25]

Hobbes here seems to assume that hierarchy preconditions the different responses of equals and unequals, so that, from his perspective, our assessment of the count's response would depend on the way we answer the question whether or not the count and the bishop are social equals. Is the count's "cheerful acceptation" heartfelt or does it politely conceal "secret hatred"? If indeed they are social equals, then the bishop's generosity not only functions as a disequalizer but also adds insult to injury by soliciting the victim's gratitude for having been newly depressed.

Notice, however, that even in describing relations between unequals, Hobbes's language insinuates a doubt about the donee's cheerfulness. "Retribution" is a strong term for the gratitude that is the honor *done to* the obliger; it is a power word, and he uses it again in 1.15 in a punitive sense to denote justified revenge. Is the donee's repayment, his discharging of the debt, a form of requital? "The obligation is no new depression": the donee is already depressed, pressed down; this inferiority is what valorizes his gratitude; he isn't expected to make a more substantial repayment; the donation reaffirms his need and inferiority, as does the honor his cheerful acceptation pays the donor. Perhaps, then, generosity is the donor's safeguard, his insurance against potential challenges to his superiority by those he may suspect of aspiring to end their depression. Even when describing hierarchically stabilized exchanges, Hobbes's rhetoric reflects apprehensiveness about the reality behind displays of deference, acquiescence, gratitude, "love," and honor. In this connection we should note that the sense of objective hierarchy is slightly obscured by his emphasis on the cognitive basis of status discriminations: "we *think* ourselves equal," "we *acknowledge for* superior."

The potential source of anxiety was more clearly delineated in the preceding chapter of *Leviathan*, which Hobbes devoted to a discussion of honor:

The *value*, or WORTH of a man, is . . . his price; that is to say, so much as would be given for the use of his power: and therefore is not absolute; but a thing dependent on the need and judgment of another. . . . And as in other things, so in men, not the seller, but the buyer determines the price. For let a man, as most men do, rate themselves at the highest value they can; yet their true value is no more than it is esteemed by others. (1.10, 57)[26]

The restriction dramatically accentuated by the economic metaphor and driven home in the concluding sentence is that honor cannot be self-conferred. It is always in the gift of another, which suggests that honor-seekers are to honor-givers as donees are to donors, and that the discourse of honor is structurally identical with the discourse of the gift. From this premise it follows that in relations of dominance and deference between honor-seekers and honor-givers the directional flow of power and obligation will be similarly ambiguated. Thus although common sense dictates that the one who receives honor is thereby elevated over those who honor, the situation is not that simple.

The question raised by Hobbes's metaphor is whether the discourse of the market differs from that of the gift or is merely its demystified form. Are all honor-seekers compelled by the very nature of the discourse to "sell" themselves? As C. B. Macpherson suggests in his remarks on this passage, Hobbes treats "valuing and honoring" as functions of "a market in power."[27] If acts of bestowing honor have the force of "transfers of power" (ibid.), does it follow that at the beginning of every such act the potential recipient is powerless in his dependence on the "buyer's" esteem?—and is thus potentially subject to the kind of humiliation associated with emasculation or effeminization?

In an important respect the model of hierarchy implied by Hobbes's passage on honor differs from that implied by the passage on benefits or gifts. The passage on gifts adumbrates—and casts a shadow of doubt on—an order in which agents theoretically occupy fixed positions as superiors, equals, and inferiors; positions from which their privileges, obligations, and functions derive; positions that predetermine the possible types or range of their responses ("counterfeit love," "cheerful acceptation"). The passage on honor adumbrates an order in which agents alternate between reciprocal functions exemplified by buying and selling, and these functions predetermine—if only temporarily—positions, privileges, and obligations. In this order every transaction is a transfer of power that equalizes or disequalizes the positional relation of the participants.

These two models of order are *pars pro toto* versions of those conceptualized by Macpherson under the rubrics of "customary or status society" and "[possessive] market society," but, contrary to Macpherson's claim that Hobbes was "deliberately rejecting" the former, I submit that, at least in the passages quoted above, the two models are depicted as interacting in asymmetrical yet dialectical relation, with emergent market-society phenomena embedded in but disturbing the dominant status model.[28] The general coordinates of this engagement and its impact on concepts of honor are laid out more legibly by Julian Pitt-Rivers in an essay on the anthropology of honor. "Every political authority," he writes, "claims the right to bestow 'honors' and it follows that those whom it honors are, so it maintains, honorable. When this is accepted by the whole population then the problem of honor presents no quandary." And (I add) when the political authority happens to be aristocratic or hierarchic, the possession of and right to honor are naturalized as hereditary. "Honor felt becomes honor claimed and honor claimed becomes honor paid" in this, the noble's paradise of honor as grazia. But, Pitt-Rivers continues,

> in a complex society where consensus is not uniform . . . honor as a sentiment and mode of conduct becomes separated from honor as a qualification for the Honors List. The two conceptions might be placed at the poles between which common usage fluctuates: at one pole we might put the notion of honor derived from conduct in the sense in which "All is lost save honor," and at the other, the titles which are piled by the usurper upon the traitors who helped him to power. Adherence to the code of honor is thus opposed to the possession of honors.[29]

Pitt-Rivers's acerb example of honors as stolen titles may remind us that in its feudal incarnation the paradise of grazia was fortified, and that from the standpoint of disenchanted outsiders such an encastellated paradise was no more than a glorified and mystified—and successful—conspiracy.

Even when the poles are closer together and the split less radical, the fall from the paradisal *fortezza* of naturalized or hereditary honor puts honor-seekers at a disadvantage. They are exposed to the dialectic of the gift and dependent on whatever political authority can back its claim to "the right to bestow 'honors'"; the strategies by which the circuit between "honor felt" and "honor paid" is closed may themselves wound the sense of honor. What was taken for granted as a preexisting disposition in paradise is now open to negotiation and the conflict of interpretations and thus dependent on performance in the everyday theater or marketplace of public speech and gesture. Grazia gives way to sprezzatura. Dispossessed of the heraldic and hereditary honors preserved in and by the fortezza, the courtier sets out heroically to find and cultivate performative honor, to invest—and risk—his manhood in the fashioning of a work of art he is then forever doomed to defend against defacement.

This version of the fall from honors to honor is the story the *Cortegiano* tells and the *Galateo* in its own way repeats, and it is also Jacob Burckhardt's story of the emergence of "Renaissance man," who sallies forth into an Italy that had "become a school for scandal, the like of which the world cannot show"—sallies forth to join

> the crowd of suitable victims, that countless assembly of highly and characteristically developed human beings, celebrities of every kind, . . . all of whom . . . gave the fullest and freest play to their individuality[.] This host existed in the fifteenth and sixteenth centuries, and by its side the general culture of the time had educated a poisonous brood of impotent wits, of born critics and railers, whose envy called for hecatombs of victims; and to all this was added the envy of the famous men among themselves.[30]

Shifting from great things to small, from Burckhardt's melodramatic overview to the tiny moment of micro-scrutiny in Chapter 4 of *Galateo*, we find the costs of individualism woven into the finest textures of everyday public life and preserved *in parvo* in a cameo that is all the more compelling for being so modest:

> having carefully observed your manners and having examined them in detail, he has found none that was not extremely pleasant and commendable except for an unseemly motion you make with your lips and mouth at the dinner table, when your chewing makes a strange sound that is most unpleasant to hear. (D, 8, altered)

> *avendo egli attentamente risguardato alle vostre maniere ed essaminatole partita-mente [i.e., una ad una], niuna ne ha tra loro trovata che non sia sommamente piacevole e commendabile, fuori solamente un atto difforme che voi fate con le labbra e con la bocca masticando alla mensa con un nuovo strepito molto spiacevole ad udire.* (Op., 374)

During their excellent rehabilitation and critique of Burckhardt's individualism thesis, William Kerrigan and Gordon Braden stress and defend the harshness of his "vision of the culture of Renaissance individualism as a zero-sum game" but argue that his "general disregard of economics" weakens the thesis. In order to suggest how it could be clarified and strengthened by translation "into economic terms," they cite Hobbes's comment on honor, which I quoted and discussed above, as a counter-example that registers the pressure exerted by economic change on traditional social bonds: for Hobbes the "natural condition of mankind"

> in many ways resembles a Bourse more than a battlefield. . . . The market-place may be individualism's field of play, but it is simultaneously the corro-sion of any secure self-respect. . . . Hobbes's specific subject is social hierar-chy, the age's most visible standard of evaluation. Talk of buying and selling gains much of its disturbing power from the acute pressure that the new economy exerts on that structure.[31]

Even if talk of buying and selling is not literal—no, *especially* if it is not lit-eral, if it has already become figurative—its presence indicates a change in the forms of symbolic capital available for investment in everyday social ne-gotiations. This change is already remarked in *Galateo*:

> Everybody wishes to be respected even if he does not deserve it. . . . It is proper to accept . . . [people] readily not for what they are truly worth but rather, as with money, for their stated value. (D, 14)

> *Ciascuno appetisce di essere stimato ancora che egli no 'l vaglia. . . . [È] convenevol cosa lo esser presto di accetarli non pere quello che essi veramente vagliono, ma, come si fa delle monete, per quello che corrono.* (Op., 380–81)[32]

> [The traditional] virtues require greater resources, lacking which they amount to little or nothing, while this [i.e., manners] is rich and powerful without any such patrimony precisely because it consists solely of words and gestures. (My translation)

> *Le . . . virtù hanno mestiere di più arredi, i quali mancando, esse nulla o poco adoperano; dove questa senza altro patrimonio è ricca e possente, si come quella che consiste in parole e in atti solamente.* (Op., 369)

The rhetorical and symbolic currency of such figures doesn't by any means reflect the destabilization of traditional social categories, but it does resemble the preemptive response to an alien virus through inoculation or through the systemic production of antibodies. In this connection I partly agree and partly disagree with Kerrigan and Braden's assessment. Though they acknowledge the existence of "an extended crisis of the aristocracy" in the Renaissance, complete with the sale and inflation of honors, they are rightly skeptical of claims about the power of a "bourgeois-state alliance" and increased social mobility to destabilize or displace the nobility. They point to "the social conservatism" demonstrated, for example, by the acquisition of land "not as a capitalist investment but as a site for an aristocratic way of life" (46–47), and they conclude that despite economic and political pressures,

> the demilitarized aristocracy keeps a lock on the social imagination, and by the end of the Renaissance, even in England, the class has not withered but *simply* had its function and membership adjusted within the new political framework. . . . The result is thus *to some extent* a circular course that changes nothing. It does, nevertheless, manage to irradiate the lives even of the unsuccessful with a sense of possibility. Social dislocation, however temporary, is also metaphorical opportunity, permanently expanding the idiom of self-representation on all levels. (47–48; my italics)

I wish to question only Kerrigan and Braden's dismissive use of "simply" and the weight they place on the modifier "to some extent." For if the new political framework is not set in stone (and is, at any rate, distinctly plural), if class boundaries are perceived as permeable, and if the adjustment of the membership is an ongoing process that guarantees a constantly changing mélange of old and new nobility—aristocrats and oligarchs, mercantile barons and baronial merchants, along with assorted burghers and humanists—doesn't the inertia of the social imaginary do more than simply sustain traditional aristocracy as a category? Doesn't that very inertia conceal and, by concealing, sustain the continuous mutation of the category even while keeping it in place?[33] Believing this to be so, I'm inclined to redirect attention away from Kerrigan and Braden's emphasis on "a circular course that changes nothing" for the elite and offers a new "sense of possibility" only to the unsuccessful. At least in terms of the social context depicted by *Galateo*, it is useful to focus on the extent to which even the lives of the successful are irradiated by a sense of possibility—the possibility of distrust, suspicion, anxiety, and paranoia, a sense sharpened by the necessity of competition and performance, and by the threat of "metaphorical opportunity" in the relatively new marketplace of manners.

My point of departure for this general discussion was the question I raised about the representation of social relations in the episode featuring Bishop Giberti and Count Ricciardo. Motivated by Elias's casual assumption that the bishop was socially superior to the count, I addressed the problem of determining how their relative status affects the way we assess the damage done by the act of donation the bishop mediates through Messer Galateo and inflicts on the count. The terms of the problem were set by the distinction the *Galateo* narrator and Hobbes agree on when they observe that the effects of gift-giving on recipients are more disconcerting for equals than for unequals. In trying to resolve the question, I drew on the idea that among individuals at various levels of the ranks that count as aristocratic the strategies and interactions we categorize as manners retain their social form even as they are modified by the force of competitive market strategies and interactions. Precisely because the latter are not conceived in fully or merely economic terms, they work simultaneously to restabilize the hierarchic model and to destabilize—to render more tentative and temporary—any aristocrat's position relative to any other, and relative to the nonaristocrats swarming up the walls of the fortezza.

The transfers of power that characterize this more labile model of interaction are concisely described by the *Galateo* narrator when he observes that "between men of equal rank it will seem that the person who is offering somehow makes himself the superior of the one to whom he is offering" (D, 58). We can install this as the basic principle of the apprehensive society of manners by hypothesizing that every social interaction involving a transfer of power starts on a level playing field. Returning at last to Bishop Giberti and Count Ricciardo with this principle in hand, I postulate that they are socially "uguali di condizione" and "di grado." Granted that the bishop's role as the count's host gives him a *potential* social advantage, the *Galateo*'s obsession with manners as an art of one-upmanship suggests that it isn't until he has seized the occasion—has ferreted out the "picciolo difetto" and sent Messer Galateo to inflict his parting "gift" on the count—that the bishop actualizes this potentiality and asserts social superiority. The episode depicts the volatile, improvisatory, and finely grained quality of the practices by which the members of a loosely defined peer group engage in continuous small-scale competitive maneuvers for social advantage in their efforts to protect or justify or secure a status, an identity, rendered uncertain by a changing sociopolitical order. This is not the green world of the aristocrat's domus placed high above the city and fenced in by its mythological paling of grazia. Grazia as noble birth has become an actor's passport, entitling him to mount the stage of courtly self-presentation and execute those maneuvers, the maneuvers Castiglione's interlocutors associate with the performance of sprezzatura.

As Elias observes, descriptions and proscriptions of disgusting behavior at table constitute the medieval residue in otherwise forward-looking treatises of the sixteenth century. And as I noted earlier, only three of the *Galateo's* thirty chapters deal with table manners. So it is all the more significant that Messer Galateo's sole appearance occurs in one of them, and that the episode he participates in dramatically reinforces the novelty Elias picks out: in making an example of a noble personage of high political rank, it "de-medievalizes" a residual scenario. For the anecdote of Count Ricciardo shifts the emphasis from the context of grazia to that of sprezzatura, which—as we've seen in this chapter—is a shift from pedagogy to surveillance, from the admonitory project of forestalling bad manners to the voyeuristic project of seeking them out. Having done this, the anecdote redirects attention from the ounce of pedagogical prevention characteristic of medieval precepts to the pound of "cure" that—under the pretense of "healing" the count and saving him from future embarrassment—further weighs him down when Messer Galateo makes him suffer the humiliating wound of gratitude for the bishop's "polite, extremely gentle, and . . . considerate" gift of reproach. Through his suave deployment of such mannerly tactics and of Messer Galateo's skill as a factor, the bishop makes himself, for the time being, the social superior of the count. The book that represents and disseminates this model of manners, the book solicited by and celebrating Galateo, is less a code of precepts than a technology of aggressive and self-protective practices, a Hobbesian war of every peer against every peer. Yet although the figure Galateo nominally celebrates plays a central part in this warfare as the bishop's factor or weapon, he is oddly underdescribed. The narrative presents nothing but the beautifully *sprezzata* surface of an older courtier, a statuesque figure about whose inwardness nothing is directly disclosed, a parody of the embodiment of sprezzatura, *il cortegiano perfetto*, constructed by Castiglione's interlocutors.

Della Casa's representations of the Hobbesian war and of the figure of Galateo not only were preceded by but also respond to Castiglione's *Courtier*. Thus during the remainder of this study the pathway to an understanding of that response will take us to and through the *Courtier*: two chapters on the discourse of gender in the latter (Part Two) are followed in Part Three by chapters that take up the question of narratorial authority and reliability in each work. But before proceeding to interpretation and moving beyond the history of manners identified with the work of Norbert Elias—and by way of making a transition—I want to conclude with a glance at a serious flaw in Elias's treatment of courtesy books.

It's clear from the foregoing discussion that my debt to Elias's landmark study is considerable, even though it has been mediated through the corrective critiques of more recent scholarship. Indeed, those critiques increase rather than diminish the value of *The History of Manners* and ensure its durability. Yet the critiques I have consulted tend to ignore the weakness I just alluded to. Elias's account of the civilizing process is based on a practice of reading that simplistically smooths out the unilinear pattern of change. Although it allows for conflict or oscillation between the residual and emergent aspects of a text, it leaves no place for the possibility of internal resistance to the text's dominant message. Elias's method is to cite and then comment on a chronological set of examples repeatedly called upon to testify to different aspects of the change in question. *Galateo* and Erasmus's *De civilitate morum puerilium* are his major sixteenth-century exhibits. Because the *Courtier* is much more than a conduct book and much less given to behavioral proscriptions, it (or its author) is mentioned only twice in passing, as an example of the general trend toward increased exposure of individuals "to the pressure of others and of social control" (*Manners*, 79–80). *Galateo* is an important member of the set because it contains passages that proscribe nose-blowing and other public exhibitions of bodily effluvia, and that are harbingers of an emergent—that is, postmedieval—anxiety about social boundary maintenance. Elias reduces each text in his series to a collection of examples symptomatic of changes in attitude and identifiable as the opinions of the time mediated through the author. The *Galateo*'s opinions are thus ascribed to della Casa as a reflector of his era.

The reason I belabor this point is that the method of quotation and commentary renders conspicuous both an odd feature of the former and the commentator's failure to notice it: Elias passes over in silence the fact that in *Galateo* the *pro*scriptions are also *de*scriptions that dwell on and rhetorically embroider what they proscribe. Disgusting things, the narrator insists at the beginning of Chapter 3, should never even be mentioned, whereupon—in a kind of perverse *praeteritio*—he spends the rest of the chapter describing unmentionable acts. If one conflates the narrator with the author, who in turn is reducible to the opinions of his era, it's hard to know what to do with the strange message this procedure conveys, namely, that this narrator, or author, or era, has a dirty mind. Elias's reductive treatment of *Galateo* and his nontreatment of the *Courtier* thus make it imperative to supplement his reading of new developments in early modern conduct with a more firmly based textual and intertextual reading of the conduct books that supply his evidence.

Two LOSING CONTROL

The Woman
Question in
The Book of
the Courtier

4.　A Perfect Gentleman: Performing Gynephobia in Urbino

My aim in Part Two is to pick out and try to defamiliarize Castiglione's treatment of a theme that is central to his book and has recently come in for a lot of attention, especially from feminist critics: the *Cortegiano*'s representation of the system and discourse of sex and gender. Their work has made it clear that although boundaries between social classes seem more permeable than boundaries between the sexes, changes in the first are intimately associated with changes in the second. And indeed, problems of gender construction and differentiation receive more emphasis in the *Cortegiano* than problems of social construction and differentiation. This is interesting if only because it reveals the fundamental reliance of the male courtier's self-definition on gender contrast and relations with women.[1]

Sprezzatura was discussed in the preceding chapters as a skill that made its practitioners aware of the importance of art in producing effects of nature. In this chapter I shift to a related question—how far does the awareness that art produces nature penetrate the veil of naturalization thrown over sex and gender?—and I take my lead from Judith Butler's argument that the "regulatory fiction of heterosexual coherence" gets defictionalized in the rule-governed repetition of performances of gender: "the various acts of gender create the idea of gender, and without those acts, there would be no gender at all." Butler emphasizes the importance of "doing gender right."[2] But so also does the *Cortegiano* in its representations of the sex/gender performances that generate the contrastive and interdependent identities of the male and female courtly subjects.

Commenting on Divine, the "hero/heroine" of *Hairspray* and other films by John Waters, Butler finds in his/her impersonations of women the implicit suggestion that

gender is a kind of persistent impersonation that passes as the real. Her/
his performance destabilizes the very distinctions between the natural and
the artificial, depth and surface, inner and outer through which discourse
about genders almost always operates. Is drag the imitation of gender, or
does it dramatize the signifying gestures through which gender itself is
established? Does being female constitute a "natural fact" or a cultural performance, or is "naturalness" constituted through discursively constrained
performative acts that produce the body through and within the categories
of sex? (x)

Courtly practices of self-fashioning and self-representation destabilize precisely the distinctions listed by Butler, and the question is whether this effect
is discernible not only in the courtiers' general discourse about the performance of courtly behavior by males in Books 1 and 2 but also in the discussions of gender relations and sex behaviors that are concentrated in the
third book but occur sporadically throughout the whole *Cortegiano*. "Like
sexuality, we might . . . say," writes Teresa de Lauretis, "gender is not a property of bodies or something originally existent in human beings, but 'the set
of effects produced in bodies, behaviors, and social relations' . . . by the deployment of 'a complex political technology.' "[3] Would it be possible to find
in the *Cortegiano* a hint of assent to—or even a glimmer of awareness of—
this proposition? Awareness, that is, of the idea that the body becomes *engendered*, is made to represent gender, through the agency of "social technologies, . . . institutionalized discourses, epistemologies, and critical practices, as
well as practices of daily life" (2)? Awareness of the idea that gender is neither
reducible to nor the product of sexual difference, but is rather a regulatory
fiction—for example, the patriarchal or heterosexual social contract—that
invests or occupies the body and the mind, inducing differential norms of
sexual behavior on the former and differential sexual attitudes on the latter?
    Ann Rosalind Jones, among other feminist scholars who write about the
factors that led to "rapid and contested social change" in the early modern
period—"centralized courts, increased nationalism, and the rise of merchant
and professional classes in the cities"—focuses on the corresponding differentiation in subject positions: "As new class identities were constructed, ideals
of feminine virtue proliferated and women became the objects of constant
scrutiny."[4] What Joan Kelly calls "the Renaissance of chastity" that attended
these changes was also a renaissance of the representation of chastity, and it
brought with it a renaissance of suspicion toward women, and of the representation of suspicion.[5] To place the accent on representation is to place it

on the discourse networks that infiltrate and modify perception even as they uphold its transcendence by marking it as prediscursive. If something more than meets the eye always meets the eye when men see women and women give themselves to be seen, this something more—call it the gaze—historicizes perception because what the discourses register and transmit are social, political, economic, and cultural changes.[6]

Since to historicize perception and its objects is to allegorize them, no perceptions of women, their properties (e.g., chastity), and their effects (e.g., suspicion) are strictly empirical; all are allegories of woman and of the variable subcategories that parcel out her functions (and their personifications) in patriarchy. Consider, for example, the following propositions cited from Lisa Jardine's chapter titled "Wealth, Inheritance, and the Specter of Strong Women."[7] Though Jardine concentrates on the situation in late sixteenth- and seventeenth-century England, the changes and contradictions she explores are more broadly applicable to early modern Europe:

> There was an area of early modern society in which apparently, although not actually, women had become frighteningly strong and independent. . . . This was the area of inheritance of property, and Land Law. (77–78)

> *Family*, particularly for the nobly born, means first and foremost in the sixteenth and seventeenth centuries the continuing kinship relations down the generations, within which the individual family group played an extremely small part. Where the demands of the two clashed it would almost inevitably be the case (the more so the more powerful and wealthy the line) that the requirements of lineage and inheritance overrode those of personal love and affection. (83)

> It is . . . a built-in feature of the European inheritance system that women are potentially powerful, albeit within a basically patrilinear system—they intrude and intervene where necessary to amend the simple law of male inheritance. (84–85)

> Not that this gives individual women power over their lives; and this is really the point at issue. They are technically strong (strong enough to have some "economic leverage," and to cause patriarchal anxiety), but actually they remain in thrall. (88)

> Female sexuality regularly represents woman's uncontrollable interference with inheritance. . . . (92)

With growing frequency in the early modern period the faintest possibility of female effectiveness spills over into outright horror and abuse of "monstrous" womanhood.... (93)

So-called irrational responses of this sort are irrational only in empirical terms; they are fully motivated by the allegorical conditions of discourse that transform perceptions into personifications. Between "the faintest possibility" and the "outright horror" falls the shadow of male fantasy engendered by a shift in discourse networks that alienates more patriarchal power to marriageable virgins and to mothers. To alienate power in this way is to preserve and amplify it but also to risk losing unconditional control over it, and thus to build male anxiety and suspicion into the discourse of inheritance. These appear in "more vehement" expressions of the "patriarchal desire to 'keep women in their place'" through a barrage of "educational treatises, pamphlets on manners, spiritual tracts, sermons and literature" that promote "the ideology of modesty and dutiful submissiveness" and "conspire to try to turn the wishful thinking of the male community into a propaganda reality" (Jardine, 62, 87).

Jardine's account of the discursive framework outlined in her six propositions makes it clear why her answer to the question "Did women have a Renaissance?" is both yes and no, with the "yes" not only registering the increased "effectiveness of women as operators within the economic system" (87) but also expressing the patriarchal fear or premonition that motivates efforts to keep women from having a Renaissance. Incompatible and contradictory representations of woman are to be expected so long as something more than meets the eye always meets the eye, so long as perceptual presentations are overdetermined by discursive representations, which are the allegories of woman precipitated out of the pressures of institutional change. The change that most concerns feminists and others writing about women in early modern culture involves a familiar paradigm shift, a reorganization of the discourse networks that alters the status of representations. What was formerly implicit and prediscursive is exposed to critical scrutiny that makes it explicit and discursive, and this is a shift in which books like the *Cortegiano* are deeply implicated. Jones observes:

Conduct books as a genre in this period illustrate an uneasy confrontation between long-standing official discourses and new social practices.... These discourses represented female character and status as fixed—eternal givens founded on nature, Scripture, and precedent. Conduct books appear to be based on a different assumption: men and women can be *produced*. They are malleable, capable of being trained for changing roles; proper instruction can fashion them into successful participants in new social settings. . . .[8]

But if they are malleable, they can be mobile, and if others can fashion them, they can fashion themselves. If woman's body is the index of woman's soul, is her sex the index of her gender? To what extent do "the new debates over women's nature" produce awareness "that femininity is a constantly changing construction, open to debate and revision" (ibid., 41, 63)? It is easy enough for us today to penetrate the prediscursive veil of naturalization thrown over sex and gender, and speak of effects of nature produced in bodies by political and social technologies and institutionalized discourses. Recent scholarship has shown how women from Christine de Pizan on engaged in protofeminist critiques that began to lift the veil. But what evidence have we for attributing an equally disenchanted sense of those effects to early modern male writers, and specifically to Castiglione?

Speculating on the possibility of a deconstructive act that could "de-literalize or re-figure the figure 'man'" in order to unveil "its violent rhetorical origins," Marguerite Waller goes on to address the issue of how

> the category "man," when it is de-figured, interpreted as literal, comes to operate linguistically in ways that compel gender discrimination. I could point out that "man," seen as working beyond rhetorical determinations, compels the subordination of the category "woman." Woman appears as the dangerous, supplemental, figural term; man as the stable, literal one. She becomes a secondary deprivileged entity, an object to be investigated; man the primary term, the subject who performs the investigation. She can be seen only in her relation to men, while men are seen as transcending such networks of relations.[9]

What Waller calls "investigation" is intensified to "surveillance" whenever the compulsion to subordinate shifts from the linguistic to the social register in response to renewed senses—motivated by changes and conflicts in class structure—of the dangerousness of the supplement. In the reading that follows I shall put the following question to the discourse of gender in the *Cortegiano*: Does it tacitly affirm and participate in the operations Waller describes, identifying its position with that of the investigative subject, or does it manage to detach itself from that position so as to include the male subject in its investigative scope?

Sprezzatura, the expression of artfulness as a conveyor of artlessness, contributes to a differential technology of behavior that produces class membership along with the ability to represent or perform specific class "natures." The gift of dissimulation is displayed as the badge of aristocracy; the natural artistry of the artful imitation of nature is the property of a proper-tied class. But as historians have often noted, the courtier's dependent political status results in peculiar social demands that call for the redefinition of norms of masculinity. The explicit if informal pedagogy enabling a man to perform as a courtier must also enable a courtier to perform as a man. Thus, linked to the idea of a performable and class-specific nature is the idea of a performable and class-specific gender. And since gender is a dialectical concept, redefining masculinity entails redefining femininity:

> Defenses of the new man in early modern Europe, whether he was a city merchant, a courtier, a member of the gentry, or a Protestant paterfamilias, required a female partner to affirm the self-representation of the rising group. . . . To imagine a woman as a carrier of class values and to *produce* her through family training, educational practices, and social rituals was to demonstrate to society at large the control the men of a particular social group had over their daughters and wives, a control often contrasted to the negligence or impotence attributed to fathers and husbands elsewhere in the social hierarchy. . . . Idealized depictions of life in the ducal palace required the presence of the court lady, trained in the witty repartee through which she elicited polished speech from the male courtier.[10]

Jones's emphasis in *The Currency of Eros* is on the strategies of negotiation by which women poets positioned themselves as "co-performers with the male poets they cite, revise, and challenge" (3). Hence her comments on defenses of women written by men are relatively brief, and she approaches the *Cortegiano* primarily as a text that registers the ideological pressure imposed on women, "the tension presumed to exist between women's talk and their chastity. . . . However carefully this link between access to women's talk and access to their bodies is repressed in courtly discourse, it remains under the surface to trouble Castiglione's idealizing group portrait" (16–17).[11] Sixteenth-century courtesy books written by men reveal lack of confidence "in women's ability to withstand the temptations of court life," or to participate with

assurance and grazia in what Castiglione represents as "a carefully choreo-
graphed dialogue between appreciative women and the men whose accomplishments they mirror back to them" (15–16). They must therefore protect
themselves by cultivating sprezzatura: to help the court lady perform the difficult task of balancing "the contradictory elements of courtly femininity . . .
a complex system of checks and balances is required in her speech" (17).

To survey works by men who "wrote to propose masculine models for
womanly behavior" (20) is a necessary first step in Jones's analysis of gender
ideologies as forces that "shape subjectivities and determine behavior" (1).
The analysis is aimed at elucidating the negotiatory strategies of early modern women writers who targeted those models and ideologies and who
may, in varying degrees, have anticipated aspects of the feminist critique. But
in order to redirect such an analysis to the male-authored texts that proposed the models, and to the question of their relation to the feminist critique, we would have to shift our attention from the pressure on women to
the pressure on men.

At one point Jones suggests that the "deep anxiety" she finds in the
courtly advice books typified by the *Cortegiano* afflicts the men responsible
for women's advancement and reputation (16). What about the male anxiety
that responds not to women's possible failure "to withstand the temptations
of court life" but to their potential success in capitalizing on those temptations, their success in using and controlling sexuality as an instrument of
courtly power? Does the *Cortegiano* reveal lack of confidence in men's ability to withstand the temptations of women, or to impose on them models of
womanly behavior that will reflect and reinforce masculine self-representation? Does it reveal traces of another anxiety? Suppose men succeed in im-
posing those models, and women as a result become expert in the virtuous
conduct of sexual speech and behavior; men would thereby extend and ensure their power to fashion women; but wouldn't they at the same time
alienate and lose control of that power to the subjects, the secret agents, they
have hidden behind or within the women they fashion?

Such worries are standard fare in the discursive expressions of male fantasy. The question is whether in any particular case the text in which readers discern the anxiety represents itself as for or against the fantasy it ve-
hiculates. If, for example, they detect the anxiety in the discussions of the
Cortegiano, their problem is to decide whether it is because the text their
reading constructs (sometimes called "Castiglione") interprets itself to them
as sharing the commitments of the discussants or because it appears to target them—to put them on display in the manner of those texts Althusser

describes as giving us "a 'view' of the ideology to which their work alludes and with which it is constantly fed, a view that presupposes a *retreat*, an *internal distantiation* from . . . the very ideology in which they are held."[12]

Questions of this sort are met head on by studies of the early modern debate about woman that center on male-authored texts. Thus Linda Woodbridge concentrates on determining the extent to which proto-feminist tendencies may be detected in the literary genre she calls "the formal controversy about women," and in which she includes Book 3 of the *Cortegiano*. She defines this genre as "largely a literary game, with very tenuous roots in real contemporary attitudes," and in this respect different from the more complex and historically grounded "transvestite controversy."[13] Though the formal controversy relied heavily on the dialogue form and often created "the illusion of real debate," Woodbridge argues that "as feminism its debate was a sham" and that the very illusion of debate "prevented serious questioning" (14, 134). The reason is that both misogynistic attacks and profeminist defenses defined female goodness and badness the same way, and both aimed to enforce the same mode of behavior.[14] Beneath their apparent disagreement they "were complementary efforts at keeping women housebound, nurturing, chaste, modest, and silent."[15]

This framework enables Woodbridge to reach carefully measured and relatively severe judgments about the "feminist tendencies" of early humanists, among whom she gives highest marks to Castiglione and Cornelius Agrippa because they came closer than the others "to embracing beliefs fundamental to modern feminism" (16, 58). Her explanation of Castiglione's success is ingenious. Of Giuliano de' Medici, the house profeminist in Book 3, she states that "even though (feministically speaking) he gets off to a shaky start," his performance improves, and at certain points he delivers himself of opinions on the basis of which "a feminist movement can be built"—for example, that antifeminist humor is no joking matter, that women are capable of military and political rule, "that God is not necessarily male," and that woman's inferiority is an effect not of nature but of male tyranny (53–57).[16] Two of these opinions, the first and the last, she attributes at different times to both Giuliano and Castiglione, from which I infer that she considers the former the latter's mouthpiece, and that if Giuliano is at times "a dubious champion" of women's rights (55), then so is Castiglione.[17] What makes the *Cortegiano* a superior proto-feminist document is that the author emphasizes the dialogical and inconclusive character of the debate, and thus "casts doubt on the efficacy of the formal controversy as a mode of improving the status of women" (58).

The compelling feature of Woodbridge's interpretation is her claim that the book achieves its success by contrary means: on the one hand it is feminist because it contains feminist opinions, but on the other hand it is feminist because, regardless of those opinions, it insists on the obstacles its own generic form places in the way of its genuine contribution to a feminist agenda, for Book 3 creates "the illusion of real debate" only to deconstruct it. The value of this account is that it sharply demarcates the perimeter within which we may explore the conflict between ideological pronouncements and strategies of internal distantiation. Its weakness is that the attribution of Giuliano's opinions to the author, and the suggestion that his performance as a profeminist advocate improves after his shaky start, won't stand up to close reading. We'll see that even the opinions Woodbridge praises for their advanced profeminist tendencies are hollowed out by antifeminist anxieties, so that unless one can show that Giuliano is not represented as a reliable mouthpiece, his failure to mount an adequate defense of woman becomes—"feministically speaking"—a failure of the text, making it difficult to sustain Woodbridge's thesis that the *Cortegiano* is a politically correct book. But the profeminist's unreliability can be demonstrated. The text consistently flags unarticulated motives that betray his uneasy machismo, his fear of losing control of both woman and his argument, his desire to use the defense *of* woman as a means to strengthen the homosocial bonds that unite the male attackers and defenders in what turns out to be a defense *against* woman. Especially in this last respect, the *Cortegiano* anticipates Woodbridge's general insight that attackers and defenders are antifeminist confederates—and not only anticipates the insight, but targets it.

What I referred to above as "unarticulated motives" escapes the specific interpretive net that Woodbridge weaves solely in terms of the concept of *misogyny*. This restriction reflects a tendency in the critical literature to use the term "misogyny" to denote the whole antifeminist position rather than merely the hostility, contempt, and dismissal expressed in conventional denigrations of woman. Yet it isn't hard to show that antifeminist discourse has a divided structure of which misogyny is but one side, and, in my opinion, the less important side for interpretive purposes. The failure to acknowledge or even label the other motive makes it more difficult to keep the dialectical structure of antifeminism consistently in view. Misogyny may be no more than the reaction to or surface manifestation of a deeper anxiety, *gynephobia*.[18] There is a gynephobia of gender and a gynephobia of sex: the former is fear of effeminization, fear of the woman within the man, and the latter is fear of impotence, emasculation, or infantilization, fear of the women outside the man; the former is fear of a threat to man's possession of the power sig-nified by the phallus, the latter is fear of a threat to man's possession of the power signified by the penis; the former is a fear of having one's status re-duced *to* that of woman but not necessarily *by women*; the latter is specifically a fear of having one's status reduced or usurped *by women*. To be unmanned by "the system"; to be politically or socially unmanned by other males or by women in positions of power or authority; to be sexually unmanned by women's insatiability, infidelity, and promiscuity: these "sources" of gyne-phobia may interact or signify each other, but they are both analytically and empirically distinct, and their conjunction in any particular case must be demonstrated.[19]

The more interesting and persuasive line of approach to the *Cortegiano*'s relation to feminist discourse has been developed by critics who take gyne-phobia into account. Joan Kelly touched briefly on it in 1977 when, in her negative response to the titular question, "Did Women Have a Renais-sance?" she associated the courtier's domination of the court lady with his subjection to the prince, noting that Castiglione "had to defend against ef-feminacy in the courtier," whose dependency on and behavior toward the prince was like that of a woman.[20] In 1978 Wayne Rebhorn also mentioned Castiglione's nervousness "about potential attacks on the courtly ideal for being too effeminate" and argued that these attacks were "reflected in the misogynistic criticisms of Ottaviano Fregoso and Gasparo Pallavicino in Books III and IV."[21] He goes on to analyze the motives behind misogyny. On the one hand, its proponents follow the conventional line: "women are the irrational daughters of Eve; they are led by passion, appetite, and their bodily needs; they have less strength, courage, and virtue than man." But on the other hand, the "hostility to women is motivated less by a confidence in the male's continuing supremacy than by a desperate urgency to fight what seems a losing battle" on two fronts. The first is the inversion of hierarchy at Urbino, where, because the court is ruled by women, the misogynists, ac-cording to Rebhorn, "clearly feel frustration and resentment" as they seek unsuccessfully "to destroy the thrones from which Emilia Pia and the duchess rule over them." The second front is the battle against woman's sexuality, fear of which is most dramatically expressed in Gasparo's diatribe near the end of Book 3: "In Gasparo's imagination women become demonic, vampire-like creatures who suck the life out of their victims without killing them"; his outburst "reveals most strikingly the sexual fear of emasculation that lies behind his, and perhaps the others', hostility toward women" (127–28).[22]

Rebhorn, like Woodbridge, follows standard practice in using the term "misogyny" to denote the whole antifeminist position rather than merely the hostility, contempt, and dismissal expressed in the conventional denigration. Nevertheless, finer distinctions are implicit in his narrative: when he claims that the courtiers feel powerless in a court ruled by women, he refers to the gynephobia of gender, whereas the other fear he mentions obviously illustrates the gynephobia of sex. Though I shall argue that his account of the courtiers' reaction to women's rule is somewhat overstated, I think his effort to articulate the structure of antifeminism makes it easier to identify the textual moves by which the *Cortegiano* internally distances itself from the profeminism it appears to espouse.

To be sure, Rebhorn doesn't explicitly take such moves into account: "Castiglione clearly sides with the Magnifico and Cesare Gonzaga in their defense of women," and if the author occasionally supports the misogynists and takes their attacks seriously, it is to communicate his "seeming nervousness" about "the inversion of traditional social roles at the court of Urbino" (126–27). It remained for Constance Jordan to show how Castiglione conducts a "subtle critique of the Magnifico's project" by displaying its gynephobic motivation. In *Renaissance Feminism*, Jordan expands Kelly's insight into the social causes of the gynephobia of gender and combines it with the woman-on-top thesis formulated by Rebhorn, but departs from Rebhorn in ascribing inversion anxiety to the house profeminist:

> The ideal courtier of the first two books has been depicted as without authority of his own and effectively powerless. His status vis-à-vis his lord is similar to that of a wife in relation to her husband; it is mirrored in the observations of Castiglione's own courtiers concerning the life they lead. Their concerns and activities, focused on providing their superiors with pleasure and diversion rather than protection or counsel, might be characterized as effeminate. Their immediate situation is complicated because they are directed by the duchess, aided by Emilia Pia, whom from time to time she deputizes (as she has been deputized) to act in her place. The conversations . . . are devoted largely to arguments that serve to console Urbino's male courtiers for the degree to which they are subjected to the women of the court. . . . The Magnifico's ideal court lady, who is so clearly inferior and subordinate to the ideal courtier, is both a repudiation of his subservience to the figure of the *domina*, embodied for the moment in the duchess and Emilia Pia, and a protection against it. That the Magnifico seeks to substan-

tiate the worth of women generally, and thus of the relatively weak figure of his ideal lady specifically, by accounts of the relatively strong figures of legendary and historical queens underscores his vulnerability. (77–78)

The importance of the kind of approach illustrated by Jordan's brief account, by Rebhorn's book, by the contributors to Robert Hanning and David Rosand's anthology,[23] and by a few other studies may be indicated by noting how easy it was for earlier critics to accuse Castiglione of being unable to sustain serious humanist objectives because of his unfortunate preference for an artificial, frivolous, and unmanly courtly ideology.[24] This preference has been attributed to the dilemma posed for him by the political instability and crisis of leadership in the Italy of the first three decades of the sixteenth century. Castiglione, as one critic of this persuasion writes, was unable "to look coldly at the Italian ruling classes in their time of failure and disaster," and either did not see or could not accept the consequences, choosing instead to leave politics behind and take "the way of evasion and unreality." A "committed member of the ruling establishment, he shares its myopia," and as a result "seems unable to draw example, guidance, or instruction from his own rich political experience," producing instead an image of the courtier "consumed in moral and even aesthetic considerations."[25]

One obvious response to this line of criticism is to acknowledge the aesthetico-moral orientation and to make a virtue of it by framing it in terms of the history of self-fashioning, and to stress the modernity of the idea of "the self as a work of art." But this is a kind of halfway house that leaves the political critique standing in the background. The achievement of Rebhorn, Daniel Javitch, Dain Trafton, and others writing in the 1970s was to demonstrate that Castiglione anticipated the criticism, and that one could detect ambivalence in his portrait of Urbino. They don't deny that his attachment to and admiration for the court he belonged to and wrote about shines forth on every page of the book. But they also find in the text signs of the perspective of the detached observer who *had* looked coldly at the ruling classes and, far from sharing their myopia, showed himself troubled by it.

This shift is of course a paradigmatic move in literary interpretation: arguing that what was previously taken as the author's participation in his subject could be demonstrated by more careful reading to be a critique of the subject. It is a move for which, obviously, I have a lot of affection and admiration. But the question that remains is whether the shift from the participation view to the critique view of Castiglione's portrait may be extended from his representation of courtiership to his representation of profeminist discourse. The work of Kelly, Rebhorn, and Jordan shows us how to make the connection. So, for example, many of the topics discussed in Books 1 and 2 support the view implied in the passage by Jordan cited above, the view that Castiglione recognized the dependency and powerlessness of the courtier class, and symbolized its "effeminacy" by showing that Urbino's courtiers chafe under women's rule. The courtiers' own anxious awareness of the problems of dependency is evident in several of the themes they directly or indirectly bring up: the apprehensiveness implicit in the accent on the defensive functions of sprezzatura (2.6–13); the dangers and dilemmas of service to princes (2.18–25, 32); the continuous threat to both the aesthetic and political autonomy of Italian court life posed by the foreign invaders (2.26, 37), and the interpolation of this concern into the discussion of proper dress (2.26–28)—as Lisa Jardine suggests, "the elaborate decorativeness of all court dress, manners and behavior" in this period "is a signal of role loss," a mark of the courtier's "growing political impotence" and "increasingly parasitic" function in governments that rely more on "financial and political acumen or professional training."[26] Jordan calls this impotence effeminacy because the courtier's status is reduced *to* that of *woman*. But that isn't the same as having one's status reduced or usurped *by women*. Therefore the second part of Jordan's statement doesn't necessarily or logically follow from the first. Does the *Cortegiano* provide evidence that the members of "this faintly effete community" need to be consoled for their subjection to the duchess and Emilia, or that they take steps to repudiate and protect against their subservience?[27]

Several features of Castiglione's presentation militate against the Rebhorn/ Jordan emphasis on gynephobic responses to the inversion of hierarchy in the court of Urbino. First, the figure of the prince discussed in the first two books is unequivocally male; it is a *dominus*, not a *domina*, who is the structural source or focus of the courtier's "effeminacy." Related to this is the sharply circumscribed position of the duchess as a placeholder ("locotenente") for her ailing husband. Would it compound or exaggerate the courtier's problem hinted at in Books 1 and 2 to have to tender service to the lord's wife? Jordan interestingly explores this dilemma, noting first that the conversation in Book 3 is in part "compensatory, guaranteeing the effeminate courtier a part of his masculinity by reserving for him at least some power—over women," and going on to observe that Castiglione's praise of the court "is equivocated by dramatic revelations of anxiety, on the part both of his courtiers, who resist the rule of women, and of the author himself, who depicts with brilliant accuracy the means by which male subordinates gain and retain control over their female superiors."[28]

My resistance to this argument is both theoretical and interpretive. Theoretically, I think a profound insight into the critique of structural contradictions in profeminist discourse is dissipated when the contradictions are attributed to a specific dramatic mise-en-scène—the court of Urbino—as the motivational ground of the courtiers' discursive performances. This approach inflates the speakers to the status of characters, psychological agents whose discourse can be explained in circumstantial or dramatic terms. It thus shifts attention from discursive to subjective agency, and from the psychology *in* discourse to the psychology *of* subjects. I prefer an approach that flips these premises and posits as the primary target of critique the contradictions inhering in unlocalized male profeminist discourse per se—inhering in the logic determined partly by the gendered source of enunciation and partly by the abstract social, political, and economic parameters of culture change. This approach would relegate Castiglione's picture of the court of Urbino to the status of an effect of the discourse, a response to its contradictions, a medium in which they can be embodied and made perspicuous.

As to interpretation, it is made clear at the very outset that the potentially sensitive area of negotiation between the courtiers and the women on top is not going to be the question of authority so much as the question of sexuality. In 1.6, when Emilia proposes the game of the evening and asks Gasparo to begin, he immediately tests her authority by retorting that she should start, and he is immediately put down by Emilia and the duchess. He grumbles back at them, wondering why "women are always permitted such exemption from labor," but goes on like a good sport to propose his game: "let each one say which virtue above all others he would wish the one he loves to be adorned with" and "let him say also which fault he would desire in the beloved: so that we may see who can think of the most praiseworthy and useful virtues and of the faults which are the most excusable and least harmful either to the lover or to the beloved" (1.7; S, 19). Richard Higgins notes that Gasparo's criterion of the "ideal fault"—its "being 'excusable' and 'least harmful' "—"reveals both a fear of these faults and an attempt to bring them into discourse and neutralize them as harmless." Higgins associates this passage with "Gasparo's demonization of women at the end of Book 3," and with his fear of the desire that makes men vulnerable to women.[29] Thus a superficial and playful challenge to authority quickly gives way to a generalized and rhetorically more covert allusion to sexual politics and erotic anxiety.

When Gasparo concludes and Emilia signals to one of the court ladies to speak next, the duchess returns to his opening complaint and finishes him off under the pretext of a mild reprimand to Emilia: "Since signora Emilia does not choose to go to the trouble of devising a game, it would be quite right for the other ladies to share in this ease, and thus be exempt from such a burden this evening, especially since there are so many men here that we risk no lack of games" (1.7; S, 19–20). The duchess thus positions the women as audience rather than participants. Yet this means not only that men will do all the talking but also that women—regardless of their deputed author-ity—will discharge the ancillary function Cesare Gonzaga would describe early in Book 3: "just as no court, however great, can have adornment or splendor or gaiety in it without ladies, neither can any Courtier be graceful or pleasing or brave, or do any gallant deed of chivalry, unless he is moved by the society and by the love and charm of ladies: even discussion about the Courtier is always imperfect unless ladies take part in it and add their part of grace by which they make Courtiership perfect and adorned" (3.3; S, 204–5). I conclude that what Wayne Rebhorn describes as "the thrones from which Emilia Pia and the duchess rule" are like papier-mâché thrones on a carnival float.[30] Their power is part of the game, consensual rather than con-tractual. The men accept the rules of the game as a challenge, and enjoy test-ing the women's mettle to see if they can maintain the authority ceded to them. Throughout the *Cortegiano* the women are represented as meeting the test with flying colors. But they are also represented as reaffirming their an-cillary status—"to serve courtiers as stimulus and audience"—while doing so.[31] It is therefore hard to take their dominance seriously enough to see it as a cause of anxiety, or as the condition that motivates and explains any an-tifeminist swerves one detects in the profeminist argument.[32]

If it is not political gynephobia per se, gender inversion per se, the courtier's uneasiness about political disempowerment displaced to—taken out on—women on top, that puts pressure on the conversation, then what is it? The obvious candidate is its alternative, erotic gynephobia, the politics of sex, and the question becomes whether the specific relations represented between the men and women at Urbino are shown to affect the argument. Ann Jones's attention to the "ambivalent demand" placed on the court lady—she "had to speak of sex" but demonstrate "sexual purity," "look se-ductive, but . . . be seen not to seduce"[33]—suggests that this is a possibility.

Jones argues that the passage introducing the duchess and describing her influence is one in which the question of sexuality troubles the initial depiction of "a world of innocent intimacy."[34] It seemed, Castiglione writes, that the presence ("conspetto") of the duchess

> *fosse una catena che tutti in amor tenesse uniti, talmente che mai non fu concordia di voluntà o amore cordiale tra fratelli maggior di quello, che quivi tra tutti era. Il medesimo era tra le donne, con le quali si aveva liberissimo ed onestissimo commerzio; ché a ciascuno era licito parlare, sedere, scherzare e ridere con chi gli parea; ma tanta era reverenzia che si portava al voler della signora Duchessa, che la medesima libertà era grandissimo freno; né era alcuno che non estimasse per lo maggior piacere che al mondo aver potesse il compiacer a lei, e la maggior pena di dispiacerle.* (1.4; C, 59)

was a chain that bound everyone together in love so that never was there concord of will nor cordial love among brothers greater than there was among all those in that place. It was the same among the ladies, with whom one had the freest and most honorable association [commerzio], for to each it was permitted to speak, sit, jest, and laugh with whom he pleased; but such was the reverence that was paid to the wishes of the duchess, that the same liberty was a very great bridle; nor was there anyone who didn't esteem it the greatest pleasure in the world to have the power to please her, and the greatest grief to displease her. (S, 16, altered)

Jones observes that the oxymoron "liberty" as a "bridle"

signals a conflict deeply embedded in the ideological complex that shapes *The Courtier*. In the gender theory Castiglione inherited from a less courtly world, "free and honest conversation" with a woman is a contradiction in terms: to be open to men's speeches is the same as being open to their embraces. (*Currency of Eros*, 16)

Castiglione's effort in this passage is clearly to deny that verbal access to the ladies of Urbino implied sexual access as well. ("Nets and Bridles," 44)

Jordan argues that when Cesare, in 3.49, praises the duchess for preferring her "widowhood" to "what seemed to all others the great grace and prosperity of fortune," her sharp rebuke indicates that "the courtiers, Cesare included, stand to benefit from any suggestion that the duchess might take a lover: at the very least, such an action would nullify any claim to authority and power she might make."[35] Does that suggestion find any resonances elsewhere in the *Cortegiano*? This question is addressed not to Jones's concern about the pressure on women at court but to Jordan's concern about the pressure the politics of gender and sex at Urbino imposes on the pro- and antifeminist arguments in Book 3. And I think a positive answer to the question is forestalled at the beginning of the first book.

In continuing and concluding his introductory eulogy of the duchess, Castiglione lays increasing emphasis on her dignity, grandeur, and heroism, ending 1.4 with the statement that she possessed "prudence and strength of spirit, and all those virtues which are very rare even in austere men" (S, 17). The passage reminds me of Lisa Jardine's account of the "saving stereotypes" by which images of Elizabeth I were assimilated "to the exigencies of male statecraft"—"portraits of female virtue so magnificent that they distract attention from their sex altogether."[36] Book 1.4 dramatizes just such an act of distraction, moving the figure of the duchess from the shadow of the medieval *mi dons*, or *domina*, into the sunlight of masculine virtue and authority and attenuated sexuality, where she can rule as a moderator in both senses of that term.[37] The distractive movement is more forcefully staged in 1.9: after Aretino aims a salvo of aggressive Petrarchisms at the hardhearted sirenic, medusan, and serpentine She, who turns out to be the duchess, and after his attempt to lure her into exonerating and explaining herself is foiled when Emilia throws that task back to him, he responds by reciting a sonnet that "was thought by many to have been improvised; but because it was more ingenious and polished than the brevity of time would seem to have allowed, some thought that it had been prepared" (S, 22–23). This failure of sprezzatura highlights the literariness of the whole move by Aretino, and conspicuously defuses the attempt to bring the duchess into the orbit of erotic warfare or male sexual fantasy. We saw that in responding to Gasparo's challenge the duchess had already positioned the women as audience rather than participants. After Aretino Emilia passes over two more suggestions for games dealing with "questioni d'amore" and settles on the proposal to fashion the perfect courtier, which further ensures that the men will be, if not on top, then at least at center stage.

Imagine an alternative in which the *Cortegiano* discourses are presided over by a prince or duke modeled along the lines of the ruler profiled in the second and fourth books, "a master who may be evil and is likely to be a despot," and who, according to Daniel Javitch, might "find intolerable" the "criticism of modern princes" entailed in Book 4 by Ottaviano's relatively "open recognition" of the autocratic pressures that necessitate the courtier's reliance on "cunning and deceit."[38] Could a discourse on the prince be conducted in the presence of such a prince as easily as a discourse on the court lady is conducted in the presence of court ladies? Would that prince be as eager as the duchess to waste an evening listening to his courtiers strut their positions on the woman question? The interventions by the duchess and Emilia at the end of Book 2 are responsible for the turn to that question, and at the beginning of the third book the duchess secures the topic by dismissing the androcentric objections of Gasparo, Frisio, and Ottaviano, which presumably dramatize the predictable masculine response to such a project.[39] It is the women on top who encourage the antifeminists as well as the profeminists to air their opinions, and who provide an interested but nonthreatening audience before whom the men can speak their minds. The women also, therefore, provide a holiday contrast to the more demanding and precarious service that is expected from courtiers—and that the courtiers describe—in the courts of male princes.

A final reason for questioning the dramatistic focus on woman power at Urbino is that it masks an ambient set of symbolic relations that indirectly but powerfully illuminate the structural weakness of the courtier's position: the surrogational authority of the duchess indexically symbolizes a lack in her absent husband, and in the opening chapters of Book 1 the symbolism is framed within Castiglione's account of the problematic relation between father and son, the former Duke Federico and the present Duke Guidobaldo. It was the warrior father who built the palace as a fortress, a thing of beauty, and a humanist haven full of "ancient statues, . . . rare paintings, . . . musical instruments . . . and rare books in Greek, Latin, and Hebrew," which he especially valued (1.2; S, 13–14). Stressing the importance of the juxtaposition of "the magnificent ducal palace" to "its present impotent and deformed inhabitant," Arthur Kinney remarks that the palace is represented not "primarily as the ducal home of Guidobaldo, but as the legacy of the former Duke Federico, who serves as Castiglione's model."[40]

Significantly, Guidobaldo's impotence isn't actually alluded to until 3.49, when Cesare Gonzaga comments on the duchess's quasi-widowhood. What we learn at 1.3 is that when Federico died, Guidobaldo was ten and motherless, and that his remarkable promise aroused the envy of "la fortuna," who set herself to oppose "così glorioso principio," and succeeded in permanently crippling him with the gout. Thus his disability is figuratively linked to a gendered displacement in Book 1, but it is attributed to sex and sexuality at a moment in Book 3 that immediately precedes several chapters devoted to the topic of erotic negotiations. In the earlier passage, the scape-goating of the personified Fortune allows the courtly author to pretend discreetly to obfuscate the source of filial disempowerment on which his account noticeably centers: the trauma of excessive paternal donation, which is conveyed in the statement that just as the son "was heir to the state, so it seemed he was heir to all the paternal virtues" and "began to promise more than it was permitted to hope for from a mortal being." The phrasing that marks the promise as dangerously hubristic associates it with the father's gifts, but it is the son who is emasculated by the nemesis that renders his body incapable of sustaining the legacy.

Castiglione tells us that although Guidobaldo "rarely succeeded in anything he tried to do," he valiantly met the assaults of Fortune with courage and dignity that won everyone's respect. He tried to emulate his father in war and peace, fighting campaigns despite his infirmity, and adding "nobilissimi e valorosi gentilomini" to the rich appointments already installed in the ducal palace. But comparison of Castiglione's profiles of the two military careers, Federico's in 1.2 and Guidobaldo's in 1.3, bears out Kinney's opinion that at their best "Guidobaldo's actions mock Federico's" (99).

Kinney argues that "Guidobaldo's imperfections . . . are described at the outset to establish the necessary reservations for the flights of imagination that follow." Specifically, the portrait warns us "not to be ensnared by the desirability of . . . [the] ideal courtier without reserved judgment" (99, 102–3). This insight takes on added force if we articulate it in terms of the distinction I made in the last chapter between the absolute courtier and the ideal courtier, the former full of grazia, the latter forced to dissimulate the grazia he lacks. In the following proportional analogy, the resemblance is less important than the play of differences it activates: the absolute courtier is to the ideal courtier as Federico is to Guidobaldo.[41] The son resembles the ideal courtier in having to compensate for a failure in donation; he differs both in his heroic, effortful struggle against adversity and in his alarming record of failures. The courtier's compensatory *virtù* is sprezzatura; Guidobaldo's is moral stamina. These comparisons make the father/son contrast a kind of proleptic parable of the problems attending the shift of grazia from God to prince and the corresponding shift in the meaning of the term from an embodied gift to a favor that must be earned, and from a reliable to an unreliable source.

The career of Guidobaldo is an admonitory travesty of the powerlessness that haunts the courtly elite, and his princely response stands out as a shining exception both to the general run of princes and to the courtiers who defend against the need for moral stamina by cultivating sprezzatura. That is, his specific virtù, suffering, and his failure fall outside the ideal of courtier-ship and stencil its limitations. They display what the courtier will have to be taught to avoid: failure, humiliation, and the need for moral stamina. But Castiglione also makes the duke the motivating force behind the pedagogy of avoidance. The narrative pattern of 1.3 is tragicomic, moving from prom-ise through pathos and adversity to a qualified happy ending, in which the duke's triumph over suffering is directly associated with the institution of the Urbino games. Having filled his house with gentlemen in whose com-pany he delighted, he was not content to spend his time engaging them in learned and witty conversation, for

> so much did the greatness of his spirit spur him on that, even though he
> could not engage personally in chivalric activities as he had once done, he
> still took the greatest pleasure in seeing others so engaged; and by his
> words, now criticizing and now praising each man according to his deserts,
> he showed clearly how much judgment he had in such matters. Wherefore,
> in jousts and tournaments, in riding, in the handling of every sort of
> weapon, as well as in revelries, in games, in musical performances, in short,
> in all exercises befitting noble cavaliers, everyone strove to show himself
> such as to deserve to be thought worthy of his noble company. (1.3; S, 15)

The happy ending of the duke's *vita*, if not of his life, is a pastoral retreat from the harsh world ruled by the dominatrix Fortune into the safer arena of ludic competition. The duke becomes a *magister ludi*, mastering in play what he had not been able to master in his struggle against the dominatrix who personifies the obstacles to his desire to internalize the paternal ego ideal ("it seemed that whatever he undertook, both in arms and in every other thing whether small or large, always turned out badly for him," 1.3). The specter of impotence is not simply exorcised but conspicuously ex-cluded, marked, by the paradigmatic substitution of words for deeds: by his "parole" he displayed his "giudicio" in evaluating performances of which he was no longer capable. This variant on Freud's *Fort!/Da!* technique transmits itself to the activities of (what Erik Erikson calls) the "microsphere" that cir-cumscribes "all exercises befitting noble cavaliers." Since the activities that take up the remainder of the *Cortegiano* are almost exclusively restricted to verbal games, devoted to fashioning the ideal courtier and "donna" in speech, the privative significance of the substitution resonates throughout.

The duke's peculiar authority derives from his "animo invittisimo" in the

face of failures and from the mastery of quiet virtues (including the aes-
theticization of military skill) with which he socializes his losses by retreat-
ing into the ludic community he organizes and governs. Because this authority presupposes the opportunity to prove himself in the face of infirmity
and ineffectuality, it is ultimately grounded in the position of weakness that
makes him an exception to the norm of dangerous princely strength embodied by his father. The verbal games he institutes are thus marked by their
origin in a position gender-coded as feminine or effeminate, and which is
thrust in the reader's face when, in the opening sentence of 1.4, the position
is reembodied in another surrogate: "Thus, all the hours of the day were
given over to honorable and pleasant exercises both of the body and of the
mind; but because, owing to his infirmity, the Duke always retired to sleep
very early after supper, everyone usually repaired to the rooms of the Duchess, Elisabetta Gonzaga, at that hour" (S, 15). However powerful or authoritative the duchess as a dramatis persona may seem to some readers, as an
embodiment of textual meaning the position she occupies in the surrogate
structure I just described is, as Finucci argues, that of a weak male.[42]

It is for all these reasons that I remain unpersuaded by the thesis that the
arguments—antifeminist in Rebhorn's account, profeminist in Jordan's—reflect Castiglione's nervousness about the Urbino power structure, and that
their peculiarities may be explained dramatistically by ascribing them to the
desire of "the effeminate courtier" to protect his masculinity and "resist the
rule of women."[43] That thesis has an oddly restrictive New Critical effect: it
promotes the irony and complexity of the fiction by reducing the arguments
to functions of a particularized mise-en-scène—the court of Urbino—the
circumstances of which motivate the performances of psychological agents—
the speakers—and account for their discursive moves. The virtues of the
New Critical position can be retained and its limits avoided by shifting the
interpretive focus from subjective to discursive agency in the case of the
relation of the speakers to their discourses, and from subjective to textual
agency in the case of the relation of authors to their texts. If I am correct
about the representation of women's rule at Urbino, it encourages this shift
by removing autocratic constraints and marking out a pastoral space in
which the courtiers may speak and argue freely. That very freedom renders
contextual motive-hunting gratuitous because it redirects the search for an
explanation of peculiarities in the argument from power relations at Urbino
to the male fantasies inscribed in sex/gender language games. The need to
control women at court hypothesized by Rebhorn and Jordan presupposes
the dual need inscribed in those language games: to control Woman and

thereby control the women who will displace and embody that specter of patriarchal discourse; to control women and thereby determine the nature of the category and subcategories of the Woman that haunts discourse.

This shift of perspective is already prepared for in *Renaissance Feminism* and may be elicited from it with the help of a few minor adjustments. Consider, for example, Jordan's trenchant formulation of the problem of authorial agency:

> Castiglione's rhetorically convoluted discussion of court ladies, women worthies, and queens makes it difficult to know how fully he intended the contradictions that both disturb and illuminate the logic of his argument. His defense fails as a defense; but whether this failure is to be understood as the pretext of a purposeful exposure of male discourse concerning women or merely as an unexamined result of his own complicity in that discourse is not altogether clear. (77)

Jordan decides tentatively if unequivocally in favor of the purposeful exposure: Castiglione conducts a "subtle critique of the Magnifico's" compensatory maneuvers (79) and the failure of the latter's profeminist argument may signify the former's awareness that "all the words and images available to his protagonists are inevitably bound up with their male interests." Thus, she concludes, his "defense of women is represented as an action that he, a male feminist, can only point to but not actually perform" (85).

The shift I mentioned may be effected by eliminating the masculine pronouns from her account or else displacing their reference from subjects (Castiglione, Magnifico) and subject positions (author, speaker) to the "male interests," the generalized male perspective that dominates both "the discourse concerning women" and the text that, in representing the discourse, internally distantiates itself from it. Although Castiglione's speakers may be exemplary figures with name recognition, and with identifiable social, political, or institutional affiliations, these have been hollowed out so that the sentiments they utter seem at most to be only contingently related to their motives and interests as empirical subjects. Whatever else Castiglione's often-discussed repetition of "ridendo" ("laughing") means or does, it reminds us that any psychological properties we impute to the speakers are severely restricted to the arena of ludic competition: they are contending for honor in a rhetorical game, and when, for example, an antifeminist criticizes or disparages a profeminist utterance, his display of animus is directed at least as much toward the logic of the utterance as toward its female referent. This doesn't mean that we have to forgo psychological analysis. Rather it means that as the speakers take up one argument after another during the discourse concerning woman, it is the discourse itself that gets characterized and psychologized. Fear, desire, contempt, condescension, veneration, suspicion, domestication, cooptation, idealization, demonization: these affects, attitudes, and practices emerge in the *Cortegiano* as properties of the generalized male fantasy that drive the discourse through diegetic patterns of meaning over which—as I shall try to show—the speakers appear to exercise decreasing control as the discussion proceeds.

The shift of interpretive focus I have been describing transfers the primary context of agency and motivation from the court of Urbino to the text of the *Cortegiano* and to the intertextual field of the discourse networks that articulate the collective male fantasy in which the text is embedded. Given the bracketing operation that provisionally disconnects agency from subjects, it seems advisable to rewrite Jordan's question about authorial agency: how fully, she asks, did Castiglione intend "the contradictions that both disturb and illuminate the logic of his argument" (77)? Since the argument I am tracking is the property neither of Castiglione nor of his fictive interlocutors, I prefer to replace "*his* argument" with "*the* argument." Not that the moves the individual speakers make and the representation of what goes on in the court and its games are to be ignored, for we shall see that the relation—or disrelation—of the ludic context to the unfolding dynamics of the discourse is vitally important. New Critical close reading of the context remains valuable, even mandatory, to the revised interpretive project, but its role has to be subordinated to a deconstructive analysis of discursive agency, one that transcends diffuse comments on Castiglione's dark view of politics or human nature. And at the general level—the level of early modern discourse networks—*Renaissance Feminism* supplies this revised project with precisely such an analysis.

One of the many accomplishments of Jordan's fine study is to show that there is drama, contestation, ambiguity, ambivalence, and contradiction within the structure of discourse concerning women because it circulates through early modern discourse networks as part of a larger set of language games that explore, defend, and question "the social and political fictions masking the real operations of power, especially (as it is perceived in the literature) of economic power" (67). Jordan's copious readings of the literature make it clear that agency and motivation are properties not only of subjects but also of the discourse, which is invested with the interests, purposes, and ideological positions of the subjects who contribute to it no less than—perhaps more than—those of the subjects who operate the discourse. Taking my cue, then, from the general interpretive framework her study provides, I shall look more closely at Book 3 in the next chapter in order to demonstrate the consequences of the reorientation I just described.

5. A Perfect Lady: Pgymalion and His "Creatura"

Wayne Rebhorn argues that both Castiglione and his spokespersons "conceive men and women as having their own appropriately different sexual characteristics." They stress the opposition between the virility of the courtiers and the "traditionally feminine virtues" they ascribe to the ideal "donna di palazzo." "Castiglione implements stereotyped conceptions by having his courtiers behave with typically 'male' forcefulness and virile aggression, while the ladies display a complementary, 'female' gentleness, restraint, and delicacy." Rebhorn goes on to note that although the "war between the sexes" in Book 2 is cast in traditional terms "as a chivalric combat in which misogynists are tagged the 'enemies' of women and the Magnifico is summoned as a knight to defend women's honor," Castiglione departs from the tradition of the "questioni d'amore" genre by focusing the debate on the "fundamental question . . . of women's nature, place, and value."[1]

The implications of the focus on woman's nature need to be spelled out with reference not only to the tradition but also to the prior construction of the ideal courtier. In Books 1 and 2 the fashioning of the "cortegiano" is oriented primarily toward an ideal of courtiership to which the display or performance of gender attributes—virility, forcefulness—is instrumental. But the fashioning of the ideal "donna di palazzo" is oriented primarily toward an ideal of femininity, or, to be more precise, toward the feminization or domestication of the female into a lady for whom "doing gender right" consists in learning how to cater to the male's erotic desire—how to speak sex and display sexuality—without losing "honor." Thus what Rebhorn calls "sexual characteristics" play a marginal role in defining the ideal courtier but a central role in defining the court lady: "The male courtier's *misura*," as Ann Jones puts it, "his graceful negotiation of a mean between extremes, is reduced for the court lady into elaborate directions for demonstrating sexual purity"—she "must be beautiful enough to attract men, but alert to the possibility that she will be criticized for doing it too well. She must look seductive, but she must be seen not to be seduced."[2] These different orientations are captured in the terminological distinction between "cortegiano" and "donna di palazzo." Since "cortegiana" is used twice at the beginning of the discussion (2.99 and 3.4), its exclusion thereafter is all the more conspicuous, and its alternative connotation, "courtesan," continues to resonate *as* a conspicuous exclusion, something to guard against, in the thirty-odd instances of a term that seems periphrastically to avoid it.[3] Furthermore, the preposition in "donna di palazzo" adds a strong genitive force of property to its topical sense: the lady is part of and belongs to the "palazzo," which is both a political institution and its architectural embodiment, and therefore she belongs in it and gets her meaning from it.[4] The term thus glances at the particular sociopolitical and economic parameters behind the production of a new gender position, while at the same time the discourse in which it is deployed reduces the meaning of the position to the expression of "appropriately different sexual characteristics."[5]

Rebhorn recognizes the extent to which the courtiers, especially Giuliano, express their anxiety about doing gender right by concentrating on the inscription of difference in woman's "body."[6] They do so in both physiological and physiognomic terms. The physiological argument is conducted from 3.11 to 3.19, and it reveals much about the character of the disputants' commitment to the theses they defend. In Chapters 11 and 15 Gasparo argues that "nature ... would constantly bring forth men if she could; and that when a woman is born, it is a defect or mistake of nature" (3.11; S, 213). Like a virile Scholastic agonist, he finds the proof of this proposition in Aristotle's *Problems*, in which it is stated that the reason " 'a woman always naturally loves the man to whom she first gave herself' " is that "in such an act the woman takes on perfection from the man." From this he deduces that women are defective because "all women without exception desire to be men, by a certain natural instinct that teaches them to desire their own perfection" (3.15; S, 217).[7] Such reasoning is fully consistent with an argument for woman's constancy and fidelity to her first love, and its purely ad hoc or point-scoring function is revealed by its inconsistency with Gasparo's repeated charge that "from women's incontinence" and promiscuity "countless evils arise, as they do not from men's"; therefore the safety of patriarchal succession can only be secured by instilling "in women the fear of infamy as a bridle to bind them as by force to this virtue" of chastity (3.37,39; S, 240–41).[8]

Giuliano defends the manhood of his argument against Gasparo's thrust with an equally Scholastic riposte in an interchange that illustrates the way homosocial bonding at women's expense is enabled by the pretense of treating the ladies with fairness and consideration while speaking on their behalf or for their edification.[9] Responding to Giuliano's paean to androgyny in 3.14, Gasparo had expressed his reluctance to "get into such subtleties, for these ladies would not understand us" and they would "believe (or pretend to believe) that I am wrong" (3.15; S, 216–17), even though, as he had said earlier, "you wish to win their favor by flattering them falsely" (3.11; S, 212). He then blithely ignores his own warning and continues dispensing the subtleties of philosophical misogyny cited in the preceding paragraph—as if to force Giuliano to respond in kind and thus, speaking over the ladies' heads, to demean them by the very manner of his defense. Gasparo's maneuver succeeds, for Giuliano meets his Aristotelian put-down with more science talk. He insists on the necessity and functional complementarity of both sexes, and on the mutuality of perfection ("even as she is perfected by him, she also perfects him"), and he proceeds to give woman's constancy and virtue a basis in nature by appealing to some now famous articles of physiological lore:

> I will attribute the cause of woman's lasting love for the first man to whom she has given herself, and of man's hatred for the first woman he enjoyed, not to what is stated by your philosopher in his *Problems*, but to woman's firmness and constancy and to man's inconstancy, and not without a natural reason: for, since the male is warm, he naturally derives lightness, movement, and inconstancy from that quality, while on the other hand woman derives quietness, a settled gravity, and more fixed impressions from her frigidity. (3.16; S, 217–18)

This explanation draws from Emilia the reproof anticipated by Gasparo:

> "For the love of God," she said, "for once leave these matters and forms and males and females of yours and speak so as to be understood; for we have heard and understood very well the ill that signor Ottaviano and signor Gasparo spoke of us, but we do not at all see in what way you are now defending us; so this, it seems to me, is to stray from the subject and leave in everyone's mind that bad impression that these our enemies have given of us." (3.17; C, 219; S, 218, seriously altered)

Emilia's rejoinder is a rhetorical tour de force because she not only plays dumb in order to fulfill—and thereby parody—Gasparo's prediction, she also shows she understands very well that Giuliano's defense is no defense, and that the straightforward misogyny of the antifeminist may be preferable to the devious chauvinism of the profeminist. For the logic of his attempt to secure woman's preeminent sexual virtue through bodily inscription is hardly damaging to the antifeminist cause: while men must pursue virtue heroically, by struggling against lightness of being, women do so by settling down passively into the grave and frigid chastity natural to their sex. Giuliano will soon reverse his field and warmly defend woman's heroic virtue, as will his ally, Cesare.[10] But when he continues his scientific explanation of woman's fine and quiet sex, natural warmth causes him to swerve once again toward the perils of gynephobia, for his praise of the female turns into a worry about the male:

> Furthermore, woman has a coldness that resists and moderates her natural warmth and renders it more nearly temperate; while in man the excessive warmth soon brings his natural heat to the highest point, and for lack of sustenance it wastes away. And thus, since men dry out more than women in the act of procreation, it frequently happens that they do not keep their vitality as long as women: thus, this further perfection can be ascribed to women, that, living longer than men, they carry out the intention of nature better than men. (3.18; S, 219)

Such arguments might well persuade Castiglione's reader to acknowledge the truth of Gasparo's response to Emilia that the name "enemy" better "fits signor Magnifico who, in giving false praises to women, shows that no true praises can be found for them" (3.17; S, 218), or at least that they can't be found in the patriarchal archive that limits the scope of the profeminist's *invenzioni*.

The physiological discourse of sex is one way to inscribe difference in the body as a basis for prescriptions about doing gender (and sexuality) right. Another is the equivalent of the modern charm school approach through cosmetic physiognomy, or pathognomy. Thus when in 3.4–5 Giuliano gives advice on how the court lady is to perform gender, he distinguishes from those qualities that both men and women share and need others that befit a man and to which a woman ought to be a complete stranger.

> I say this of bodily exercises; but above all I think that in her ways, manners, words, gestures, and bearing, a woman ought to be very unlike a man; for just as he must show a certain solid and sturdy manliness, so it is seemly for

a woman to have a soft and delicate tenderness, with an air of womanly sweetness in her every movement, which, in her going and staying, and in whatever she says, shall always make her appear the woman without any resemblance to a man. . . . And I . . . think that beauty is more necessary to her than to the Courtier, for truly that woman lacks much who lacks beauty. Also she must be more circumspect, and more careful not to give occasion for evil being said of her . . . for a woman has not so many ways of defending herself against false calumnies as a man has. . . . I say that, in my opinion, in a Lady who lives at court a certain pleasing affability is becoming above all else, whereby she will be able to entertain graciously every kind of man with agreeable and comely conversation . . . [but so as] to cause her to be thought no less chaste, prudent, and gentle than she is agreeable, witty, and discreet.(S, 206–7)

This is a physiognomic project: instructions for training a female mind to make its face the index of the lady's mind.

But such a project is of course problematic. If, in "the early modern period, the female body is the site of discourses that manage women," does it follow, as Karen Newman claims, that "by continually working out sexual difference on and through the body, the social is presented as natural and therefore unchangeable, substantiated, filled with presence"?[11] What Giuliano recommends and enjoins may be described in Butler's words as *"a corporeal style"* of gender, "an 'act', as it were, which is both intentional and performative, where *'performative'* suggests a dramatic and contingent construction of meaning," and one explicit enough to cast doubt on Newman's claim.[12] For the instability of the arguments on both sides of the controversy indicates that the increased scope given to explicit pedagogy, accompanied by the correlation of class transformations with the development of new gender positions (the court lady, the queen, the bourgeois wife), places both the physiological approach to sex and the physiognomic approach to gender in question, especially since they are deployed in the service of a conduct-book agenda based on the premise that "men and women can be *produced*."[13] From this premise it is a short step to the conclusion that a corporeal style of "true gender is a fantasy instituted and inscribed on the surface of bodies,"[14] and in *Renaissance Feminism* Jordan has scrupulously and persuasively documented the extent to which much early modern feminist writing anticipates that conclusion.

One of the differences between anti- and profeminist positions is that the latter, in promoting the inscription of virtue, entrusts to women the task and privilege of making the female body, in Newman's words, "the site of discourses that manage women." This may be illustrated by the conflict between Gasparo's and Cesare's philosophies of the bridle. For Gasparo, we recall, women's "fear of infamy" is "a bridle to bind them as by force to this virtue of chastity," but for Cesare "a bridle to women generally is their love of true virtue and their desire for honor, which many whom I have known in my time hold dearer than their own life" (3.39, 41; S, 241, 244). This is more than a contrast between negative and positive opinions as to what should be inscribed. The antifeminist in effect assumes that only men operate the discourses that manage women and thus finds it necessary to manage them from the outside by oppression, deceit, or the force of persuasion. The strategy exemplified by the profeminist is to alienate the operation of managerial discourse to women, who are enjoined to inscribe the fantasies on their own bodies from within. Yet a program for managing women by giving them more autonomous powers of self-representation is also a program for raising the level of anxiety and suspicion in males who want to retain control of the power they alienate. And my argument is that discourse about gender and sex in the *Cortegiano* is not merely structured by this anxiety but structured to *dramatize* the anxiety. The text depicts the double bind of profeminism in narrative terms by placing increasing emphasis on the effect of gynephobic motives on Giuliano's performance (as we shall see). But it also shows that anxiety and suspicion together are an important part of the game: the male courtier wouldn't be without them.

"All women have a great desire to be—and when they cannot be, at least to seem—beautiful," Count Ludovico proclaims out of his wisdom at 1.40, and he goes on to discuss the proper method of painting the face.[15] He praises the "grazia" of a woman "who paints (if at all) so sparingly and so little that whoever sees her is uncertain whether she is painted or not." But he is most impressed by one who, "not ugly, is clearly seen to have nothing on her face, it being neither too white nor too red, but has her own natural color, a bit pale, and tinged at times with an open blush from shame [vergogna] or some other mishap [?—accidente], with her hair artlessly [a caso] unadorned and in disarray, with gestures simple and natural, without showing effort or care to be beautiful. This is that careless [sprezzata] purity most pleasing to the eyes and minds of men, who are ever fearful of being deceived by art" (C, 98; S, 65–66, slightly altered). One wonders why the example of "vergogna" is given, and what some other "accidente" might be, and by the time one reaches the adjectival form of "sprezzatura," one wonders whether this isn't as artful a performance of nature as the ideal courtier himself is capable of. "Sprezzata" reminds us that men respect and admire such skillful dissimulation as much as they fear it, and that women who have learned their lesson well are to be desired and admired and doubly feared (and therefore doubly desired, and triply feared) for their ability to conceal the truth behind a veil of physiognomic self-dramatization.

The veil gives back to men the fantasy they have inscribed on woman's body and mind through the discourse in which they persuade women to alienate and embody the fantasy so that the ideal courtier, like Pygmalion, may see himself limpidly reflected in the gaze he constructs as his ivory beloved. This aspect of 1.40 has been persuasively demonstrated by Finucci, from whose account I depart only in placing more emphasis on what she describes in passing as "man's fear of castration."[16] For of course the men know that the women know how to wear the veil, play the ivory doll, and withdraw behind the mirrors they make of themselves. As the count adds new examples, his rhetoric conveys the connoisseur's smug and sagacious mystery of women's ways, but at the same time it betrays a *frisson* of pleasure at the possibility of being duped by an artlessness he knows is artful. His account of the proper way for a woman to let her hands and legs be seen registers this confusion. In the following passage, does he more admire the spontaneity of disclosure or the calculated theatricality of the performances that display it?

> The same is true of the hands, which, if they are delicate and beautiful, and are uncovered [mostrate ignude] at the proper time, when there is occasion to use them and not merely to make a show of their beauty, leave one with a great desire to see them more and especially when they are covered with gloves again; for whoever covers them seems to have little care or concern whether they are seen or not, and to have beautiful hands more by nature than by any effort or design.
>
> Have you ever noticed when, in passing along the street to church or elsewhere, in play or through whatever cause, it happens that a woman raises just enough of her dress that she unwittingly shows her foot and often a little of her leg? Does it not seem to you to possess the greatest grace, if she is seen at that moment in a certain elegant feminine attitude, dressed in velvet shoes and dainty stockings. Certainly to me it is a pleasing sight, as I believe it is to all of you, because everyone thinks that such elegance of dress, when it is where it would be hidden and rarely seen, must be natural and instinctive with the lady rather than calculated, and that she has no thought of gaining any praise thereby. (1.40; C, 99; S, 66, modified)

"The discursive process molding femininity," Finucci writes of this passage, "here both neutralizes and immobilizes woman's form into an ordered and erotic image, as well as objectifies it through a technique of descriptive dismemberment" (52). This predictable emphasis on the violence of the blazon diverts attention from something more interesting and ambivalent going on in the count's prose. Since "mostrate ignude" strongly implies an act of exhibition ("displayed in the nude"), it frustrates the attempt to insist on the polar opposition between unintended display and "per far vedere la lor bellezza," reducing it to the difference between the sprezzatura of successfully masked exhibitionism and *affettazione*, or failed sprezzatura. In the second paragraph, the studied casualness produced by the repeated disjunctions—"o per le strade andando alle chiese o ad altro loco, o giocando o per altra causa"—is transferred through "accade che" to the act of display, which is carefully measured enough ("tanto della robba," "just so much of the dress") to suggest that "unwittingly shows" ("senza pensarvi mostra") may be part of the act. Thus the message the lady beams through the count's description is, "I have no thought of gaining praise by this conspicuously unintentional exhibition of desirable body parts." In his fantasy of her self-representation the dissolution of the polarity, art vs. nature, or calculation vs. spontaneity, constructs an aporetic barrier behind which unpenetrated or undecidable motives materialize in the form of the hiddenness and mystery of woman's mind. The construction, however, is troubled by two of the definitional aspects of "sprezzatura" I discuss in Chapter 1: (1) the ability to show that one is not showing all the effort one obviously put into learning how to show that one is not showing effort; (2) the ability to show that one is not showing what one really desires, feels, thinks, and means or intends. It is the first that forces its way through the count's description and raises a question about what it is—art or nature—that he admires. But the second, which he ignores, raises more serious questions. The mysterious *she* who makes her face the index of *his* mind by withdrawing behind the mirror that reflects his fantasy becomes the tain of the mirror, the ghost in the machine, the secret agent in the black box—a Pygmalion, perhaps, in her own right.

This *she*, however, is not a prediscursive she but the creature of his discourse, the unrepresented self or subject produced as the logical effect of his representation of her self-representation. Teresa de Lauretis provides me with the schema for describing the movement between the represented and unrepresented female subject of male discourse: "*not* . . . a movement . . . from the space of a representation . . . to the space outside the representation, the space outside discourse, which would then be thought of as 'real' . . . or again, from the symbolic space constructed by the sex-gender system to a 'reality' external to it," but rather "a movement back and forth between the representation of gender (in its male-centered frame of reference) and what the representation leaves out or, more pointedly, makes unrepresentable."[17] The unrepresented *she* materializes as the hidden agent to stir up renewed desire and anxiety, renewed efforts to penetrate the veil and capture the excess in representation; the excess is continuously reconstituted "outside discourse as a potential trauma which can rupture or destabilize . . . any representation" (3) and which thereby motivates the renewal of the efforts to contain it. It is because Finucci ignores this possibility in her eagerness to demonstrate Castiglione's erasure of woman that her otherwise valuable interpretation of the episode needs to be revised.[18] I have argued that this dialectical movement in the *Cortegiano* should be interpreted not as an effect of the particular sex-gender relations fictively represented in the court of Urbino but as a function of the dynamics of the sex-gender discourse those relations are constructed to facilitate. The efforts of containment are dramatized by the rhetorical structure of the so-called war between the sexes, which is displaced, first, to a speech war between male courtiers who take up opposing sides of traditional arguments on the woman question, and second, to the internalization of that conflict within the discourse of male profeminism. In what follows I shall explore the effects of the second displacement on the rhetorical and narrative features of Giuliano's performance in Book 3.

Giuliano's performance in this Book is initially elicited as a response to a salvo of antifeminist sentiments. At the end of Book 2, Gasparo and Ottaviano turn the discussion from the account of jokes conducted by Bernardo Bibbiena to an attack on women, and as a result the duchess assigns their defense to Giuliano because he is "held to be the defender of women's honor" (2.97; S, 194). He responds that in order to do the job properly and give women an even break it would be necessary to follow the example set by the fashioners of the ideal courtier and imagine an ideal "donna di palazzo" (2.98). This move already subverts his express concern for equal rights because the differential repetition ("as the Courtier, so the Lady") consigns the lady to a secondary and specular relation to her counterpart. Her specularity is confirmed when Giuliano initiates his defense with a tactic familiar in the Raphael/Castiglione circle: he eschews the example of Zeuxis for a more radical example in stating that since he doesn't know where to find a model for his perfect court lady, he will speak of her "as I would wish her to be; and when I have fashioned her to my taste, and since I may not have another,

like Pygmalion I will take her for my own" (3.4; S, 205). This sounds a genially but clearly competitive sennet: it is a competitive challenge to the
fashioners of the ideal courtier, whose Zeuxian reliance on external models
he will overgo, and it differs from their project in asserting more arbitrary
and thoroughgoing proprietary rights in his creation.[19]

The allusion to the Pygmalion story is casual enough to discourage the
energetic interpreter from unlocking it and letting its meaning seep into the
text of the speaker's profeminist discourse. In its Ovidian context, on which
I comment more fully below, the meaning is complicated by the tale's contribution to a pattern that characterizes its fictive narrator, Orpheus, to whose
storytelling most of *Metamorphoses* 10 is devoted. The string of stories with
which he regales the birds and beasts after having lost Eurydice and rejected
women for boys reflects his misogynist standpoint. He makes Pygmalion's
idolatry a reaction to the impiety of the "obscene Propoetides" whom Venus
turned first into prostitutes and then into stones: "Pygmalion had seen these
women spending their lives in shame, and, disgusted with the faults which in
such full measure nature had given the female mind, he lived unmarried and
long was without a partner of his couch."[20] The hasty generalization from an
unrepresentative sample to all womankind establishes the meaning of Pygmalion's ivory love: she is both the product and the symbol of his misogyny.
In the most notable medieval revivals of the story—*The Romance of the Rose*,
the *Ovide moralisé*, and Christine de Pizan's *Letter of Othea to Hector*—this
Orphic theme drops out and emphasis is redirected to such "diverse exposi-
tions" (Christine) as the sins of idolatry and lechery and a more pious allegory of creation. Clearly the original Ovidian context has greater relevance
to the debate in Book 2 than to any of these latter-day occurrences, but one
would need more than Giuliano's single passing reference to Pygmalion to
demonstrate a specific allusive relation. As luck would have it, the reference
is preceded by another clue, which, dropped at a critical transition point,
supplies the energetic interpreter with new hope.

When Gasparo begins insulting women near the end of Book 2 and
Bernardo chides the listening ladies for letting him get away with it, "at a
sign from the Duchess, many of the ladies rose to their feet and all rushed
laughing upon signor Gasparo as if to assail him with blows and treat him as
the bacchantes treated Orpheus, saying the while: 'Now you shall see
whether we care if we are slandered'" (2.97; S, 193–94). The allusion is to the
attack of the Cicones on "nostri contemptor" in *Metamorphoses* 11.1–43, and
this cue to think of Ovid's misogynist narrator makes it more probable that
the mention of Pygmalion a few paragraphs later will flag the same con-

text.[21] The energetic interpreter may want to go a step further and formal-
ize these relations into a proportional analogy: *Gasparo : Orpheus :: Giuliano :
Pygmalion* (or *Gasparo : Giuliano :: Orpheus : Pygmalion*), which would make
the profeminist idealization of the court lady an episode within the antifeminist argument. I'm not sure it helps to push the relation that far, but Giuliano's performance as Pygmalion takes it a good part of the way.

Like Pygmalion, whose ivory love is represented as the contrast and exception to defective female nature, Giuliano begins by defining his "creatura"
primarily through negative prescriptions that will distinguish and insulate
her from the run of actual ladies at court and their failings: "let her take care
to avoid this and not to do that, let her not fall into the errors or vices so
many other women fall into." At 3.4–9 and again at 3.54–59 his message is,
"I would not have her be like other ladies, therefore let her safeguard the
ideal from the faulty practices in terms of which and against which she was
imagined in the first place." Yet it is interesting that between these two passages—from Chapter 12 to Chapter 52—the "donna di palazzo" is mentioned only twice, once by Cesare as the price of his admission into the discourse at 3.40. At 3.11, as we have seen, pressure by Gasparo diverts the
course of discussion for eight chapters from gender to sex and sexuality,
from the specific femininity of the court lady to the general role of the female in the politics of reproduction. After the friar interlude at 3.19–20 Giuliano returns to take up an earlier challenge in which Gasparo urged him to
descend from generalities to particulars in order to persuade his audience that
the ideal was not "impossible and miraculous" (3.7). His response is oddly
off target: from 3.22 to 3.36 he tries to prove that he is not "speaking of mir-
acles" and that "there have always been . . . and still are women quite like the
Court Lady I have fashioned" by citing examples of women quite unlike the
court lady, examples of women who behaved heroically and showed themselves "capable of the same virtues as men" (3.21; S, 223) in domestic and
political crises.

If there is a rationale governing this long digression from Giuliano's an-
nounced project, it isn't easy to discern, and perhaps the simplest hypothesis
will be the most helpful. There are two discussions, the first about sex, the
second about gender: from 3.11 to 3.19 the debate centers on arguments
about sexual difference based on traditional (Aristotelian and Galenic) physiology; from 3.22 to 3.36 the focus is on women who—as mothers, wives,
daughters, sisters, warriors, and rulers—display male-identified virtù (Machiavellian in some cases and martial in others) and who in many cases would
qualify for membership in Lisa Jardine's category of "saving stereotypes."[22]

Excluded from both the first discussion of sexual difference and the second discussion of gender similarity is any reference to the specifically erotic dimension of sex and gender relations, the dimension that dominates the construction of the court lady. Both discussions are conspicuously traditional in orientation, based chiefly on ancient sources, and the examples of good or strong women illustrate aspects of what Constance Jordan calls "symbolic androgyny": "Persons who were sexually distinct were seen to be capable of being behavioristically androgynous; the more carefully their androgyny was described, the less close seemed the link between sex and gender."[23]

My hypothesis is, first, that since physiology offers a battleground more favorable to the misogynist position, the shift to heroic women is a move in the other direction, a strategy that aims to weaken the link between sex and gender, and second, that this move paves the way for a safer return to an account of the subtle and precarious negotiations of the erotic relation in which sex and gender are closely linked. As an antitype to the Pygmalionist ideal proposed at the outset, the ancient fantasy of the heroic woman is paradoxically the site of a pastoral retreat from that dangerous linkage, the site of a straightforward, traditional, easy, and expansive profeminist narrative that defers the embattled and erotic climax of Giuliano/Pygmalion's discourse. But at this point a consideration arises that adds a wrinkle to the hypothesis. The legends of good women are also legends of strong women, and the safety of the pastoral retreat depends on keeping them good. Giuliano shows how the profeminist does this: his heroic examples use their strength to defend patriarchal interests. "In herself," Jordan remarks, "the virile woman tended to reaffirm patriarchal values. Her excellence is seen in her masculinity—that is, her rationality, courage, and physical strength" (137) and it is also seen in her devotion to, her willingness to sacrifice herself for, marriage, family, and political order. But of course this phantasmatic woman can be scary. The tales of good women are haunted by the specter of the virago. Produced in the profeminist reaction to the misogynist's subordination of gender to sex, the woman warrior who embodies the hyperdevelopment of gender power freed from the bonds of anatomical sex easily shades over into the virago, figure of gynephobic fantasy.

The virago takes more forms than that of the ferocious battle ax. Like the patient Griselda, she can by the very strength of her goodness (and not merely by the goodness of her strength) shame, disempower, emasculate the men she nominally serves no less than those she polices. A variety of these spectral forms hover about Giuliano's stories, and they include those listed by Arthur Kinney:

The lesson of Alessandra, which appears to honor courage and fortitude, actually emphasizes impiety and ruthlessness [3.22]; the Trojan women ostensibly honored for their part in founding Rome are characterized by their trickery and deceit (3.29); and the Sabine women learn that it is wiser and more expedient to accept the fact of their rape than to seek justifiable revenge (3.30). Imitatio is surely implied yet just as surely denied by the careful reader, who will *not* follow the Trojan women into crucial acts of betrayal or Sabine women into acquiescence to rape.[24]

The sensitive profeminist may suspect that Kinney's "careful reader" is a misogynist and that the spirit of Gasparo lurks behind the moral skew implicit in the contrast between "*appears* to honor" and "*ostensibly* honored" on the one hand and, on the other, "*actually* emphasizes impiety" and "*characterized* by . . . trickery." Giuliano would object that Kinney distorts his meaning, but any sensitive misogynist with minimal training in the pragmatics of language use could reply that Kinney's censure responds to the utterance meaning, not to the utterer's meaning. He could then go on to remark that Giuliano, like a good humanist, made the mistake of drawing his examples from classical literature, and that since such traditional resources of apparent or ostensible profeminism were infiltrated by antifeminism, whoever took up the former would be unavoidably saddled with the latter, whether or not she or he knew it, meant it, or wanted it. The contradiction lay in the utterance, not the utterer; the agency responsible for it was discursive, not subjective.

The fantasy I just spun out has very little to do with Kinney's utterance, to which I now return. Or, to be more precise, if the utterance betrays residual misogyny, the utterer doesn't intend it because his interpretation of the *Cortegiano* is free of any concern for the problematics of gender. Indeed, as Kinney notes, the examples and judgments he cites are drawn from an essay by Dain Trafton, the major thesis of which is that in Giuliano's legend of good women the emphasis on gender is a smoke screen. Trafton argues that Giuliano, like a good courtier, speaks in ambages and uses the stories of good women to deliver a discreetly Machiavellian warning: "the courtier, and the prince whom he instructs, must not allow the elegant, civilized sublimations of the court to obscure the fact that cruder passions and ugly dangers inform the outside world of politics; those passions and those dangers cannot be laughed away with raillery but must be subdued by bold cunning and force," and "political success" in these enterprises "requires a degree of freedom from morality."[25] According to this view, Giuliano's political realism extends so far as to sanction not only the courtier's resisting princely tyranny by force but also, in extreme cases, tyrannicide and usurpation; for this reason Castiglione/Giuliano prudently conceals these "dangerous ideas" behind the "tales of good women" (42). Trafton thus removes them from the context of the debate about women, insisting that the tales are "intended to have a general applicability to both sexes" (33); that is, the women really stand for men.

Trafton's insistence on the contiguity of the tales of good women to dangerous ideas is nevertheless very suggestive, and the passage by Kinney provides a way to resituate the contiguity in the debate about women. Though the passage is a condensed paraphrase of Trafton's insights into the examples Kinney cites (compare Trafton, 35–37), it shifts attention from the Machiavellian message of the examples—what is morally blameworthy may be politically laudable—to their moral obtuseness—what is represented as laudable may also be read as blameworthy. The shift implicates a more basic perspectival difference: Trafton identifies the speaker's views and performance with those of the author but Kinney wedges them apart, arguing that Castiglione revealed his skeptical assessment of humanist methods and optimism by dramatizing them in Giuliano's unreliable interpretation. This wedging operation is an important move, but as Kinney performs it, it is theoretically too casual and thematically too unfocused, and in order to preserve its interpretive value its rhetorical structure has to be made more explicit.

The ironic wedge that marks Giuliano's moral obtuseness is produced by Kinney's repetition of skewed lessons exemplifying the pattern "surely implied yet just as surely denied"—implied by the speaker, Giuliano, but denied by ("the careful reader" of) the text. The pattern belongs to a well-marked family of tropes the most ancient and familiar of which are *occupatio* and *praeteritio* and the general structure of which I have tried to characterize by calling them tropes of *conspicuous exclusion*. In Kinney's example, the text promotes dissonance between some obvious meanings of a statement and a focalizing strategy that excludes them, with the result that resistance and curiosity are aroused in readers who find themselves confronted by an apparently wrong or gratuitous interpretation. As I noted, the legends of good women are also legends of strong women, and what the trope problematizes is the subordination of "strong" to "good" not only in Giuliano's account but also in the classical tradition of profeminist discourse he mobilizes. The reader for whom the negative features of the examples are conspicuous, and therefore conspicuously muffled or ignored, is encouraged to wonder whether the selectivity of profeminist interpretation is defensive. Were the narrative to foreground those negative features, the account of "virile women" who tend, in Jordan's words, to "reaffirm patriarchal values" might be transformed into an account of viragos who imperil them. The effect of the conspicuous exclusion of this possibility is to insinuate into the profeminist reading of good women a strain of suppressed gynephobic anxiety. It is as if the reaffirmation of patriarchal values can't be taken for granted when those legends are put into play.

Such an approach provides a context for the constructive revision of Trafton's thesis by bringing the thesis into contact with the argument of feminist historians that courtiership was perceived as disempowering and effeminizing. When Trafton mentions "the emphasis on arms that emerges from a proportionally large number of the Magnifico's examples," and remarks that the women in the examples "benefited their countries because they understood (often better than their men) the need for martial virtue" (38), one thinks immediately of the unwarlike character of both the ideal courtier and those who fashion him. Thus John Hale extends his snide description of Castiglione as "a well-horsed and expensively armored man of peace" to the interlocutors in the *Cortegiano*, who are shown to share their author's troubled awareness that they and their fellow Italians, "the direct descendants of the all-conquering Romans, were regularly being thwacked in battle by the 'barbarian' nations they still affected to despise."[26] Prominently featured in the second as well as the fourth book, the thwackability of Italian males throws its shadow across the parade of woman warriors who, according to Trafton, furnish Giuliano with a vehicle of displacement for "dangerous ideas" about the need to venture forth from the sheltering "arts of courtiership per se—the jousting, the dancing, the loving, even the giving of good counsel— . . . and call upon sterner political virtues" when the common good demands it (42). But I don't think the *Cortegiano* represents these ideas as dangerous primarily because they offend the moral sense, as Trafton and Kinney argue. Rather they are dangerous for a reason strongly implied by the form (if not the intent) of the following statement by Trafton: "Like the good women whom the Magnifico praises, the courtier must be prepared to be killed and to kill; he must exhibit the heroic spirit of Hercules, who, according to Ottaviano, 'waged perpetual and deadly war' against tyranny (4.37)" (42). The dangerousness of such ideas rubs off on the women who vehiculate them and who, in doing so, usurp the manly function and expose the enervated masculinity of the courtly ideal. But to read this into Trafton's statement is to render all the more striking his correlation of the good women with Hercules.

Though Trafton concedes that Ottaviano's reference in Book 4 compares Hercules to good princes rather than to courtiers, he insists that the general theme, resistance to tyranny, binds all these figures together (44), and I agree, with one modification: the heroism of Hercules, good princes, and good women represents both a challenge and a rebuke to the figure of "il cortegiano perfetto" developed in the first three books. Ottaviano strongly insinuates in 4.3–4 that unless the portrait is augmented by the political virtues he is about to discuss, there would be little difference between the courtier and the "donna di palazzo"; the social graces prescribed for the former "serve merely to make spirits effeminate [effeminar gli animi], . . . whence it comes about that the Italian name is reduced to opprobrium, and there are but few who dare, I will not say to die, but even to risk any danger" (4.4; S, 289).

Ottaviano here makes explicit a theme in a minor key, various notes of which are sounded again and again but with a gingerly touch, hinted at and then left behind to echo as dissonant vibrations of anxiety. At 1.43, for example, while defending the value of letters and of the imitation of classical heroes for the courtier's military education, the count pauses to consider the objection that "the Italians with all their knowledge of letters have for some time shown little valor in arms." This, he acknowledges, "is only too true." It is "the true cause of our ruin." But since it is the fault of only a few, it would be "shameful to publish it," therefore "it is better to pass over in silence what can't be recorded without pain, and, avoiding this subject, which I broached against my will, to return to our Courtier." This is conspicuous exclusion with a vengeance, though here it is practiced by one of the interlocutors rather than by the author. A similar move occurs at 2.23 after Federico, pressed by Ludovico Pio to justify the courtier's obeying whatever the prince commands, even if that means killing a man, replies that he ought to obey his lord only "in things that are useful and honorable to him." When Gasparo asks "how one can discern things that are truly good from those only apparently so," Federico demurs: "I don't wish to get into that, for there would be too much to say, but let the whole matter be consigned to your discretion." At such moments, one critic observes, the author "raised for an instant the veil that concealed the hideous moral reality and then rapidly dropped it again."[27] It would be more correct to phrase the insight in the present tense of the text and redirect it from the author to the interlocutors. For these are moments in which the author represents his courtiers' own bad-faith attempts to disown or ignore knowledge of their true condition. Conspicuous exclusion is conspicuous evasion. The passages reveal an authorial perspective that allows the reader to question the idealized portrait of the courtiers on which the *Cortegiano* generally and dominantly insists.

These instances make explicit the drift of Ottaviano's comment at the end of Book 3 that the protracted account of the court lady prevented the company from "hearing many other fine things that remain to be said about the Courtier" (3.76; S, 281). But it also gives a mordant twist to the mandate Giuliano received from the duchess at the end of the second book and tries to carry out in the third: her desire to have him fashion a court lady "equal in worth to the Courtier" (2.100) is now in effect revalued by Ottaviano into a fear that the courtier is no different from, no better than, the "donna di palazzo," a point he expressly makes at 4.45. Ottaviano's concern betrays political gynephobia, the gynephobia of gender specifically centered on the fear of being unmanned in the sense of politically disempowered, whether by men or by women, but a fear that is obviously intensified when the masculine role is performed by strong women.

Giuliano's attempt at heroic pastoral is interrupted at 3.37 when the misogynists bring up the question of sexual incontinence in women and thereby redirect attention from gender to sex. At this point Cesare Gonzaga steps in to relieve Giuliano, and spends ten chapters illustrating women's heroic chastity and continence in the face of men's erotic aggression. This moves the discussion via a relatively safe passage toward the erotic reintegration of sex and gender. At 3.51 Cesare confesses—with some justice—that he and Giuliano have been spouting clichés in defense of good women, and concludes that they were needless because everyone knows how much power men have invested in those women by (in effect) playing Pygmalion, idolizing them as objects of desire and as stimuli to noble deeds, virtues, and manners. This peroration, together with comments by Gasparo and the duchess, prepares for Giuliano's resumption of the Pygmalion role he began with, and prompts Federico Fregoso to return to the context of that opening move and ask for more on the topic Giuliano first brought up, that is, "what you stated to be the main business of the Court Lady," her mastery of the "discourse of love" ("ragionamenti d'amore," 3.53). Giuliano accordingly shifts from the larger context of gendered behavior to focus on the interlocutory strategies of erotic talk. Finucci claims that in this stretch of Book 3 "the reasoning . . . soon becomes empty and repetitive," but in fact from 3.52 until Gasparo's diatribe at Chapter 74, Giuliano's conduct of the argument changes in several significant ways, and the major result of the shift is that the profeminist's concern to fend off misogynist arguments gradually diminishes while the gynephobia that underlies the profeminist position betrays itself.[28]

(1) When Giuliano returns to his creation after a hiatus of thirty chapters, he begins to refer to her as "la mia donna" (3.52, 54, 57, 59) and "mia creatura" (3.54). The first reference is especially interesting: he pretends to have said enough about her and states with mock truculence that "as for me, I am content with this lady of mine; and if these gentlemen don't want her as I have fashioned her, let them leave her to me" ("quanto per me, contentomi di questa mia donna; e se questi signori non la voglion così fatta, lassinla a me": 3.52; C, 252; my translation). This rhetorical tour de force stages the contentious and cajoling defensiveness of (a) the artist daring his auditors not to praise his creation, (b) the lover daring them not to admire and desire the woman who belongs to him, and (c) the orator daring them not to ask him to continue speaking. By this point it has become clear that the pro-feminist argument together with the imaginary "donna" are instrumental to the proprietary, erotic, and competitive—and homosocial—motives of courtly debate.[29]

(2) From Chapter 54 through Chapter 59, while he concentrates on the dangers posed by men's lust and deceit, Giuliano speaks of his "creatura" as would a protective father, guardian, or lover. When he is twice accused of being too "austere" in his prescriptions (3.55 and 58) one begins to sense in his solicitude a touch of jealousy that eroticizes the concern he expresses for his "creatura." Along with a desire to protect her from unworthy suitors he betrays an anxiety to distinguish her from the majority of women ("infinite donne," 3.57), who fall short of the ideal. Here I think the Ovidian context of the Pygmalion story illuminates the subversive implications of that anxiety. The ivory statue, as I noted, is both the product and the symbol of Pygmalion's anxiety. Giuliano's defense of his "donna" participates in this structure to the extent that it is a defense not only against untrustworthy men but also against untrustworthy women: at the beginning of his account (3.4–9) and again at 3.54–59 he produces his court lady contrastively by isolating her virtues from the defects of actual court ladies. In this respect, his pro-feminism is contaminated by antifeminism. But the latter is unstable: it oscillates between impatience with the weakness of most women on the one hand and, on the other, an express interest in containing their sexual power over men and breaking down their resistance to male stratagems. In the twenty chapters concluded by Gasparo's diatribe the emphasis of the discussion shifts from the first, misogynist, tendency toward the second, gynephobic, tendency. From Chapter 54 through Chapter 59 negotiations between Giuliano and other discussants center on the problem of empowering the "donna" while ensuring that her conduct of the discourse of love will con-

form to the needs and desires of the ideal courtier and hence to the institutional requirements of the "palazzo." That Giuliano's fantasy construction responds specifically to the misogynist strain in the discourse is signified by the cessation of references to the "donna di palazzo" after 3.60, precisely when an intervention by Aretino marks the shift toward gynephobic attention to woman's power, a shift that correlates with the third of the three major changes in Giuliano's conduct of the argument.[30]

(3) Just when Giuliano's solicitude toward his creature begins to hint at eroticized possessiveness, he shifts the center of discourse from the court lady back to the courtier as lover. After Giuliano and Roberto da Bari agree that she must not be so guarded as to deny access or encouragement even to her ideal male counterpart, Roberto praises him for having "taught her how to love, which is something these gentlemen have not done for their Courtier," and Aretino responds that "it would be more to the point to teach the Courtier how to make himself loved rather than how to love" (3.60; S, 266–67). With one exception, the topic from this moment until Chapter 74 is no longer how the "donna" is to receive and deal with the lover's advances but how the courtier is "to win his Lady's favor" (3.72).

The exception is critical, because it consists of Emilia's major contribution to the discourse, a spirited interchange with Aretino in which she efficiently puts down his Petrarchan double-talk about the ungrateful women who have victimized him. Her advice to him takes us well outside the bounds of the male perceptions that have dominated the book so far:

> "He who begins to love must also begin to please his beloved and to comply entirely with her wishes, and by hers govern his own; and he must see to it that his own desires serve her, and that his soul is like an obedient handmaid, nor ever think of anything except to transform himself into the soul of his beloved, if that is possible, and to reckon this his highest happiness; for they act so who truly love."
>
> "Precisely," said the Unico, "my highest happiness would be to have a single will govern both our souls."
>
> "Then it is for you to act accordingly," replied signora Emilia. (3.63; S, 269)

Aretino's gallantry concedes too much, since according to her formulation the "voglia sola" will be the beloved's, and it is not she but he who must make it happen: "A voi sta di farlo." Her idea of psychic union is a skewed and truncated echo of the Neoplatonic commonplace the distortion of which

Bembo will set right with a vengeance in Book 4 when, as Rebhorn astutely observes, he provides the courtier "with motivations and goals that . . . remove him from the influence of women" by arguing that he should love and serve them "only as the first step in transcending them altogether."[31] The crucial phrase in Emilia's counterattack is the command that the lover's soul must be "come obediente ancella": his courtly service to the master mistress is voluntarily to lower himself—his soul—in class and gender to the status of a serving woman. Emilia thus touches on man's deepest fear, fear of effeminization, fear of the woman within, the gynephobia of gender that threatens him even more than does fear of impotence or emasculation, the gynephobia of sex.

The men immediately backpedal away from this pitfall with a series of relatively brief comments by Bernardo, Cesare, and Gasparo that returns command of the discussion to Giuliano, and that dramatizes a movement in which the profeminist and antifeminist bond together against the threat of disempowerment. But the gynephobic motive continues to betray its force beneath the apparently masterful knowledge of the *ars amatoria* displayed by Giuliano and his fellow experts from 3.65 to 3.74, when it ruptures the complacent surface of discourse in Gasparo's virulent diatribe. Their attention having shifted from the "donna" to the courtier, they discuss how the lover may break down the woman's resistance to love and breach her defenses; how he is to avoid losing control, being deceived, risking public exposure, and being outmaneuvered by less worthy rivals; how, in short, lovers are to keep conflict among men from transferring the power of sexual choice and discourse to the beloved.

A good example of subversive gynephobic interference occurs at 3.66, when Giuliano returns to the fray after Emilia's challenge. He begins to strut his mastery of courtly love by bringing into play the traditional armory of scopic weapons, the traditional imagery of war, sorcery, and disease, associated with the metaphoric pathology of optical infection and psychic inflammation. But his control wavers when he echoes the transformation of souls Emilia had mentioned and tries to analyze it in the following ophthalmological fantasy:

> If the form of the whole body is beautiful and well proportioned, it attracts
> and draws to itself anyone who looks upon it from afar, bringing him
> closer; and as soon as he is near, the eyes dart forth and bewitch, like sorcerers; and especially when they send their rays straight into the eyes of the
> beloved at the moment these are doing the same to the other's; because the

spirits meet, and in that sweet encounter each takes [or catches—piglia] the other's qualities, as we see in the case of a diseased eye, which, by looking fixedly into a sound eye, communicates its own disease to it. Thus, it seems to me that in this way our Courtier can in great part make his love for his Lady known. (3.66; C, 263; S, 271–72, slightly altered)

If the attribution of agency is confusing, I think it is because the description is itself confused by competing motives. The woman appears to be the first agent, though there is momentary doubt when Giuliano mentions "the eyes of the beloved thing [or one]"—"negli occhi della cosa amata."[32] The infection (see "piglia") is then described as mutual, but in the simile that follows, though it is possible that the infection travels simultaneously in both directions, the terms of the image make it unlikely, and, influenced by the previous emphasis on the woman's agency, the simile suggests that she is infecting the lover. The final sentence, however, blithely and anomalously—and too conspicuously—ignores those implications to restore power and agency to the courtier. Thus the passage as a whole insinuates a Medusan threat and stages an effort to fend it off in an unconvincingly apotropaic conclusion.

It is, however, the lover who initiates the process, and what Giuliano here characterizes pejoratively through the metaphor of disease he has praised at the beginning of the chapter as an appropriate conquest strategy: after noting the discretion demanded of a lover who would write or speak his way into a woman's confidence (3.65) he states his opinion that

the method [via] that the Courtier ought to follow in making his love known to the Lady would be to reveal it to her by actions rather than words, for it is certainly true that more of love's affection is sometimes revealed by a sigh, by a reverence, by timidity [si conosce in un suspiro, in un rispetto, in un timore] than by a thousand words; next, by making his eyes be faithful messengers in bearing the embassies of the heart, since they often reveal the passion within more effectively than the tongue itself, or letters, or messengers; and they not only reveal thoughts but they often kindle love in the beloved's heart. (3.66; S, 271)

This prescription is followed by Giuliano's scientific explanation of the effect of the optical transmission of the vital spirits generated near the heart. The emphasis on the mechanics of the process may steer us away from the contradiction in the above passage, but it doesn't obscure it: one can't *make* one's eyes reveal one's passions; one can only make one's eyes "reveal one's passions" in an artful display of nature. The contradiction expresses the effect of the dissimulative norm of sprezzatura, the theatricality of which is accentuated by Giuliano's placement of the indefinite article not only before "suspiro" but also before "rispetto" and "timore," transforming dispositional attitudes into discrete acts that perform them. The contradiction also invades Giuliano's logic, for, since the figure of messengers bearing "ambasciate" implies written or spoken messages, and therefore intentional rather than involuntary communication, it further underlines the *disegno* or calculation behind the delivery of spontaneous passion, the efficiency ("efficacia") of which is increased by not appearing to have been scripted. Having thus delivered himself of these ambages, Giuliano participates in the same courtly deception by attributing the lover's performance to physiological mechanisms. That is, his own performance is inscribed in a traditional bad-faith discourse of erotic conquest, and the result of the bad faith emerges at the end of the ophthalmological fantasy when the power of infection is confusedly assigned to the woman. The concluding apotropaic avoidance of this outcome suggests the possibility that the bad-faith discourse may be infected by bad conscience.

The whole of the speech containing the ophthalmological fantasy is marked by the assault imagery of courtly and Petrarchan conventions, and in this it doubles back to a moment near the end of Book 2 in which the battle between pro- and antifeminists begins, because its resonance chimes rhetorically with a speech by the profeminist Bernardo at 2.94. Bernardo has just insisted that "un gentilomo di valore" should be sincere and truthful in love as in all other things, and that since treachery to an enemy is judged abominable, to betray the woman one loves should be considered a much more serious offense. He goes on to express his belief

> that every noble [gentil] lover endures so many toils, so many vigils, exposes
> himself to so many dangers, sheds so many tears, uses so many ways and
> means to please his lady love [l'amata donna]—not chiefly in order to pos-
> sess her body, but to take the fortress of her mind and to break those hardest
> diamonds and melt that cold ice which often subsist in the tender breasts of
> these ladies. And this I believe is the true and sound pleasure and the goal
> aimed at by every noble [nobil] heart. Certainly, if I were in love I would
> prefer to know clearly that she whom I served returned my love from her
> heart and had given me her mind—without my having any other satisfac-

tion from her—than to possess her and have all her substance [goderla ed averne ogni copia] against her will; for in such a case I would consider myself master of a dead body. (2.94; S, 191–92, altered)

Gasparo's dismissive response, "whoever possess a woman's body is always master of her mind" (2.95; S, 192), well illustrates the function of misogynist speech in this discursive economy: by its open contempt of women it functions like a lightning rod to divert criticism from the subtler form of antifeminism that underwrites the profeminist position.[33] In the love-war convention Bernardo citationally deploys, the true lover is one who redirects rape action from the body to the mind and justifies his violence as retaliation for the suffering inflicted by and from "la ròcca," which is the chastity, the virgin power, alienated to "these ladies" through patriarchal inscription intended to keep female sexuality from interfering with inheritance. Their double bind reflects their double power, sexuality and chastity, the former feared and castigated by the antifeminist, the latter praised and castigated by the profeminist. When the true lover breaks into the fortress, the spoils of his conquest are her "voluntary" return of his love and "gift" of her mind.[34]

It is to this conception that the discussion returns in its final phase in Book 3, after Giuliano's defense of woman has turned into an attack on woman and into an account of the strategies by which the fort may be won. Perhaps because the antifeminist tendencies in his discourse become more pronounced at this juncture, Castiglione reactivates Gasparo's lightning-rod function by assigning him the long invective at 3.74–75. The diatribe is all the more surprising in view of a tonal change in his interventions that begins in Chapter 51 when he genially—and rightly—notes that "if I had not contradicted signor Magnifico and messer Cesare, we should not have heard all the praises they have given to women" (S, 256). Of his next six interventions before the diatribe, five are either mildly positive concessions or apparently nonpolemical questions that further the argument.[35] Such complicity heralds an intensification of the antifeminism always latent in Giuliano/Pygmalion's profeminist discourse. It also accentuates the homosocial character of the discussion at precisely the moment in which the shift of attention from the newly empowered "donna" to the courtier's erotic stratagems gives the speakers a topic that motivates male bonding.

Giuliano makes the homosocial turn explicit in his final contribution at 3.73, which responds to a request from Gasparo: "now that the Courtier knows how to win his Lady's favor and how to maintain it, and knows how to deprive his rival of it, it is for you to teach him how to keep his loves [amori] secret" (3.72; S, 277, altered). This returns to an earlier opinion expressed but not elaborated during Giuliano's discussion of the risks that confront lovers: "Love affairs that are brought about by common talk risk causing a man to be pointed at in public. . . . Therefore if our Courtier would follow my counsel, I would urge him to keep his loves secret" (3.67; S, 273). As we shall see in a moment, Gasparo's superficially benign effort to elicit more information on this topic packs a hidden punch, but Giuliano takes it up in good faith. He explains that the best way for the lover to maintain secrecy is not to blurt out his passion to his beloved in private, since that may arouse her suspicion, but to seek the help and mediation of "some loving and faithful friend . . . who, besides helping with favors and counsel, often repairs the mistakes made by the blind lover, and always observes secrecy and attends to many things to which the lover himself cannot attend. Moreover, a great comfort is felt in telling one's passions to a cordial friend and in unburdening oneself of them; and similarly, to be able to speak of one's pleasures to another greatly increases them [accresce molto i piaceri il poser comunicargli]" (3.73; S, 278, altered). In this passage the conflict between pro- and antifeminist tendencies stands out. On the one hand, Giuliano's emphasis falls on the danger posed to the liaison by male gossips, and on the beloved's justified doubts as to the lover's tact or sincerity. But on the other hand, there is a significant change in the form of the classic triangle, the orientation of which is at first heterosexual—*lover > (friend) > beloved*—and then homosocial—*lover > (beloved) > friend*.[36] As the instrumental role shifts from the friend to the beloved, her power is contained, and the grace she bestows on the lover, the intimacies she shares with him ("i piaceri"), provide the matter for erotic disclosures that increase the intimacy of the friends. Prompted by Gasparo, Giuliano continues to relish in the role of *magister amoris* a new and improved version of the Ovid he and Bernardo had dismissively mentioned just before his explanation. In doing so, he exposes his infidelity to the cause of the "donna di palazzo."

The profeminist's abandonment of the Pygmalionist project is certified by Gasparo's repetition of Giuliano's phrase "a tener secreti gli amori suoi" ("to keep his loves secret").[37] If "amori" merely means "affections," Singleton's translation, "loves," is misleading, but it is not misleading if the plural form implies that the courtier is a philanderer eager to avoid the deleterious effect of gossip on his campaigns against those bastions of chastity whose resistance offers the most exciting challenge. The concern for secrecy, however, may just as easily glance at women's promiscuity—at adultery and the liaisons of courtly love, or at premarital infidelity—and regardless of what Giuliano means to stress, this is where Gasparo takes it. He uses Giuliano's statement as a springboard to his long indictment of women, whose greatest pleasure is to collect and victimize lovers, flaunting their power to "make men miserable or happy, and bestow life and death upon them as they choose," and who perversely enjoy reducing "the poor lover to sheer desperation and to acts that make public what with every care ought to be kept most secret" (3.74; S, 278–79).

This takes us very far from the court lady and seems to have nothing to do with Giuliano's arguments. Yet at the beginning of the speech Gasparo makes it clear that he is taking a leaf from Giuliano's book: the cause of poor lovers' public disgrace is "vain ambition conjoined with madness and cruelty in ladies, who, as you yourself have said, seek to get as many lovers as they can." The reference is to Giuliano's denunciation, in 3.57, of "an error into which countless women fall, who ordinarily desire above all else to be beautiful: and since having many lovers seems to them a proof of their beauty, they put all their efforts into getting as many of them as they can" (S, 263). Giuliano has just reassumed the function of Ovid's Orphean Pygmalion and is characterizing the sins of the Propoetides from which he will safeguard his "creatura." In spite of Gasparo's rhetorical pleasure in paranoid exaggeration, the theme he batters away at is essentially the same as the one Giuliano lightly glides over, and the former's acknowledgment of his debt to Giuliano not incorrectly links his arguments to those of the profeminist. They are reactions to the same gynephobic fantasy.

This complicity is both implied and obscured by the summary comment of Ottaviano at the end of Book 3 that Gasparo slandered women "more than he should have" while Giuliano and Cesare gave them "perhaps a little more praise than they deserved"—in addition to which, he adds, they went on so long that "we have lost the chance to hear many other fine things that remain to be said about the courtier" (3.76). To accuse them of this double excess—partisanship and prolixity—is to find them guilty of a failure in *sprezzatura*. Ottaviano's comment reveals not only his own competitiveness and homosociality but also those of all the participants in a rhetorical contest that uses the discourse concerning woman as a vehicle of performative self-display. The comment reminds us that the speakers are not represented as having a deep personal investment in the woman question, which they treat as a performance opportunity. Their views of women are instrumental to an epideictic exercise in which they seek praise for their polemical skills. This makes all the more noteworthy the implication in Ottaviano's remark that the speakers protest too much. To have worked through Castiglione's complex and nuanced organization of diegetic patterns in the debate encourages the reader to take both the implication and the substantive issues more seriously than do the participants. Such dissonance between the reader's and the speakers' perspectives introduces the element of structural irony that allows one to entertain the possibility of internal distance between the text and the fiction it represents.

In this ironic space the norms, logic, agency, and dynamics of a cultural discourse driven by male fantasy become perspicuous. The ludic quality of the dramatic situation both conceals and enables the unfolding of a self-divided account of the sex/gender system that builds to a climax in which the profeminist argument is shown to be rooted in gynephobic anxiety. My reason for taking issue with the emphasis Rebhorn and Jordan place on the motivating political structure of the situation—a court ruled by women—is that it obscures the contrast between woman as the product of the textualized operations of male fantasy and the benign embodiments of woman who supervise the discussion, provide the attentive audience indispensable to any performance, and occasionally intervene with critical comments and procedural suggestions. The detextualized or embodied women who are dramatic personae seem more manageable, less powerful and dangerous, than the variety of specters that flit through male discourse using their sexuality and chastity to disempower men. That the dramatic context is ludic and the "actual" women nonthreatening is an important clue both to the phantasmatic character of those specters and to the textual critique of the disrelation between ludic aims and discursive meaning.

In Chapter 4 I cited and briefly discussed several statements by Lisa Jardine that profile discontinuities in women's actual, potential, and imagined or represented power over property and inheritance, over their own lives and sexuality, and over men. During my reading of the discourse concerning woman I picked out of the various arguments advanced by the participants a program of physiognomic and pathognomic (and physiological) inscription the aim of which is to make the behavior, speech, and appearance of *women* index the categories of *woman's* mind formulated by male fantasy—and formulated, as Jones, Kelly, Jardine, Woodbridge, Jordan, and others have shown us, in the service of erotic, legal, economic, and political interests. I now conclude with a question that was suggested to me by one of Jardine's statements, her reference to the effort of patriarchal agencies "to turn the wishful thinking of the male community into a propaganda reality" through ideological inscription.[38] If the element of wishful thinking is both conspicuous and successful, does it give rise to what may be called *representation anxiety*? Is there bad conscience in men about the representations they inscribe and the self-representations they induce on women? Or, to put it more accurately, is bad conscience inscribed and detectable in their discourse concerning women? Is there anxiety, too, about what lies behind the "propaganda reality"—uncertainty about the new "hidden" reserve their inscriptions create, the reserve of power, desire, and self-representation they may now suspect to be obscured by the "reality," a reserve that may include, perhaps as a closely guarded secret, the wishful thinking of the female community?

My affirmative answer to this set of questions leads me to correlate representation anxiety with gynephobic anxiety. The salient interpretive episodes that constitute my evidence for the correlation are as follows: (1) the implication of the count's discussion in 1.40 of women who "unwittingly" allow glimpses of their hands and ankles; (2) the traces of gynephobia registered by conspicuous exclusion in Giuliano's legends of good women; (3) the shadow, behind the Pygmalionist ideal proposed by Giuliano, of all the women who, like Ovid's Propoetides, fall short of the ideal and motivate its construction as a desperate defensive measure; (4) the disappearance of Pygmalion's ideal "donna" under the pressure of requests by other speakers that Giuliano return to the topic of erotic relations, and the consequent shift of perspective in which the discussants cheer the lover on with advice on the best way to diminish risk and conquer Ladies in erotic campaigns; (5) Bernardo's description of true love as mental rape in 2.94, and the reverberation throughout Book 3 of profeminist rhetoric that—to borrow a phrase from Teresa de Lauretis—"weaves the inscription of violence . . . into the representation of gender";[39] (6) the convergence of the pro- and antifeminist positions within the gynephobic force field of male fantasy, a convergence reinforced by the intensified representation of the male courtiers homosocially huddling together at the end of the third book.

"If the inner truth of gender is a fabrication and if a true gender is a fantasy instituted and inscribed on the surface of bodies, then it seems that genders can be neither true nor false, but are only produced as the truth effects of a discourse of primary and stable identity."[40] However radical such a formulation seems, it doesn't lie beyond the pale of a culture famous for its revival of skepticism and cultural relativism, for its critique of traditional essentialisms, for the demystifying effects of its technologies of representation. Much of Constance Jordan's book is devoted to exploring early modern feminist contributions to the critique of "rigid categorizations of gender that are based on sexual difference"—to "what today we call the cultural construction of gender," a construction in which gender was envisaged "not only as distinct from sex but also as flexible."[41] "The truth effects of a discourse of primary and stable identity" are precisely the target of the feminist challenge Jordan examines: its object "is to reveal that the hierarchy of creation and its reflection in human society, which is distinguished by its ranks of persons and . . . by their sex, is not naturally or divinely instituted" but is fictive—indeed, is doubly fictive, for the discourse of hierarchy conceals the fictiveness "of sex-determined gender" by concealing the fictiveness of the claims to divine or natural institution (67).

In the passages of the *Cortegiano* I have discussed, an attempt both to construct the norms and to regulate the performance of sex- and class-determined gender goes on right under the reader's eyes. The motivation behind the attempt and the problems it entails are outlined in the six episodes I cited as evidence for the correlation of gynephobic anxiety with representation anxiety. Yet I remain unconvinced that I have secured the argument for the kind of discursive irony that produces internal distance, that is, the argument that the text's relation to these anxieties is one of critique rather than participation. This is a roundabout way to avoid asking the question some form of which still troubles me even though merely to think the question is to commit the mortal sins of intentional fallacy and abuse of the author function. Do gynephobia, homosociality, and the antifeminist contamination of the profeminist argument appear in the text as the unintended consequences of the logic of male profeminist discourse circulating through the author's culture, or does he intentionally display them?

I assume, of course, that I can ask such a question without suffering excommunication because my concern is strictly with the author as a textual property or discursive function. Rephrased to express this concern, the question becomes, Does the text represent the performance of the author as subject to the same constraints and contradictions as those he inscribes in the performance of his fictive interlocutors? Is his representation of the interlocutors also an act of self-representation, and, if so, is it troubled by the bad conscience of representation anxiety? Is his performance marked by the gynephobia of gender and by signs of the sociopolitical disempowerment the portrait of Urbino's courtiers reveals? Finally, does the text offer the reader a perspective *on* this author, a position of internal distance from which to hold him up to critical scrutiny? The *Cortegiano* invites these questions because its parerga are prominent: there are several passages of authorial self-representation, the dedicatory letter or proem and the prefatory chapter of each book. These have often been casually discussed, primarily from the standpoint of genetic speculation about the historical author. Only once, to my knowledge, has authorial self-representation as such been singled out for sustained interpretation—in a very strong and valuable reading by Wayne Rebhorn, in *Courtly Performances*.[42] Rebhorn demonstrates decisively that a coherent pattern of motivation and characterization projects the author into the fictional limelight. In Chapter 6 I shall follow his lead, first discussing the prefatory chapter of Book 3 and then exploring the other *parerga* through a running dialogue with his interpretation of the author.

Three MISSING HERCULES

Unreliable
Narrators in
The Book of
the Courtier
and Galateo

6. Internal Distance: At Home and Abroad with Castiglione's Author

As a rhetorical performance 3.1 is a tour de force that produces its effect chiefly through a cunning deployment of the figure of Hercules, by means of which the author dramatizes his relation to readers with respect to a central problem in his portrait of Urbino. The problem has been well described by Arthur Kinney: on the one hand, the guests at Urbino, with their "shallow manners" and "trivializing talk," "ignore both the serious theological and political struggles" of the day, but on the other hand, "we cannot forget the fact that Castiglione also chooses to immortalize these very guests" and to preserve their discussion from oblivion in order "to teach a tarnished present." Relying on Ghino Ghinassi's reconstruction of the stages of composition, Kinney advances the genetic hypothesis that the fourth book, the last major addition, "rescues *Il Cortegiano*" from the "superficial concerns" of the earlier drafts.[1] Genetic explanation, however, is theoretically suspect, and is usually a symptom of interpretive default unless it is introduced ex post facto to lend contingent rhetorical support to an intrinsic or nongenetic reading. So, for example, someone who has already worked through a reading of textual irony in 3.1 and decided that its approach to the problem posed by Kinney is studiedly subversive will be happy to note Ghinassi's deduction that 3.1 was written later than the elegiac preface in 4.1–2. This gives aid and comfort, if little more, to the critic intent on showing not only that the *Cortegiano*—as we have it today—rescues itself from superficial concerns, but also that the rescue operation begins on page 1, and that the text represents both the concerns and the rescue in continuous dialectical encounter. In the discussion that follows, my effort to show that the Herculean extravagance of 3.1 obviates recourse to genetic explanation will not be so rigorous as to keep me from mentioning—and enjoying—the fruits of Ghinassi's research: the *Cortegiano* "was begun in 1514 as a relatively traditional commentary on *il valore delle donne*."[2] It is precisely such a traditional discourse, developed into a profeminist defense against misogyny, that the present state of Book 3 and its prefatory chapter place in question.

Addressed and dedicated to Alfonso Ariosto, 3.1 opens with a good humanist gambit, "Leggesi" ("one reads," or "we read"), and the subject of our text is the most subtle and ingenious method used by Pythagoras to deduce the size of Hercules' body from the size of his foot, with which the hero measured off a 625-foot-long stadium that was larger than other stadia of the same nominal length because the latter were measured by the smaller feet of ordinary mortals. The author urges Ariosto to apply the same Pythagorean reasoning to "this small part of the whole body" to prove the comparable superiority of the latter, the court of Urbino, "to all others in Italy, considering how much these games, which were devised for the relaxation of minds wearied by more arduous endeavors, were superior to those practiced in the other courts of Italy" (C, 205; S, 201, altered).

On the face of it, this labored analogy seems to have no other function than to allow the author to flex his humanist muscles by citing an account of the ancient paragons of mental and physical machismo. We should note that the object of admiration is not Hercules' feet but Pythagoras's feat, and that a moment's thought will disclose not only the triviality of that so-called feat but also its dubious empirical truth value. For presumably all Pythagoras had to do was apply a standard ratio, conventionally 6:1, to get the proportion of the body to the foot. And whether or not he was correct in the case of Hercules is undeterminable, since Hercules, if he ever existed, was no longer around, and since, being an anomalous figure or figment, his proportions (if he had any) may not have conformed to the standard. Why, then, does Castiglione puff up the achievement of the sage who is about to serve as a model for the ideal interpreter of the textual traces of the court of Urbino? Conceivably a skeptical—non-Pythagorean—reader might suspect she or he was being sent up, and deduce from his or her suspicion that Pythagoras was not reconstructing the Herculean body but inventing it, making a mythic cipher materialize as the embodiment of a conventional proportion. How, then, will that skeptical reader respond to a Pythagorean interpretation of the textual traces of Urbino?

It will be objected that all this misses the point of Castiglione's opening, which is not a personal reflection but a citation. Its first word is "Leggesi." The act of citation is performed with a discreet show of learning. Castiglione's subtext is the opening chapter of Aulus Gellius's widely read *Attic Nights*, and Gellius, who modestly or defensively refers to his work as a collection of "trifling pleasures" ("delectatiunculas"), begins the chapter with an attribution to Plutarch's treatise on Hercules ("Plutarchus in libro . . . conscripsit").[3] Since Castiglione echoes Gellius's Latin with several direct Italian equivalents, his subtext is easily recognizable, so that the laconic "Leggesi"—the refusal to follow Gellius's example and name the source—is a nicely "sprezzata" move: marking and making light of his erudition in the same gesture, he tactfully flatters his readers by showing confidence in their ability to identify the source. This is a courtier's game, a display of urbanity—of Urbinity—that not only illustrates and preserves the practices the author is praising; it becomes clear a little later in the chapter that it also mediates them by picking out a select readership of "nobili cavalieri e valorose donne" capable of appreciating the game, a readership the founding member of which is Alfonso Ariosto. But something else will become clear as well: the elite lectorial community mobilized, as it were, to reproduce Urbino's values is gradually displaced to make room for a more skeptical readership, brought into play by a strange metamorphosis of the Hercules analogy.

According to Rebhorn, the analogy poses no problem because the author "directly and unambiguously" extols the court, "equating Urbino's superior stature to Hercules' superior size and thus actually relating it to the more than human world of heroes."[4] This pledge of allegiance to the elite community ignores a rhetorical tactic that makes the author's comment on the court ambiguous and indirect. Castiglione begins by establishing three proportional analogies, or Herculean ratios:

1. *Hercules' foot : Hercules :: this book : Urbino court*
2. *Hercules' foot : Hercules :: Urbino's games : Urbino court*
3. *Hercules : other mortals :: Urbino's games and court : other games and courts*

In the passage from which I draw these ratios, the first two are less clearly distinguishable. The first is no sooner suggested than it slides syntactically into the second:

> *Voi adunque, messer Alfonso mio, per la medesima ragione,* [1] *da questa piccol parte di tutto 'l corpo potete chiaramente conoscer quanto la corte d'Urbino fosse a tutte l'altre della Italia superiore,* [2] *considerando quanto i giochi, li quali son ritrovati per recrear gli animi affaticati dalle facende più ardue, fossero a quelli che s'usano nell'altre corti della Italia superiori.* (3.1; C, 205, emphases mine)[5]

Once the ratios are picked out, it becomes possible to detect the volatile meaning traces of high-energy troping—after, that is, we decelerate the passage to the snail's pace that enables us to board it and move about inside it, for otherwise we get only a blurred view of the rhetorical mechanisms responsible for the sprezzatura of authorial self-representation. The primary mechanism is the mapping of the Herculean foot/body relation onto the relations among the book, the games, and the court. Since the foot/body relation is metonymic (or synecdochic), its influence complicates what would otherwise be a mimetic sign/referent relation by making the book a part of what it represents, and the syntactical slide from book to games confirms the complication. For example, when the identification of "questa piccola parte" with *Il libro del cortegiano* assimilates the book to the court as an organic or contiguous part (its foot), or as the trace of the part (the foot size), the Pythagorean reader is offered several partitive possibilities. The book is part of the court in the sense that it is a representation and memoir of some of its activities or in the sense that it is itself a courtly performance, a product and epitome of the Urbino style. The latter sense segues into another as the first ratio slides into the second: the relation of book to game is more than that of sign to referent; as a courtly performance, the book is the record or trace structure of one of Urbino's "giochi," an indexical sign of literary activity and the cultivation of letters. But this implies that the book does more than merely reflect Urbino's superiority; rather, it is the superior quality of the book from which one deduces that of the court. Readers are allowed a glimpse of this tactful yet distinctive gesture toward self-promotion before it gets swept under the rug of the second ratio. The rest of the prologue plays with other views of book and author, not all of them consistent.

Having made these initial maneuvers, the author begins to subject his ratios to a torquing pressure that turns them awry. If the games depicted in his book are so fine, he continues, "imagine what the other worthy pursuits [operazion virtuose] were to which our minds [gli animi] were bent and wholly given over" (C, 205; S, 201)—that is, the pursuits or performances not set down in his book.[6] This reference to things left unexpressed is amplified in the final section of the prologue. After a passage defending the credibility of his account, which I shall discuss later, he urges his future readers to model their Pythagorean practice on the following exemplar: no latter-day reader "of the marvelous things of the ancients does not form in his mind a certain higher opinion of those who are written of than the books themselves seem able to express, though they are divinely written." If in the future his own work proves "so worthy of favor as to be seen by noble cavaliers and virtuous [valorose] ladies," he hopes they "will suppose and firmly believe that the Court of Urbino was far more excellent and adorned with singular men than we can express in writing." After this he steers the prologue into a safe conventional harbor, the harbor of authorial apology provided by a blend of the topoi of inability and inexpressibility: "if we had as much eloquence as they [the singular men] had worth, we should need no other proof to bring those who did not see it to believe our words" (S, 201–2).

The harbor is less safe than it would have been, however, had his hope for the future not been spun about by the crosscurrent of the ancient analogue, which says that although the old books were "divinamente . . . scritti"—inspired, or consummately eloquent—it seemed that "non possano esprimer" opinions of their subjects as high as those entertained by later readers. Just what *are* these mysterious constraints? The phrasing seems carefully calculated not to attribute them to authorial self-deprecation, and this leads one to wonder whether the readers made more of the subjects than the written material warranted. The same suspicion is extended to the *Cortegiano* by the author's echoing phrase "che noi non potemo scrivendo esprimere." The echo allows the ancient analogue to throw the shadow of a doubt over the apologetic force of the inability topos. Is the apology directed toward a lack in the author's writing or toward a lack in the court and courtiers he writes about? The shadow also falls on the motives he attributes to the "nobili cavalieri e valorose donne" he singles out as the readers he most wants to reach. In appearing to flatter them in advance for their goodwill, is he also implying that they ennoble and valorize what they read by way of flattering themselves? Is it to compensate for some lack in themselves that he enjoins them to this effort of imaginative supplementation? Caught between the innuendo about ancient writing and the inability topos, the cause and meaning of that effort are placed in question.

A harder look at the use of the inability topos in this context intensifies the question. The topos is a paradigmatic instance of sprezzatura, and it thus takes us back to the first two Herculean ratios, which imply that as a courtly performance the *Cortegiano* is a product and epitome of the Urbino style, one of Urbino's games—indeed, a *ludus ludorum*. Under the rule of sprezzatura, the display of inability is a signal of, a claim to, high ability. The author is a *magister ludi ludorum*. His performance most closely and adequately imitates what he represents when he claims to fall short, when he dissimulates the adequacy of his account. Therefore the statement that the court and courtiers must be better than he says they are is to be taken as false. Not that they are worse, but that he is better; he is one of them; his performance is good courtly practice. If the writing does justice to the subject, and the ideal

readers of the future are still invited to provide lectorial enhancement, perhaps the invitation is merely an ornament of the inability topos. Or perhaps
not, since the influence of the ancient writing analogy suggests that readers
may find something lacking not in the author but in the subject; for ancient
authors wrote "divinamente." Perhaps the sprezzatura of inability operates
according to a seesaw principle, with the courtly author on one end of the
seesaw and the courtier he writes about on the other, and with the down
and up positions respectively signifying inability and ability. Then if the author politely goes down to send the courtier up, when the topos is decoded
(inverted) to send the author up, the courtier must bump down. On this
principle, the author may activate the topical seesaw to reveal that he is concealing a lack of some sort in the courtier, to invite lectorial enhancement
from readers moved to form "una certa maggior opinion" than the one they
find in the book, and to clear a space for other readers who are not so
moved and who may interrogate the author's invitation.

So wonderfully slippery a set of maneuvers brings into focus another
Herculean ratio, the fourth in our series,

4.   *Hercules' foot : Hercules :: the imitation of Urbino in the book : the
      reader's enhancement of it*

Comparison with the first ratio, *Hercules' foot : Hercules :: this book : Urbino
court*, shows that the analogical force of the whole Herculean body has been
redirected from the writer's model to the reader's enhancement. Reviewing
from this new standpoint the request to the Pythagorean reader to "imagine
the other *operazion virtuose*" not represented in the book, one is inclined to
shift the emphasis from "imagine the *other* worthy pursuits" to "*imagine* the
other worthy pursuits." It is the reader's interpretive fantasy that now receives the epithet "Herculean." But not, as I suggested, every reader, only the
noble reader with whom the authorial figure Wayne Rebhorn depicts as a
"nostalgic courtier" forges a courtly alliance.[7] The reader—or, to deperson-
ify, *the reading*—that emerges from the decelerated passage through the Herculean ratios is one constructed by that passage to go against the grain of the
nostalgic courtier's representation of himself and his subject, and to reject
the privileged lectorial standpoint provided for those who, in imitation of
the nostalgic courtier, would transform the text into an idealizing mirror in
which to recover or reaffirm themselves.

"Imaginate quali eran . . . l'altre operazion virtuose": Singleton's rendering of the last two words as "worthy pursuits" obscures the problematic
force of the invitation, since the noun may denote both performances and

works, while the adjectival form of *virtù* shares the noun's double meaning, "virtue" and "power." The skeptical emphasis adhering to the fourth ratio produces doubt about the Herculean fantasy, that is, it produces doubt about the Pythagorean claim or desire to restore the missing Herculean body of Urbino, or at least to measure and visualize the corporeal source of the mythic "operazioni" and "virtù" assigned to the names "Hercules" and "Urbino." How this skeptical reading problematizes the *Cortegiano*'s image of Urbino may be made clear by reflecting on the implications of the third ratio, *Hercules : other mortals :: Urbino's game and court : other games and courts.* One wonders, for example, in what way, according to what criteria, "these games, which were devised for the relaxation of minds wearied by more arduous endeavors, were superior to those practiced in the other courts of Italy." What could those endeavors be?

At this point I would like to return to Dain Trafton's thesis about the political implications of Giuliano's legend of good women, because it will illuminate the comparison focused by the third ratio. Through the analogy contrasting Urbino to other courts, Trafton argues, "the *Courtier* reminds its readers that the games it records, refined and fascinating though they are, do not represent the real business of courtiers." In the "greater and harsher world" of Italian politics, "the heroic energy and force of a Hercules (the whole man, not just the foot) are needed," and, I add, they are not to be found in what Thomas Greene describes as "this faintly effete community."[8] One is thus led to question the view that the author is innocently "equating Urbino's superior status to Hercules' superior size and thus actually relating it to the more than human world of heroes."[9] A glance at the discursive material stored up in the name "Hercules" indicates a less benign structure of allusion.

In both his classical and early modern manifestations, Hercules is an ambivalent figure who, beneath a glossy coat of idealization, retains a core of undomesticated and dangerous fury: "in spite of allegorical interpretation the stories of Hercules continue to suggest terrifying excesses as well as superb self-mastery ... and one sometimes has the impression that a somewhat subversive meaning asserts itself under the cover of the respectable official interpretation."[10] The displacement of beneficent moral or political power into the strength of the primitive club-wielding justicer may jeopardize its beneficence; the repressive violence necessary to protect weak men from gigantic forces of evil may seem indistinguishable from those forces. If Hercules is officially an exemplar of the *vita activa* he may also under certain circumstances betray his other role as a figure of phallic overcompensation who reflects his origin in the straits of gynephobic fantasy, an origin also expressed by the notoriety of his transvestite bondage.

None of this would be particularly relevant to the *Cortegiano* if Hercules appeared only in the two casual references we find in Book 4, where he is mentioned by Ottaviano and Bembo.[11] But things change when the interlocutor is the author rather than one of his characters, and when the context and circumstances of the reference to Hercules—introducing the discourse on women—invites suspicion. As will later be the case with Ottaviano's tyrant killer, Hercules and his phallic foot are brought into contact with what is clearly not a "more than human world of heroes." The effect of the ratios on the Hercules/Urbino analogy is to produce a recoil from similarity to contrast. The physicality, anger, and excessive violence never fully purged by allegorical cleanup crews from the exemplar of the active life are momentarily aroused by—and reinforce—the conspicuous inappropriateness of the comparison between Hercules and the "faintly effete community" of Urbino. This analogical strain engenders the specter of phallic overcompensation, for the anxiety to which the specter corresponds *is* appropriate to the constraints on the discourse of courtiership exhibited or implied during the preceding two books. By its hyperbolic expression, the caricature of a virile and violent agent of justice measures the depth of the discursive hole it fills.

It is the discourse of Urbino's "cavalieri" and "donne" that the *Cortegiano* represents, and it is the "cavalieri" and "donne" of the future that the author singles out as the readers he hopes to persuade to continue the discourse by magnifying their counterparts. Both sets are thus inscribed in the discourse of Herculean enhancement, which is also a discourse of self-interpretation and self-representation. The rhetorical maneuvers of the prefatory chapter of Book 3 constitute an oppositional set of readers by providing clues that will encourage them to resist an enhancement rooted in the fear of being unmanned, the courtier's fear made explicit by Ottaviano, his fear of finding himself inadequate to what seem to him to be the Herculean dimension of the ever "more arduous endeavors" demanded by the "greater and harsher world." From this I conclude that the figure of Hercules is used to run up a danger signal, and that the slippage in the four ratios inscribes in the text a disclaimer of responsibility for or commitment to the enhancement it superficially encourages.

I have not as yet discussed the one statement in 3.1 that offers most resistance to this conclusion. After mentioning but not itemizing the unrepresented "other worthy pursuits," the author goes on to assert that regarding the superiority of Urbino he dares confidently to speak in the hope of being believed, for I am not praising things so ancient that I am free to invent [fingere], and I can prove my claims by the testimony of many men worthy of credence who are still living and who personally saw and knew the life and the customs that once flourished in that court: and I consider myself obliged, as far as I can, to make every effort to preserve this bright memory from mortal oblivion, and make it live in the mind of posterity through my writing. (S, 201–2)

This passage chimes with the inability topos that concludes the chapter, and between these two moments is the discussion of lectorial enhancement. The passage differs from the discussion because it says that unlike praisers of ancient things, the author could not lie and get away with it, while the point of the discussion is that his book will resemble books about ancient things in relying on future readers to make more of Urbino "than we can express in writing." If in the first case what is at stake is the truth of "questa chiara memoria" to which reliable eyewitnesses can testify, do we take this truth to be identical with the truth that, in the second case, readers are urged to enhance?

Given the subversive seesaw of the inability topos and a defensive note of overprotestation in the first passage, one feels the force of the message conveyed by the comment on divinely written old books: their truth is never as glorious as later readers make it. Against the extension of this charge to the *Cortegiano* the author mobilizes his courtly rhetoric, his courtly eyewitnesses, and his courtly readers.[12] All together will testify that his memory is true, its "chiarezza" no enhancement, its nostalgic yearning justified. Yet at the same time, in the interpretive sea-change they undergo during their passage through the Herculean ratios, all testify that the author, as a nostalgic Urbino courtier writing about his dead fellow courtiers, is committed to preserving not only his sense of them but also their sense of themselves, committed to dissimulating (as they dissimulate) their weakness, committed to participating in the enhancement of the object of memory even as he insists that he doesn't. The urgency of commitment expressed by "io mi tengo obligato, per quanto posso" speaks as much to *this* necessity—the necessity of enhancing the truth—as it does to the necessity of merely transmitting it.

Later on in Book 3 Gasparo will remark of Giuliano's ancient legends of good women that "God alone knows just how these things happened; for those centuries are so remote from us that many lies can be told, and there is no one to gainsay them" (3.33; S, 235). This is a nastily disenchanted variation—but a variation nonetheless, a family member—of the author's "no one reads of the marvelous deeds of the ancients without forming a certain higher opinion of those who are written of than the books themselves seem able to express, though they are divinely written." Perhaps Hercules, Pythagoras's admirable calculation, Plutarch, Aulus Gellius, and *Cortegiano* 3.1 constitute a lectorial chain of supplemental enhancements, or "lies." But if so (and there is no way of telling), they are lies that reveal the truth about the interpretive fantasy that motivates them: the truth of the desire for supplemental enhancement, the desire to compensate in reading or rewriting for what the written testimony of the past seems unable to express. Castiglione looks back through Gellius (and Plutarch) to the intellectual power displayed by Pythagoras in calculating the physical size of Hercules. An odd detail suggests the character of the chain: in Gellius's account, the stadia are 600 feet long;[13] Castiglione overgoes his pretext by adding another twenty-five feet, which in turn enlarges the fabled Herculean foot and body—if, of course, there ever was such a thing, and if it conformed to Pythagoras's proportions. This little *aemulatio* registers the phallic impetus driving through the chain of successive efforts to capture or supplement or otherwise dominate the past, and it suggests to me that the truth of Hercules' foot, as of the phallus it displaces, is profoundly illuminated by the following inversion of the formula expressing the truth of Pinocchio's nose: the bigger it grows, the more it lies.

The lesson I draw from the parable of supplementarity I have explored in this section is that Hercules is missing. There is a gap where an origin should be, and anxiety about the gap is expressed by filling it with the mythic caricature of virility. The first chapter of Book 3 stages a parody of authorial sprezzatura in which the name of Hercules and the moves implicit in the argument collaborate to engender the problem of narrative authority and representation anxiety. The author who picks out his ideal readers, the noble and the valiant, can't avoid picking out others, if only by the logic of conspicuous exclusion. Those readers who refuse the invitation to supplement his inability with lectorial enhancement, and who thereby mark the invitation as an act of authorial self-parody, are then invited to look for the traces of the anxiety that motivates it, and all the traces lead to the theme of disempowerment. They lead back to the impotent duke who founded the games and forward to the powerlessness of the profeminist argument to purge itself of the antifeminism it opposes. Thus at least in the case of 3.1 we can point to a textual agency, a coherent and therefore "intentional" structure of logical, narrative, and rhetorical or dialogical moves, that continuously interrogates the simple positivity of the portrait of Urbino and its courtly games.

This interpretation of 3.1 may support a claim that the failure of the profeminist argument is prepared for and signaled by the engendering of authorial self-representation. But it still isn't clear that what holds for Book 3 holds for the rest of the *Cortegiano*. Since we know from Ghino Ghinassi's research and his publication of *La Seconda Redazione del "Cortegiano"* that Book 3 was composed after the others, its critical perspective on the author's performance could conceivably be a new development. Can we find support elsewhere in the book—that is, in the other parerga—for the effects I have been describing? In approaching this inquiry it will be well to forestall possible confusion over the question of the order in which the books were composed. The parerga contain definite, if inconsistent, statements about the conditions and motives of composition, statements about the author's relation—including his temporal relation—to the events he portrays. In the proem dedicated to Michel de Silva, he writes that, intending to publish the book after a delay of many years, he "started to reread it" (Proemio, 1; S, 2). And he goes on to describe the sadness caused by the death not only of many who participated in the conversations but also of Alfonso Ariosto, to whom the four books are dedicated. Book 4 begins with an account of the bitterness he felt when, "thinking to record the discussions held on the fourth evening following those reported in the previous books," he remembered that "untimely death deprived our court" of three of the participants shortly after the discussions took place (4.1; S 285).

This gives us a sketchy chronology. The proem is the last in the series, the result of a rereading preparatory to revision of the rough draft he dashed off many years ago, shortly after the death of the duke and not long after the conversations took place.[14] Book 4, the first of the books to establish temporal distance from the event, precedes the Proem. He gives no detailed indications of the changes he made between the rough draft and the final version except to imply that the exigency of immediate publication kept him from revising as much as he would have liked. It would be a mistake to assume that the differences between the genetic story Ghinassi tells and the one implied by the few clues the author gives should be ignored; they serve to emphasize the point that what I am concerned with is a fiction of genesis contained within the fiction of authorial self-representation. Whether or not the genetic clues illuminate the history of the text, they illuminate the self-interpretation of the author, and this is how I shall treat them in the discussion that follows.

★ ★ ★

"I can prove my claims by the testimony of many men worthy of credence . . . and I consider myself obliged . . . to make every effort to preserve this bright memory from mortal oblivion, and make it live in the mind of posterity through my writing" (3.1; S, 202). The note of urgency and defensiveness in this passage is neither isolated nor arbitrary. If it marks the passage as an appeal for credibility and not simply as a claim to it, the letter to Silva offers a pragmatic reason why the author should display anxiety. New information in 1.1 complicates the reason. In 2.1–4 his sententious wisdom about the effects of aging on judgment and memory hints at yet another refinement of the reason. The problem of the author's dependency on the reader, brought to the fore by the Herculean ratios, is featured in 4.1–2, where it anticipates discussion of the ethical and political problems raised by the courtier's dependency on the prince.

The author begins the proem to Silva by explaining that because, after Duke Guidobaldo died, "l'odor" of his virtues

> was fresh in my mind, and the delight that in those years I had felt in the loving company of such excellent persons as then frequented the Court of Urbino, I was moved by the memory thereof to write these books of the Courtier: which I did in but a few days, meaning in time to correct those errors that had resulted from my desire to pay this debt quickly. But Fortune for many years now has kept me oppressed by such constant travail that I could never find the leisure to bring these books to a point where my weak judgment was satisfied with them. (Proemio, 1; S, 1)

It was because Fortune's assaults were reinforced by another Bad Lady, who betrayed her trust and threatened him with loss of control over his text, that he decided to revise and correct ("revedere" and "castigare") as much of it as time would permit, and to publish it.[15]

Castiglione depicts himself in the same threatened position he assigns to Guidobaldo in 1.3 and, a little farther on in the Proem, to Ottaviano Fregoso, whose *disgrazie*, "so steadfastly endured, were indeed enough to prove that fortune, as she ever was, is even in these days the enemy of virtue" (Proem, 1; S, 2). The meaning of "disgrazie" is illuminated by Ullrich Langer's perception that fortune is not only a figure for but also a product of the arbitrariness of despotic power: Ottaviano's disgraces are caused by princely disfavor and ingratitude.[16] The bitter irony of this is sharpened when we remember that the author's thought of Ottaviano's death through (princely) "disgrazia" is motivated by his rereading of Ottaviano's exhortation to courtiers to become counselors and moral reformers of princes—an exhortation and argument delivered in a manner that suggests Ottaviano does not have high hopes for the success of the project.

The tactful displacement of despotic power to "la fortuna" may be no more than a rhetorical reflex, a conventional trope of self-censorship, but it is precisely this "no more than" that makes it a significant move. For if it is casual or arbitrary with reference to the specific user of the trope, that only means he has let himself become the conduit through which a linguistically grounded structure of male fantasy imposes itself on his narrative and engenders his anxiety, modulating it through the filter of gynephobic discourse. Trying to avoid blaming princes, who are also the symbols, sites, and agents of patriarchal authority and law, one avails oneself of what is expressly a mere personification, an anamorphic condensation, of a host of unspecified but safely alterior forces and causes. It is thus that woman appears, in Marguerite Waller's phrase, "as the dangerous, supplemental, figural term" that represents not only the evil some men do but also the kind of victimization others suffer: infantilization, emasculation, by the specter of the powerful, hostile, deceitful, and irrational virago that haunts the material—that is, rhetorical—conventions of discourse.[17] Note, however, that the individuals who courageously oppose fortune—Guidobaldo, Ottaviano, the author—can still be characterized as heroes, or at least heroic underdogs. The subject of emasculation is not the individual but the structurally constrained sociopolitical position he occupies. As La Fortuna, the agent of emasculation is the hyperbolic personification of all the unofficial powers possessed by or ceded to women as sex objects, wives, and mothers.

All but one of Castiglione's references to fortune fit this pattern, but that one is perhaps the most interesting. When Guidobaldo "began to promise more than it was permitted to hope for from a mortal being," so that men judged Federico's "begetting such a son" his most notable accomplishment, fortune stepped in and crippled his body (1.3). Here the author's phrasing directs attention to the problematics of father/son rivalry, "A son was expected to emulate his father," writes Coppélia Kahn, "in the sense of following his example and carrying on what was begun. But . . . emulation . . . almost always shades into ambitious rivalry for power or honors . . . which is frequently contaminated by envy."[18] It is as if the motherless son's threat to paternal donation is punished by the virago who exercises her arbitrary despotic power on the father's behalf but in such a way as to diminish his legacy. As Thomas Greene points out, the creative male figure, Federigo da Montefeltro, the founding father, is dead. In his place there exists a vacuum. Duke Guidobaldo, the putative male leader, is indisposed and absent. He never enters the stage, the game space of the drawing room, and he fails to play the centrifugal, out-thrusting role that his father had played and that would open up the rigid enclosure of the court's withdrawal.[19]

Greene's emphasis is on the practices by which this court, protected against fortune's assaults by its benign "feminine enclosing presence," acknowledges but resiliently contains the threats and challenges, "the insecurities and inconsistencies" (12) that beset it. He remarks that "the quality of laughter in the book," defined by "the beleaguering force of enclosure . . . has its own purity and its own courage even if that courage falls short of the full lucidity which would render this purity impossible" (14). While I endorse and admire this subtle, supple characterization, my emphasis obviously tends in the opposite direction, since I believe that although the author also endorses and admires what Greene praises, the text that represents this author is by no means saturated by his endorsement and admiration. On the contrary, it depicts not only his portrait of Urbino but also his relation to the portrait, as I tried to show in the preceding discussion of 3.1, and it marks this relation with insecurities and inconsistencies that redirect the reader's attention to a vacuum *in the portrait*. The representation of the author hints at his anxiety about a certain rigidity of enclosure and desire of withdrawal that affect his memory of Urbino and may distort his portrait.

The first traces of anxiety appear in his account of the series of distractions that forces him to rely on a temporally distant retrospect. It isn't clear whether the errors caused by the elegiac impulse to turn out a quick draft are errors of style or errors of factual recall, but the new information in 1.1 will point toward the latter. One of the problems caused by the delay, as he ruefully notes in the prefatory letter, is that most of the participants he writes about have died, and this renews the elegiac impulse that, added to "the threat to my book," moves him finally to have the book "printed and published in such form as the brevity of time permitted" (Proemio, 1; S, 3). The apologetic tone conveys the strong implication that he is still dissatisfied with his portrait of the court, and in the sentences that follow, the implication is restated in the form of the inability topos, which temporarily, and conspicuously, shelves the question of accurate recall. But we have been put on notice that he is powerless to recall the event as if from a standpoint within it, and that the temporal distance may not translate into a critical distance, since the years between have suffused his memory with bitterness and nostalgia.

The question of accurate recall is reopened in 1.1 by two new pieces of information. (1) The author gives a different account of the origin of the book, attributing it to a request from the dedicatee, our old friend Alfonso Ariosto, to "write my opinion as to what form of Courtiership most befits a gentleman living at the courts of princes" (1.1; S, 11). Now a thematic purpose either replaces or is added to the elegiac purpose. These two purposes are easily reconcilable but it is obvious that they call for different emphases, and that the motive of factual recall may be subordinated to the coherence of thematic explication. (2) He appears to take this possibility into account and defend against it when he states that his book will not "follow any set order or rule of distinct precepts, as is most often the custom in teaching anything whatever." Instead, he will follow "the fashion of many ancients," and,

> renewing a pleasant memory, we shall rehearse some discussions that took place among men singularly qualified in such matters. And even though I was not present and did not partake of them, being in England at the time when they occurred, I learned of them shortly thereafter from a person who gave me a faithful report of them; and I shall attempt to recall them accurately, in so far as my memory permits, so that you may know what was judged and thought in this matter by men worthy of the highest praise, and in whose judgment on all things one may have unquestioned faith. (1.1; S, 12–13)

The news that the *Cortegiano* is a secondhand rather than a firsthand account should startle anyone who has just read in the prefatory letter that the author, moved by the duke's death, dashed off a hasty draft that he intended to correct. Now we learn that he will revive a pleasant memory by trying to recall, as accurately as his memory permits, the faithful report given by an eyewitness shortly after the conversations took place.[20] Since the duke was alive when they were taking place, the report must have been part of the memory that moved the author to write his draft; yet the qualification "in so far as my memory permits" suggests that he lacks a verbal transcript of the report, and that the reconstruction Ariosto is about to read has recently been composed, many years after both the event and the report. In the meantime, the pleasant memory has receded behind a screen of bitter memories not only of his own vicissitudes but also of the death of so many whose loss has "left me in this life as in a desert full of woes" (Proemio, 1; S, 2).

This unexpected change in the author's genetic account raises several questions. The most interesting is the question of the author's absence, but since the meaning I attach to that piece of news derives from aspects of authorial self-representation I have yet to discuss, I defer my comments on it until the end of this chapter. A more manageable question at this point concerns what it means for a report to be "fidelmente" narrated, and on what grounds the absent author would deem it faithful. The question has nothing to do with the conventions of historical representation; we can assume that verisimilitude was an enabling fiction, that modern standards of transcription (the "faithfulness" hyperbolically represented by taped conversations and film) are irrelevant, that interpreters imitated what they took to be the "truth" of the past by freely reconstructing its setting, detail, rhetoric, and so on.[21] Within this permissive historiographical framework, the question raised by Castiglione's author centers on the psychosocial factors that may have affected the report. They include the influence of the reporter's interests and desires on his memory and attention; they also include ad hominem or (in Aristotle's sense) ethical considerations—for example, does the author equate an Urbino eyewitness with a "nobile cavaliere" who could be expected to have the right take on the matters he reports? His characterization of eyewitnesses in 3.1 suggests that this is the case. The eyewitness would be faithful to an interpretation he shared with the author. But the author has already displayed his own vulnerability to motives that induce him to submit his account to "castigatio," which for him as for his humanist predecessors denotes the act of emendation that restores a corrupt text to integrity.[22] And even within the safe confines of a consensual community, reports may differ, as he is careful to note in 2.5: when the lately arrived prefect asked what had been said on the previous day, "as often happens, he got a variety of answers, because some praised this and some that, and many disagreed also as to what the Count's opinion had really been, since everyone's memory had not fully retained what had been said" (S, 95). Given the author's criteria for "fidanza," however, all these responses could be equally faithful, regardless of how much they conflicted, and—more important—regardless of how inattentive the respondents had been to the detail of what they heard; the quality of "fidanza" is an a priori property of the members of the club.

Another question raised by the revised account in 1.1 concerns the author's statement that "alla foggia di molti antichi . . . recitaremo alcuni ragionamenti" ("in the fashion of many ancients we shall represent some discussions"). This allusion to classical exponents of the dialogue genre flags an intention to engage in literary aemulatio, activates the pun lurking in "recitaremo," and sends scholars rushing to their Platos and Ciceros, especially—in the case of Castiglione's parerga—to the *Orator* and *De Oratore*. In the era of high scholarship the threat posed by the conspicuously citational performance was that it tempted readers to place the authorial expression of personal sentiments in quotation marks by centering on their emulative function, and thus on the author's learning, ingenuity, and rhetorical mastery. This threat has more recently been displaced by another, one that challenges even the most sophisticated readers of citational performances: the danger that the critic will confuse the author who is the cause of self-representation with the author that is its effect. It used to be acceptable practice to phrase this as a distinction between author and speaker or persona, or between the author at the desk and the author in the text, but since this distinction begs the question of the "social text" that includes both the reader or critic and the author at the desk, new approaches to literary history treat the latter on the model of the author in the text, thus preparing the stage for the act of prestidigitation that will make both vanish. However, the application of the concept of intertextuality to both social and literary texts has often tended to obscure the difference between the two. And whether the difference is reintroduced in a relativizing manner or a heuristic mood, it is essential to an interpretive practice that centers on interactions between fields of textuality that are theoretically—and empirically—distinguishable.

When it comes to the interpretation of "imitatio" and "aemulatio," which constitute an intertextual field of explicit citationality, it is useful to replace the distinction between the author at the desk and the author in the text with a distinction between authors in literary history and authors in intertextual diachrony. That is, it is useful if one is to deal not only with examples in the field but also with prior approaches to it. "Authors in literary history" names the version of the field constituted by high scholarship and left unquestioned by the New Criticism, which narrowed attention to the intertextual field of allusion. It is by foregrounding the distinction between the two categories that we may confront and overcome the confusion they often suffer in practice, and thus work toward a clearer grasp of the way citational performance reveals the agency of the author in the text. In the example that follows, I shall try to show that this approach leads to a strange if not unexpected result: the portrait the interpreter draws of the author in history—of Castiglione at the desk—turns out to be a portrait that the text subjects to critique, and it is largely through citational allusion that it does so; this result suggests the pressure of a textual agency that can't be identified with the interpreter's portrait of the author at the desk.

In his discussion of the author as nostalgic courtier, Wayne Rebhorn uses the *Cortegiano*'s Ciceronian echoes to develop a persuasive contrast between Castiglione and Cicero. The burden of difference is that although both authors represent themselves as nostalgic, "Castiglione seems much less concerned with the complex, concrete historical situation of his beloved Urbino when compared to Cicero, who carefully relates the characters and events he describes, as well as his own situation, to the larger developments of Roman history."[23] I note in passing the somewhat peculiar construction "when compared to Cicero"—reading innocently along, one expects the comparison implied by the "less" phrase to be completed by a "than" phrase ("than Cicero is with Rome")—because it adumbrates a crucial interpretive move that I shall consider in a moment. Rebhorn goes on to argue that the contrast implied by persistent allusion and variation highlights Castiglione's tendency to ignore "much of Urbino's history," his vagueness "when alluding to historical events involving its relationships to other Italian states," and his silence about his own diplomatic activities. His prefatory letter "raises a series of puzzling questions" of historical fact but leaves them unanswered, giving only a "somewhat vague" impression "about what happened to the court of Urbino during the time he was writing and revising . . . and he is equally vague about his own personal relationship to it" (103).

Rebhorn uses this citational contrast in support of the following two theses: first, Castiglione transforms Urbino into a strangely remote and ahistorical Arcadia for which he—like the sad shepherd of pastoral—nostalgically mourns; second, his "horrified vision of a universe overwhelmed by the absolute tyranny of death and fortune" prevents him from fully accepting either the pastoral vision with its "complacency about time and death" or Cicero's "historical vision" focused on the meaningful efforts of human agents, a political vision of "Roman patricians engaged together in a tragic struggle for the survival of the state" (103–8). Castiglione's response to the stark vision is not merely to "brood passively and helplessly about" the lost Arcadia but to memorialize it in elegy, "to compose a fitting and enduring monument for the dead." Thus, Rebhorn concludes, Castiglione resembles Proust, "that greater master of nostalgia," in relying on "art, not religion, . . . to recapture lost time, to resurrect a dead past, and to achieve . . . a momentary intimation of immortality" (114).

This emphasis on the interaction of nostalgia, idealization, and memorial desire is obvious enough, and not in itself new. It has often been remarked by scholars writing about the relations between the composition and meaning of the *Cortegiano* and its author's political career. In 1973, for example,

José Guidi persuasively demonstrated how political changes between 1508 and 1528 both account for and are effaced by the portrait of Urbino's golden age.[24] But Rebhorn's interpretation is distinguished from others by its evidentiary mode—sustained close reading informed by the convergent legacies of New Criticism, genre criticism, and the interdisciplinary coalition of cultural and art history that emerged in the 1950s and 1960s under the rubric of Renaissance studies. For me, this approach, with its distinctive focus on the *Cortegiano*'s generic affiliation, produces a compelling interpretation, and one to which I am deeply indebted.

The nature of the debt, however, is not simple, and in today's critical climate it isn't even simple to describe. To say that my debt to Rebhorn includes the opportunity to make adjustments in certain aspects of his vision that I can't fully accept—to say this is to invite the charge that so courtly a way of phrasing an introduction to the critic's favorite pastime, trashing precursors, is snide at best. But the charge reflects simplistic assumptions about critical encounters, for example, that they should be zero-sum and two-dimensional affairs dominated by agon and epideixis, that they should either be a central form of action in the polemical genres classified as theory or else be relegated to footnotes in more workaday jobs of interpretation, and that footnotes are the appropriate environment—cramped, marginal, of modest eight-point stature—in a word, adequate for listing credits, briefly thanking creditors, and compactly (if less briefly) dismissing competitors.

Such conventions make it harder for those working in interpretive genres to do in public what most of them do in their preparatory negotiations: map the traces of the continuous exercises in triangulation that involve critics in often complex journeys as they circulate back and forth between "secondary" and "primary" texts. In the present case my reading of authorial self-presentation in the *Cortegiano* was influenced by and filtered through the formulations and terminology of a single critical study. But at the same time that I tracked the portrait of Castiglione's author through Rebhorn's reading I discovered something in his formulations and terms that resisted his deployment of them and suggested a different reading. It is this whole negotiatory process that constitutes the proper sphere within which to define indebtedness and express gratitude, and to do so with no implication of irony. In what follows, I shall try to show, through a dramatization of the process, how impossible it is to dissociate my view of the *Cortegiano*'s authorial performance from Rebhorn's view of it and from my view of his view of it.

I begin by recalling the distinction I mentioned above between the sentence Rebhorn didn't write, "Castiglione seems less concerned with history than Cicero," and the sentence he did write, "Castiglione seems less concerned with history when compared to Cicero." The comparison shaped by the first formulation is between two authors in literary history, two writers at their desks, Castiglione and Cicero. The comparison shaped by the second formulation is more complex: it is between Castiglione contrasted to Cicero and Castiglione not contrasted to Cicero, and the difference Cicero makes is that Castiglione seems less concerned with history than he would have been had the contrast not been drawn. Rebhorn treats this as a strong or marked contrast, one that implies a judgment—"less concerned than he *would* have been" = "less concerned than he *should* have been." But where does this judgment come from? Is it Rebhorn's judgment on the author in literary history or is it his description of a judgment passed by the text on its author?

His trenchant analysis of the effects of citational contrast and his subsequent argument linking the ahistorical Castiglione to the sad shepherd running back to paradise clearly indicate the latter. But that leads to a further implication: some textual agency must be imagined as producing an attitude toward Castiglione's bad attitude toward history; some textual mechanism must be transformed magically, animistically, into an intentional force, personified as another author, another Castiglione, the one who uses Cicero to suggest that Castiglione seems less concerned with history than he should be. If we rely on such hypostatizing devices to put into play the concept of authorial self-representation, we find ourselves confronted in this case with a divided figure of agency and desire, or with two authors, one of them behind the deployment of Cicero, the other its target. Thus Rebhorn's comparison is not between two authors in literary history but between two authors in the text.

I have been unpacking what I believe to be the logic of his comparison in order to demonstrate the structural necessity of divided agency to his reading of the *Cortegiano*. For me, the strength of the reading lies in its directing us toward that structure. Yet in the course of developing the argument about the nostalgic courtier who flinches from history, Rebhorn loses sight of the other author. As he dwells on the sad shepherd's attempt to recapture lost time in an ahistorical image and resurrect a dead past by idealizing it, the author whose contrastive imitatio casts a cold eye on this attempt vanishes, or is assimilated to his target. This disappearance or conflation protects the shepherd from intratextual criticism, and it is confirmed by

Rebhorn's final laudatory comparison of two authors in the literary history of nostalgia.

In order to restore the distinction Rebhorn began with, I turn back once more to his account of the Ciceronian *imitatio*, which has special interest for me because the intertextual action he describes has the form of conspicuous exclusion, a trope often found in the neighborhood of the act of conspicuous allusion that converts a source or influence to a meaning effect. The effect is clearly and compactly registered in the following remarks by Carla Freccero, whose argument is similar to Rebhorn's but whose focus on the political dimension of the effect is sharper:

> The characters in *De oratore* are all dead at the time the dialogue is being narrated, and at least two of them . . . were killed for political reasons. They are orators reduced to political impotence, just as Castiglione's characters (although he does not mention it) are courtiers deprived, in the context of despotic and distant rule, of their role as counsellor to the prince. The explicitly political context of *De oratore* resembles the undiscussed situation of Castiglione's courtiers, as aristocrats whose class status is threatened by the changing political circumstances of the Italian peninsula.[25]

Freccero goes on to develop a persuasive account of the devices by which the undiscussed political dilemma is conveyed through displacements that in turn have an impact on the medium of displacement, noting, for example, that "through the discourse on women, Book III attacks both the papacy and the courtier's 'new' position" (273), and that passages seemingly about the problems and virtues of women are vehicles for discussing the problems and virtues of courtiers (268–79).

Freccero's more penetrating analysis of conspicuous allusion/exclusion can be used to strengthen Rebhorn's attempt to show that the shadow of Cicero falls across—and marks—a path not taken by the nostalgic courtier on his journey toward Arcadia, a shadow that continues to trouble the reader who might prefer to take it. It is the shadow of the *metapastoral* attitude, which I have characterized elsewhere—and at length—as the intertextual critique of pastoral escapism. More specifically, in studies of pastoral from Theocritus to Marvell I have identified a strain of strong, or disenchanted, pastoral that targets—by parody, mimicry, and ironic citation—a variety of discursive genres linked together by a common project: they all justify or promote the desire for eternal power, pleasure, and happy consciousness in a permanent glorified body by representing it as the pursuit of moral, religious, aesthetic, philosophical, erotic, or ascetico-contemplative transcendence; a transcendence effected through the sublimation of life into art, body into soul (the body's glorified state), the human into the divine, speech into song, and love into literature.[26]

It may be straining generic limits to classify all these projects and practices as pastoral, since they aren't confined to literature that displaces its self-reflection into the vehicle of the idyllic or rustic landscape peopled with shepherds. But since Rebhorn's focus on the pastoral aspects of the *Cortegiano* is illuminating, and since the idyllicism his focus picks out transcends the generic confines, I shall use "pastoral" and "metapastoral" loosely to denote a particular structure of desire and the critical perspective on it. I have called this structure "the paradise principle" and demonstrated that when viewed through metapastoral glasses it appears not simply as a positive longing for the paradisal state but as a dialectical interplay between fantasies of paradise and equally excessive fantasies of disorder, an interplay in which idyllic desire and misanthropic or anthrophobic anxiety entail each other, exacerbate each other, as two sides of the same dynamic. Indeed, the extent to which the logic of this pastoral principle governs such an apparently non-pastoral example of the desire of transcendence through sublimation as Bembo's speech in Book 4 tells us much about the way the text problematizes that performance.

Both the rapturous Neoplatonic ascent Bembo describes and the corresponding intensification of the rhetoric of rapture with which he describes it are threatened with demystifying quotation marks by the conspicuous citationality of the discourse—its clear echoes of Ficino and Plato, and his reference to its source in the historical Bembo's own text, *Gli Asolani* (4.50). The idea of a grace beyond the reach of art is thus revealed as the product of an art that dissimulates self-limitation and self-transcendence—as, in a different mode, the author does when he executes the inability topos. Bembo presents and appears to participate in an experience structured by the semantics of logocentric and physiognomic truth claims (see especially 4.57). But the presentation is hollowed out by the intertextual resonances that mark it as citation and thus *re*presentation. Were this a gratuitous and isolated effect, a metapastoral critique of the speaker and his performance alone, it would be trivial; he could well be enraptured by the Neoplatonic discourse of rapture. It is the discourse itself, the powerful tradition of the Neoplatonic and Christianized misreading of the *Symposium*, that the critique targets, and it does so by positioning it in such a way as to make it an escapist response not only to the difficulties of the political activism promoted by Ottaviano in Book 4 but also to the erotic difficulties of Book 3. In fact the shift of attention from the former to the latter is itself interpretable as a regressive move to escape the potential trauma of exposure to princely politics.

The shift is engineered by Gasparo, who resituates the problem of the old courtier within the context of the woman question, to which Bembo responds not so much with a homosocial as with a theosocial solution. And in spite of its aspiration, the speech remains immured within the parentheses of the woman question. After Bembo concludes he seems "quasi . . . astratto e fuor di sé," rendered "come stupido" (C, 332) by the power of the Platonic/ Ficinian/Bembonian subtext he recited. The very increase in mystical discourse—which, as J. R. Woodhouse notes, differentiates the final draft from the *Seconda Redazione*—revives the irony of logocentric performance more broadly featured in the latter when an interlocutor begs Bembo to "tell us, then, with your living voice what you have written" and Bembo replies, "you would perhaps wish me to recite a book here?"[27] Emilia's good-humored attempt to bring Bembo back to his senses is less deflationary than his response: if his soul forsook his body, it "would not be the first miracle love has worked in me"—this arch allusion to previous love affairs shows us Bembo has returned (4.71). And his subsequent refusal to continue (because the citational afflatus has left him) is followed by a series of comments that land the discussion back in the debate between Gasparo and Giuliano, so that Book 4 ends with a promise to revert to the woman question on the next night.

Given this context, the traditional discourse of transcendence that incorporates the "Platonic" slander of the body with Christian contempt of the world is unmasked as a higher idyllicism, as a logocentric confusion of mediated (discursive) with unmediated (prediscursive) inspiration, and therefore as a desire not to abandon but to retain the body and its pleasures in the glorified state known as "soul."[28] Bembo's speech, in short, is a script written by the paradise principle. Addressed to aging courtiers, it offers them a metaphysical nostrum, the revelation of a blameless and trouble-free love that would bring them the "somma felicità," keep them from looking foolish, and not distract them from continuing to instruct the prince (4.50). But what Bembo goes on to describe is for all practical purposes a misogynistic and apolitical escape from the fickleness of women and princes to God, the private—indeed, secret—bliss of intercourse with the beauty "hidden in the inmost secret recesses [*secreti penetrali*] of God," and the promise of "true rest from our labors, the sure remedy for our miseries, . . . safest refuge from the dark storms of this life's tempestuous sea" (4.69; S, 355). This performance is also colored, as we shall see, by the author's critique in 2.1 of the bitterness of old men nostalgic for the lost pleasures of youth. Bembo metaphorically restores those pleasures in the safer paradise of spiritual bliss.

In metapastoral representations of the paradise principle, idyllicism is often found masquerading as idealism, and misanthropy as the morally justified *ressentiment* of the world-class victim. Within this general framework metapastoral discourse stages traditional debates over the relative merits of polar opposites in order to ambiguate the terms and deconstruct the polarities. In its citational performances of traditional arguments for or against youth and age, city and country, ambition and retirement (or action and contemplation), eroticism and antieroticism, profeminism and antifeminism, it shows how they infiltrate and contaminate each other, and how the threat of contamination is defended against by ever more strident assertions of the purity of each position.

I introduce this framework here for two reasons. First, it makes explicit the structure that governs what I can now call Castiglione's metapastoral representation of the nostalgic courtier, and, as we shall soon see, it will enable us to analyze the way the *Cortegiano* uses the diachronic youth/age opposition to perform its critique of the author's nostalgia. Second, it makes explicit the structure that governs the terms and relations of Rebhorn's analysis and will thus enable us to reorganize those terms and relations in order to realize the full power of his interpretation. Rebhorn, as we saw, sets three factors against each other, the pastoral idealization of Urbino, the implied Ciceronian critique of its ahistorical escapism, and Castiglione's fantasy of disorder, which, as Rebhorn describes it, is not so much misanthropic as misocosmic: "Arbitrary, perverse, irresistible, death and fortune are the ultimate powers in Castiglione's universe; they reduce cosmos to chaos and negate the very possibility of forming any scheme, any order at all. . . . Castiglione's horrified vision . . . separates him from the pastoral tradition" and "also helps explain why he refused to follow Cicero's lead and establish a historical scheme" (111).

Rebhorn's argument that the vision overwhelms the idyllic defense thrown up against it doesn't quite square with the metapastoral perception that the defenses and the vision are the complementary fantasies of a single principle.[29] If the theory of pastoral I outlined is valid for Castiglione, it suggests that what helps explain the refusal of historical specificity is not the separation from the pastoral tradition but, on the contrary, the nostalgic courtier's submission to it—submission to the paradise principle that is the source of the horrified vision no less than of its idyllic complement. Furthermore, the refusal of a historical *scheme* seems to me to be less relevant to the *Cortegiano* than the refusal of another historical function, the accuracy with which the past is recaptured. And this is indeed where Rebhorn's real emphasis lies: his comments on Castiglione's selectivity, vagueness, and tendency to idealize the past support the view that the *Cortegiano* represents the intrusion of elegiac and eulogistic desire as one of the pressures that impose limits on memory. The comments make available all the interpretive materials with which to make a case for the metapastoral reading Rebhorn occasionally gestures toward. The problem remains of trying to determine whether and how Castiglione flags the author's refusal of history and submission to the paradise principle. I turn now to explore these issues in a passage that makes them perspicuous, the dedicatory chapters of Book 2.

In 2.1 the author criticizes the tendency of the aged to "praise bygone times and denounce the present," which he attributes partly to the fact that, having been deprived of youthful capacities and pleasures, they fail to see that "the change is in themselves and not in the times" (2.1; S,89, 91). The cause of the fallacy, then, is in his opinion chiefly physiological: age "deprives the blood of a great part of the vital spirits; wherefore the constitution is changed, and these organs through which the soul exercises its powers become weak" (89–90). He concedes the debilitating effects of senescence and describes them in heightened language that conveys the sympathy of one who well understands how the sense of loss could induce the fantasy that youth is a golden age and that the rest of life is doomed by the body's nature to be a fall from *illo tempore*. But he goes on to spend the remainder of the first three chapters criticizing the old men for their poor logic, faulty historical perceptions, misplaced bitterness, and obtuse self-righteousness. This is the longest of the four prefatory sections, twice as long as the elegiac lament for the dead that opens Book 4, and almost as long as the dedicatory letter to Silva. To ask why this should be and what the preface is really about quickly resolves itself into the question, *Who* is it about? Is it about the old men or about the author? Is so long and energetic a diatribe presented to the reader as a set of authorial reflections to be accepted at face value and even admired for their spirit and sagacity? Or does its form, rhetoric, and argument redirect attention from the critique of old men to a critique of the critique? The reason these questions are not real but rhetorical is that my reading of the preface has been influenced by Rebhorn's—less by its argument than by its form, and in particular by the odd way in which it duplicates the form of the author's prefatory argument.

Rebhorn begins with a concession similar to the author's: he preemptively grants that insofar as Castiglione's "nostalgia for Duke Guido's court" leads him to see it "through rose-colored glasses," he is to some degree vulnerable to the charges he levels at the old men. But like Castiglione, Rebhorn goes on to enumerate, and to accentuate, the differences that manifest the author's superior insight. First, "Castiglione presents himself as a much more balanced and reasonable judge" than those he scolds, and his "very scolding" demonstrates his sure grasp of the source of their misapprehension, proving that the nostalgia "which colors his entire work . . . has not blinded him to reality or perverted his judgment." Second, although both the author and the old men "yearn for a more beautiful, fulfilling past," Castiglione differs in that "he refrains from projecting his sense of loss into a moralistic condemnation of the present," preferring to contrast "Urbino's past glory . . . with his own very personal isolation" rather than "with its subsequent decline" (100–101).

Such an *apologia pro suo auctore* places a strange filter between its object and our view of it. It makes the author's performance appear to be an example of the same exculpatory strategy. As a result, both the performance and Rebhorn's account of it seem less persuasive, and this is an enabling clue to a more suspicious interpretation. But because his account presupposes a weakness in the author's position and proceeds to defend against it as if the author needs help, it blocks consideration of the possibility that the author may be displaying the need for exculpation—displaying, that is, a threat of inculpation that he doesn't want explained away. This clue extends the preemptive concession of nostalgia from Rebhorn's argument to the author's, and changes the significance of his polemic against the old men. For now the polemic assumes the value of a diversionary maneuver responding to— and defending against—the suspicion that "his own nostalgia . . . [may] lead him to a distorted presentation" of Urbino (100).

An important feature of the maneuver, and one I wouldn't have remarked had not Rebhorn's emphasis picked it out, is the author's tendency to minimize what he has in common with the old men—they both distort the past—while dwelling on their distorted treatment of the present. This is diversionary because the chief problem addressed by the parerga of the *Cortegiano*, by the orientation of its pastoral nostalgia, and by Rebhorn's study as a whole, is the problem of the distorted representation of *the past*, not of *the present*: "I consider myself obliged, as far as I can, to make every effort to preserve this bright memory from mortal oblivion," and to do so in a narrative to whose truth reliable eyewitnesses can testify (3.1). The representation of the present is largely—and conspicuously—irrelevant to this project. Thus when Rebhorn dwells on that theme after dismissing the problem of the past in a briskly executed concessive/adversative sequence,[30] he produces what amounts to a parodic foreshortening of the diversionary maneuver more discreetly pieced out by the author over the course of the first four chapters of Book 2. And the effect of parody provides me with a key that opens the way to the text's metapastoral perspective on the polemic of the nostalgic courtier. That is, if I take Rebhorn's account to be not merely an exposition of the author's performance but a kind of caricature that places the author's exculpatory strategy in relief by foreshortening his argument, then the account becomes the model of an ironic perspective *in* the text. It helps me imagine a metapastoral author who throws himself "ridendo," with wry gusto, into the pastoral author's vexed representation of himself as an expert in comparative nostalgia.

The traces of metapastoral mimicry are clearest when viewed through the magnifier of close reading, and they appear early in 2.1. Since their target is the author's pastoral gerontology, I begin with an outline of its thesis. The author opens the chapter on a reflective note, wondering why it is that "la età matura," which in other matters tends to make human judgment more perfect, should so corrupt it when it comes to comparing the present with the past that old men invariably praise "i tempi passati" and denounce the present without realizing that if history always went downhill we should long since have hit bottom (C, 115). Since references to this erroneous judgment exist in ancient writings, he assumes it is universal and must therefore be "proprio e naturale" to the aged. This assumption gives him permission to locate its cause in the body and display his confident mastery of psychobiology: because the bodily organs of the soul weaken with age, "not only the body but the mind also is enfeebled," and thus memory is more easily vulnerable to distortion. The appeal to physical determinism justifies any senior citizen who claims to be powerless to correct the distortion.

From this point on the author appears to forget his reference to the beneficial effects of "la età maturita" on all other mental functions. Concentrating his attention on the exception, he treats it as the rule and reduces "i vecchi" to personifications of an anomaly for which they are to be pitied (because they can't help it) and blamed (because they stubbornly and irrationally persist in denouncing the present).[31] However, his position with respect to the old men becomes uncertain and his credentials as critic, psychobiologist, and gerontologist become suspect as soon as he continues with his explanation:

Thus, in old age the sweet flowers of contentment fall from our hearts, as in autumn the leaves fall from their trees, and in place of bright and clear thoughts there comes a cloudy and turbid sadness attended by a thousand ills. So that not only the body but the mind also is enfeebled, and retains of past pleasures merely a lingering [*tenace*] memory and the image of that precious time of tender youth in which (while we are enjoying it), wherever we look, heaven and earth and everything appear merry and smiling, and the sweet springtime of happiness seems to flower in our thoughts as in a delightful and lovely garden. (2.1; S, 90)

Although the first-person plural has general force, the sentiment is pumped up and personalized by the rhetoric of Poetic Feeling. The author makes it clear that the parade of elegiac clichés signifying pastoral nostalgia is not citation or mimicry, as in "thus"—*they say*—"in old age the flowers fall," but his own opinion: "for my part, I do believe . . ." ("estimo io per me," C, 115). He himself buys into a theory that affirms the glory of "quel caro tempo della tenera età" and justifies the bitter reaction to its aftermath on basically physiological grounds. His science, in short, is a pastoral science, one that excludes the more balanced view of "la età maturita" he began with so as to conform with the logic of the paradise principle. For it is the expectation or desire of eternal youth and immortal happy consciousness that produces not only the unbalanced bitterness of old age but also the unbalanced glorification of youth, and not only these paired fantasies but also the pastoral science that naturalizes them.

In this connection it should be noted that the context of the phrase "no other than a lingering memory" ("né . . . altro che una tenace memoria," C, 115–16) makes "tenace" hard to translate, and Singleton's "lingering" (90) doesn't catch its range of implications. Partly because it means "tenacious" or "stubborn" and partly because it is often idiomatically used to modify the faculty ("avere la memoria tenace") rather than its product, "tenace" here glances at a possible displacement: a memory tenacious of past pleasures clings to *their* traces rather than to *others*, but the mind ascribes tenacity to *their* power and its *own* feebleness. That the pastoral theory validates the ascription and that the author confidently expresses and fervently espouses it expose his authority as a critic of "i vecchi" to metapastoral scrutiny. One is almost tempted to ask how old he is and whether his age would qualify him for membership in the class of old men by the standards of his era.[32] But such a genetic consideration is irrelevant to an interpretive practice focused strictly on the textual indices that establish his relation to the old men. He may well be, if not a very senior citizen, then at least what in today's parlance would be called "mature," but the point is that on the one hand he opposes the old men as a "they" to his editorial "we," and on the other hand the logic and rhetoric of his performance identify his general perspective with theirs. Inasmuch as the opposition implies that he is not an old man, the identity of viewpoint disproves the pastoral theory, since his nostalgia can't be attributed to physical decrepitude.[33]

The contradictions and limits of the author's commitment to pastoral science and poetry appear more forcefully in the lines following those I just discussed. He expresses the counterfactual wish that

> when the sun of our life enters the cold season and begins to go down in the west, divesting us of such pleasures, it would perhaps be well if along with them we might lose their memory too; and, as Themistocles said, discover an art that could teach us to forget. For the senses of our body are so deceitful that they often beguile the judgment of our minds as well. Hence, it seems to me that old people in their situation resemble people who, as they sail out of the port, keep their eyes fixed upon the shore and think that their ship is standing still and that the shore is receding, although it is the other way round. For the port, and similarly time and its pleasures, stay the same, while one after the other we in our ship of mortality go scudding across that stormy sea which takes all things to itself and devours them; nor are we ever permitted to touch shore again, but, tossed by conflicting winds, we are finally shipwrecked upon some reef. (2.1; S, 90)

At first the author continues to sympathize with the plight of old men, for he and they together are subject to the fate of "nostra vita" and the power of "i sensi del corpo nostro" to deceive all who live long enough. But the use of the third person in the nautical figure that follows brusquely pushes "i vecchi" away and assimilates them to "quelli" whose landlubberly incomprehension converts their ship of mortality to something like a ship of fools (C, 116). Their naïveté exerts the pejorative pressure of caricature on the erroneous judgment they illustrate.

This is an unexpectedly contemptuous picture of those depicted in the author's preceding sentence as victims of the deception he attributes to the aging process.[34] But I think a motive for the shift to caricature may be glimpsed in the final sentence. Returning to the inclusive "we" and the rhetoric of personal involvement, he feelingly complains that after "we go flying [fuggendo]" away from the port of youth and pleasure in the ship of mortality,

our storm-tossed voyage inevitably ends in shipwreck. Once again his attitude coincides with that of the old men, for the lament participates in precisely those sentiments that the author goes on to criticize in the next three
chapters: the pessimism of the aged, their embittered idyllic desire, their
sense of loss and disempowerment. As Marina Beer notes, the fantasy of dread
and powerlessness expressed by "fuggendo n'andiamo l'un dopo l'altro per
quel procelloso mare che ogni cosa assorbe e devora" is his fantasy as well as
theirs.[35] Thus the effect of caricature in the nautical analogy strikes me as a
diversionary tactic with a scapegoating function. It conspires with the uneasy waver between critique and pathos to flash a metapastoral signal sending the reader news of a problem: what motivates the author's investment in
his attack on old men?

The logic of the paradise principle that drives pastoral discourse is a logic
that conforms in some respects to what Julia Kristeva calls "abjection." The
principle produces its complementary fantasies, the idyllic and the horrific,
by excluding and alienating (abjecting) the deathly powers exerted by the
weakness of the body. "Necessarily dichotomous, somewhat Manichaean,"
the subject constituted by pastoral discourse "divides, excludes, and without,
properly speaking, wishing to know his abjections is not at all unaware of
them," for the abject is excluded in a strange manner, "not radically enough
to allow for a secure differentiation between subject and object, and yet
clearly enough for a defensive *position* to be established." The opposition is
thus "vigorous but pervious, violent but uncertain."[36] Castiglione's pastoral
author abjects the seductive dangers of his nostalgia into a safely distorted
caricature. Yet his critique of the aged abjects is performed with a degree of
rhetorical vigor that suggests he doesn't feel impervious to the boomerang
effect.

"Vigorous but pervious": this precisely describes the combination of force
and fear with which the author prosecutes the critique. The force is more
obvious than the fear, and my reading of the fear as the inner lining of the
force derives, as I noted earlier, from my interpretation of the language
Rebhorn uses to distinguish the author's nostalgia from that of the old men.
What gives me permission to treat Rebhorn's account as a model of metapastoral mimicry is his insistent repetition of terms that stress the author's
rhetorical self-consciousness. In the following sequence of predications Rebhorn's language gradually intensifies our sense of the author's anxious and
tautly focused effort at self-presentation: Castiglione "*establishes* an implicit set
of contrasts," "*presents himself* as a much more balanced and reasonable judge"

than the old men, "*shows himself* able to discriminate," and, by "scolding" the old men for being unaware of the effects of nostalgia, he "*demonstrates*"

> his own self-consciousness about it. The effect of all these contrasts is not to deny the latter's nostalgia, which colors his entire work . . . , but *to show* that it has not blinded him to reality or perverted his judgment. Castiglione *places his nostalgia* within the context of a reasonable, discriminating, self-conscious personality and thus *makes himself* a difficult target for the mockery and censure he directs at the old men. (100–101; my italics)

Against the background of the passages in 2.1 I just examined, this characterization conveys the pressure of the author's self-scotomizing impulse to defend against the suspicion that he may be too easy a target. He is especially vulnerable when "scolding" the old men, since his scolding seems to be as self-righteous as theirs, so that in the act of criticizing their failures he exhibits them as his own. Thus the transfer of Rebhorn's compact and foreshortened scenario to the text enables us to precipitate out a screen of metapastoral impersonation that targets both the performance anxiety of the pastoral author and the uneasy conscience with which he defends himself from the boomerang effect of the attack on his senile abjects.

This conclusion, however, only revives the question I asked earlier: what motivates the author's investment in the attack? The short answer is, his desire to defend his nostalgic portrait of Urbino, but the gap between the question and the answer needs to be filled in by an outline, at least, of the strategy that connects the attack with the desire. An economical way to do this is to review the sequence of propositions of which the author's pastoral gerontology consists: (1) youth and its pleasures are the golden age of life; (2) owing to physiological decline, life after youth is a stormy journey ending in shipwreck; (3) it is natural and understandable, if unfortunate, that the effect of proposition 2 on old men's judgment and memory leads them to confuse the quality of youth with that of the past in which it occurred and the quality of old age with that of the present in which it occurs; (4) since propositions 1 and 2 lead them mistakenly to conclude from 3 that the past is always better than the present—a theorem with absurd historical consequences—they praise the morality and customs that prevailed during their youth and censure those that prevail during their old age; and this is stupid.

Propositions 1 and 2 flow from the paradise principle as the logical consequence of the interaction between idyllic desire and its misanthropic or misocosmic complement. The author lays them down primarily to pave the way for the critique in 3 and 4, by dwelling on which he dramatizes his superiority to the old men. As Rebhorn notes with approval, he pays special attention to their irrational tendency to condemn the present: "While both he and they yearn for a more beautiful, fulfilling past, he refrains absolutely from projecting his sense of loss into a moralistic condemnation of the present" (101). But first, since the portrayal of the present is not what the author is concerned about, the condemnation contributes to the pattern of diversionary moves that fend off criticism of his treatment of the past. And second, he doesn't emphasize that he shares the old men's yearning in 1 and 2; this is revealed only by the elegiac rhetoric with which he discusses the propositions. The first consideration points toward the real problem, the desire for "a more beautiful, fulfilling past" that troubles his portrait of Urbino, while the second suggests that in downplaying his own submission to the paradise principle in 1 and 2 and accentuating its perverse effect on the old men in 3 and 4, he is evading the real problem. Because the diatribe is conspicuously irrelevant to the problem, I deduce from its length no less than from its intensity that it has the force of a strategic misdirection. And because he himself apologizes for its length, I think the reader is encouraged to suspect that, in Kristeva's words, "without . . . wishing to know his abjections [he] is not at all unaware of them": after harping on point 4 for two chapters, he confesses that "questo discorso" is "forse ormai troppo diffuso ma non in tutto for di proposito" (C, 119) "perhaps already too copious but," he insists, "not on the whole irrelevant to his subject."

The "proposito" is his portrait of Urbino, with which the remainder of the long sentence that constitutes 2.4 deals, and which has been linked to the critique by the comparisons introducing 2.2 and 2.3:

> Of courts therefore they speak as of all else, declaring those they remember to have been far more excellent and full of outstanding men than those we see nowadays. (S, 91)

> Therefore, when our old men praise bygone courts for not having such vicious men in them as some that are in our courts, they overlook the fact that their courts did not contain some men as virtuous as ours—which is no marvel, since no evil is as evil as that which is born of the corrupted seed of good; hence, as nature produces much greater talents now than she did then, so those who aim at the good do far better now than did those of former times, and those who aim at the bad do far worse. (S, 93)

Alluding to these arguments in 2.4, he announces his intention to return "to the discussion that took place concerning the Courtier, from which we readily understand the rank held by the Court of Urbino among other courts, and what manner of Prince and Lady they were who were served by such noble spirits, and how fortunate all could count themselves to live in such a society" (S, 94–95).

It is in the very next chapter, however, that a seed of doubt is planted about the evidentiary basis of the portrait by the author's report of the response to the prefect's question concerning the debate of the previous evening: "as often happens, he got a variety of answers, because some praised this and some that, and many disagreed also as to what the Count's opinion had really been, since everyone's memory had not fully retained what had been said" (2.5; S, 95). After this, as Rebhorn observes, "Castiglione's own reliance for his account of the ideal courtier upon the supposedly accurate memory of an unidentified individual invites raised eyebrows at the very least, and it underscores the fact that *Il Cortegiano* is a fabrication by directly flouting the laws of probability Castiglione otherwise respects" (55). But why should it do this? Rebhorn argues that it is to underscore authorial or artistic power. I think it is to underscore authorial or artistic or courtly weakness. But I arrive at that conclusion only after coming to realize how much Rebhorn's argument reflects, and thus elucidates, a similar argument for power in the text—an argument for the power of a pastoral representation and for a courtly readership, a horizon of courtly expectations and reception, that will make it come true; but an argument the text metapastorally questions as a compensatory and idyllic appeal for help from the compensatory and idyllic desire of readers. This is what I mean by saying that the text underscores or thematizes authorial weakness and, as before, I find it most useful to approach the theme via Rebhorn's defense of the pastoral argument for power.

Centering on the contradiction between the author's feint toward "historical authenticity" and the "feeling that . . . [he] is gilding Urbino's lily," Rebhorn notes that the stretch between these tendencies has divided Castiglione's readers into two camps, and he tries in a lengthy discursus (55–90) to show how the problem can be made to vanish by shifting from modern to Renaissance expectations. First, he reminds us, Castiglione's "contemporaries assumed that when one wrote history, one created a work of art that was in some measure an ideal reconstruction of reality and not a literal transcription of it," so that it would be normal practice for him to wish to commemorate his subjects both "as real people" and as "ideal types" or exemplars (57, 55). But second, although "humanist historical theory and practice" are influential in a "general and approximate fashion," Castiglione nowhere calls his work a history; he calls it a portrait ("ritratto") and conceives of it "as a painting rather than a history" (58–59). This gives Rebhorn permission to develop in detail the argument that, as in High Renaissance painting, Castiglione poses the relation between the mimetic and idealizing tendencies as one not of contradiction but of the harmonious reconciliation of opposites. He provides just enough information to make his characters recognizable as historical personalities, but otherwise simplifies and stereotypes them to the specifications of the "representative types" of a particular class: "Just as Raphael painted his *Castiglione* both to do honor to the individual and to celebrate an ideal type, a representative of nobility and courtliness, so Castiglione depicted characters who are at the same time historical realities differentiated by their personal attributes and ideal types serving to illustrate just how ideal courtiers and ladies behaved" (80).

These comments may seem obvious enough not to need so much citation, but my aim is to show that Rebhorn both ascribes to Castiglione and himself embraces the interpretive principles of a particular early modern ideology, the one I have called mimetic idealism.[37] Mimetic idealism resolves the tension between the claims of mimesis and those of idealization by relying on a thesaurus of traditional, chiefly classical, arguments—among them, for example, the argument that art is superior to nature in its selectivity, and therefore closer to the real idea that nature strives for but generally fails to realize. The art of self-fashioning and its product, sprezzatura, fit comfortably under this description, and Rebhorn's demonstration that the author represents himself as a courtly performer, a master of literary sprezzatura, lends support to the notion that in his artful pretense to be "natural"—that is, truthful and accurate—he fashions an idealized but still faithful and recognizable portrait of Urbino.

Nevertheless, sprezzatura has a negative as well as positive dimension, and the tension between mimesis and idealization is too real and stubborn, too central to early modern discourses and technologies of representation, to be resolved by arguments that don't explain it so much as explain it away. To ascribe mimetic idealism to Castiglione on the grounds of the argument from period mentality assumes what has to be proved. Granted that there is a place in the *Cortegiano* for both of Rebhorn's opposing camps, those who read it as "a valid mirror of its culture" and those who focus on its "unrealistic, idealizing character" (56–57), it is at least conceivable that the text may be disobeying Renaissance rules and refusing to resolve the conflict in the mode of mimetic idealism. It's even conceivable that it keeps the two camps in conflict in order to *represent* the desire of resolution inscribed in mimetic idealism so as to question its validity.

Nothing in Rebhorn's account blocks that possibility. Consider once more his basic characterization of the split: on the one hand, Castiglione implies that the ideal really existed, was historically instantiated at Urbino, by giving his portrait "the appearance of being real discussions carried on by real people," and on the other hand, in various ways he "emphasizes the improbability of his fiction and declares that his *Cortegiano* is indeed a work of art" (54–55). By this emphasis and declaration, the author conveys the message that he freely composed his portrait, selectively improved on the nature of life as he knew it at Urbino, so as to bring out its best features and, "with little significant distortion of reality," made it not merely an example but a model and paradigm of "the ideal civilization" (89–90). But why should the emphasis on improbability work only to heighten the portrait of an ideal reality? Why couldn't it, very simply, undermine it by indicating its improbability? This is the alternative I now turn to explore.

Far from reconciling the incompatible representational emphases, the parerga continually thrust the incompatibility in the reader's face and, in doing so, they make it serve a particular configuration of premises: (1) there is no question that the *Cortegiano* represents itself to its readers as imitating real discussions by real people; (2) there is no question that it represents these people in simplified exemplary form as members of an idealized class; (3) it does indeed seem to flag their exemplarity as historically authentic, and thus encourages readers to conflate premise 2 with premise 1 in accordance with the formula of mimetic idealism; (4) there is no question that many clues to the improbability of the fiction are sprinkled throughout the text; (5) these clues raise questions not about premises 1 and 2 separately but only about premise 3. In other words, the *Cortegiano* pretends to portray real people and pretends to portray them as really ideal, but pretends also to portray their idealized reality as improbable, and pretends, finally, to offer clues to a less ideal and exemplary if inexplicit portrait of the real people. The first two pretenses (premises 1–3) produce the pastoral perspective, which is identical with that of mimetic idealism, while the last two (premises 4–5) open up the metapastoral critique of the first two.

To conclude that the interaction of all these pretenses or premises constitutes the fiction of the *Cortegiano* is to remind oneself that the first premise is no less a pretense than the others, so that the real people who come to life in its pages have only a pseudo-mimetic or pseudo-referential relation to their counterparts beyond the book.[38] The author's inconsistent statements about his relation to the events he purports to describe conspicuously confuse the reader's sense of the genetic process of composition. To Rebhorn's perception that this confusion produces skepticism as to the author's claim to historical accuracy I add that the accuracy is nevertheless something on which the author insists. The effect of this contradiction is to persuade us to take the first premise seriously but alter the meaning we attach to it. That is, the purpose served by the fiction of historical representation is no longer primarily mimetic. The mimetic baseline becomes an allegorical device. It is allegorical in that it enables the author to represent both himself and his subjects as the imaginary sites of real discourses, and by "real" I mean rooted in the changing social and political arrangements from which the discourses derive their structures of interest and motivation, their contradictions, their agency. As I tried to demonstrate in my account of the discourse of gender in Book 3, these are the discourses by which the interlocutors represent themselves to themselves and each other, and by which they represent to themselves and each other their views of their relation to the changing arrangements. And since the discourses have their own objective structures of interest and motivation, they are neither fully controlled nor fully understood by the subjects who put them in play.

It is in these terms that I return to the parerga in order to explore the relation between the fifth premise mentioned above—the premise that clues to the improbability of the fiction problematize the pretense to portray historical figures as really ideal—and my claim that these clues underscore authorial weakness rather than power. I begin with the passage that led Rebhorn to focus on the analogy to painting:

> I send you this book as a portrait of the Court of Urbino, not by the hand
> of Raphael or Michelangelo, but by that of a lowly painter and one who
> only knows how to draw the main lines, without adorning the truth with
> pretty colors or making, by perspective art, that which is not seem to be.
> And, although I have endeavored to show in these conversations the quali-
> ties [le proprietà] and conditions of those who are named therein, I confess
> that I have not even suggested, let alone expressed, the virtues of the Duch-
> ess, because not only is my style incapable of expressing them, but my mind
> cannot even conceive them. . . . (Proemio, 1; S, 3)

Successive expressions of modesty and inability help the author ensconce himself in the rhetorical ethos of the reliable truth-speaking portraitist of the court: no cosmetic flourishes, no false illusions, no effort to conceal his inability by mendaciously expressing the inexpressible. But while protecting his integrity and sharing with us the standard he will hold himself to, he nudges us to be on the lookout for adornments that strain beyond the limit at which "the ideal reconstruction of reality" (Rebhorn, 57) could still be considered an authentic reproduction. In tracking his performance through the parerga, we might keep in mind that in one sense of the phrase "ideal type," there could be an ideal type of the disempowered courtier, and that the portraitist could adorn this figure of need by painting into his image the pretty colors of imaginary power. Rebhorn doesn't discuss this possibility, but the parerga keep it before us. They detail the circumstances and suggest the motives that prevent the truth from being undistorted by the kind of adornment I just exemplified, motives that lead the author to present idyllic distortion as idealized mimesis, provoking him to a variant of that art of forgetting which, he remarks in 2.1, Themistocles longed for.

The aim of the Themistoclean art, the author tells us there, is to "teach us to forget" the pleasures whose loss makes us bitter. The author's variant is to teach us to forget death and loss, or to diminish their pain, by revising the pleasurable image of the past, even if that means replacing the real past with a fiction. The pastoral art of forgetting makes that which is not seem to be by making that which was or is seem not to be. It is an art of pretending to have lost what actually may never have been there to begin with, pretending to recapture and resurrect what the artist creates. Arthur Kinney argues that the portrait of Urbino "omits much that is damaging" because Castiglione's is "an uncompromising view of art that will teach men to forget what is painful" and "admit what elevates."[39] These words give aid and comfort to a view of his art the pastoral author would like his readers to ratify, but they ignore the many signals that lace the parerga with the metapastoral suspicion that his may be a compromised view of art, a view that commits the artist to gilding Urbino's lily while pretending not to.[40]

The often-stated opinion that the author "makes his mask reflect the qualities prescribed for the ideal courtier" (Rebhorn, 92)—an opinion I endorse and have tried to substantiate in this study—supports a positive reading of this view by mapping it onto sprezzatura. In the basic formula, "look how artfully I pretend to be natural," "natural" for the author becomes "accurate" or "truthful." In the formula that relates the ideal courtier to the absolute courtier, "look how artfully I pretend to have grazia," "grazia" for the author denotes not only the gift of fluent expression but also the gift his book receives from the sprezzatura and grazia of those it commemorates, for if their virtù is true, his share in it enables him effortlessly to be accurate or truthful. In both formulas the accent on pretense raises questions, but in neither formula need the pretense jeopardize the presumption of accuracy, since the accent tends to fall reflexively on the equation of the author's artfulness with his pretense of artlessness or effortlessness. His use of the inability topos may contribute to this effect inasmuch as the message "I am incapable of saying how good they are" conventionally cues the reader to applaud his mastery of literary craft and courtly demeanor without arousing the suspicion that he is only pretending to tell the truth.

There is, however, a negative reading of authorial sprezzatura, one toward which we are directed by two features I discussed earlier. The first is that sprezzatura signifies a lack of the grazia it dissimulates. The second is that when the concept of grazia shifts, during the course of the discussions, from God and nature (inherited grace) to the prince, from an ascriptive to a performative source and relation, the political dilemmas of courtiership are brought into the foreground. The foreign invasions, the crisis in political leadership, new and unstable relations of autocracy and dependency—these conditions, to which Castiglione frequently alludes, lead scholars to describe the disempowerment of the courtly elite as effeminizing. The failure of the traditional ascriptive fantasy and the transfer of grazia into the gift of princes are the symbolic and institutional sides of the same structural change. Both appear in the *Cortegiano* as targets of opportunity, but that appearance is qualified by many statements indicating that both are also sources of anxiety. It has often been pointed out that the moral idealism informing Ottaviano's political counsel to courtiers in Book 4 is enclosed in the parentheses of a counterfactual hypothesis and is represented as an attempt to make the best of a bad thing. Opportunity gives way to anxiety as the discussion turns more and more to the problems posed for courtiers by the perception that most of the princes who dispense political grazia are lacking in its ethical counterpart, so that it becomes increasingly difficult to imagine how the courtier fashioned in Books 1 and 2 could succeed. Ottaviano argues that the political task calls for a Theseus and Hercules, not for the cool reserve of a literate, witty, mannerly dissembler of grazia who sits a horse well and defends his honor in duels (4.37–46). The courtier is therefore advised to yield his title to the figure of an older, wiser counselor on the model of Aristotle and Plato (and even Plato failed), but one no longer capable of competing with his juniors in the activities and performances essential to successful participation in the daily social life of the court. The political impotence of the young courtier is replaced by the old courtier's ineptitude in love play, and this sad conclusion, engineered by Gasparo, motivates Bembo's idyllic flight to the hidden higher mysteries (4.46–51). Trapped in the vacuum between two regimes of grazia, the old and the new, the sprezzatura celebrated and imitated by the author as nostalgic courtier transmits its aporia to his performance.

It is to this dilemma that his scapegoating or abjection of the old men speaks. The argument he ascribes to them is that the morality prevailing in their dotage is a corruption of the morality prevailing in their youth. The author doesn't pursue the argument to its logical conclusion: if they were right, it would mean that they failed to transmit their high moral standards to the next generation, and that they would be blaming their own failure on their children and successors. This parable of self-disempowerment and bad faith doesn't seem to apply to the author, which may be why it isn't mentioned. The reason I mention it is that it illuminates the author's disempowerment behind his bad-faith abjection of the old men. His laborious riposte to "their" argument is that those who live in the present are more competent in both virtue and vice than their predecessors. But since this riposte is made in the context of an implicit comparison between the courts of their youth and Urbino, it only serves to remind us that his portrait of Urbino accentuates the virtue and suppresses the vice, obeying the principle he criticizes in the old men, albeit in inverted form. And since it is a portrait of Urbino's past relative to the author if not to the old men, his relation to it is identical with their relation to the courts of their youth—so that the principle may not be inverted after all, and his abjection again fails.

The conclusion I mentioned above—that by their criticism of the present the old men betray their failure to communicate their virtue—may not come into the author's discourse in 2.1–4, but since it concerns problems of morality, empowerment, and pedagogical responsibility, it is an idea that pertains not only to relations between seniors and juniors but also to relations between courtiers and princes, and thus, as we have seen, to the central issue of Book 4. A canceled echo of the old men's theory of decline may be heard in 4.2 when the author claims that Urbino "continues to produce the same [good] effects" and hopes "that good fortune will so continue to favor these virtuous achievements that the blessings of the court [casa] and the state shall not only not decline [non sia per mancare] but rather increase at a more rapid pace from day to day" (S, 287; C, 274). The substitution of the paired terms "la casa" and "lo stato" for "la corte" seems to be calculated because it follows a list of courtiers who, having been associated with Urbino, went on to successful careers in church and state: they went from "la casa," the dynastic household and extended family, to positions in ecclesiastical and ducal formations of "lo stato." The need to negotiate this change is marked by the distinction: in the political retrospect of Book 4, the Urbino depicted in 1–3 is reduced to an idyllic "casa" from which the courtiers must be weaned if they are to justify and transcend the aesthetic self-fashioning in which "creati si sono" (4.2) in the Montefeltre/Gonzaga household. The difficulty this negotiation causes not only to the courtiers trying to imagine and articulate it but also to the author trying to imagine and articulate their effort is inscribed in the two prefatory chapters of Book 4.

The author begins Book 4 with an elegiac retrospect that, in the fictive time scheme he elaborates, precedes the Proem's longer and more comprehensive lament for the ending of an era. The shipwreck metaphor introduced in 2.1 reappears at the start of the retrospect. This time it is voiced not as the author's generalized reflection, an expression of his pastoral view of life, but as a sentiment specifically prompted by the recollection of the untimely death of three courtiers shortly after the discussions took place. One of these was Gasparo Pallavicino, which makes more interesting the oddly abrupt and unmotivated statement in 4.3: "It seemed, then, as signor Gaspar Pallavicino used to relate [raccontar soleva], that on the day following the discussions contained in the preceding book . . ." (C, 275; S, 287). Since "raccontar soleva" denotes a habitual or recurrent activity, anyone who recalls the reference in 1.1 to the author's anonymous source is entitled to presume that he has finally been identified in this statement, and that the news of Gasparo's early death is to be connected with the problem of a memorial reconstruction made many years after the event. The abruptness and brevity make the statement conspicuous while keeping it rhetorically unmarked, and its effect is to push a button lighting up the circuit of references that problematize the author's claim to accuracy.

After commemorating the three courtiers, the author writes that had they lived, their eminence would have given all who knew them "clear proof of how praiseworthy the Court of Urbino was, and how adorned it was with noble cavaliers—as nearly all that were ever reared there adorned it." Then, before giving a list of some of those who went on to successful careers in church and state, he ventures a strange comparison that I shall come back to later: "For truly there did not come forth from the Trojan horse so many lords and captains as from this court have come men singular in worth and most highly regarded by all" (4.2; S, 286). At the end of 4.2, before referring to Gasparo and after expressing the hope that Urbino's blessings will increase,

he announces that he will "continue with the discussions about our Courtier, in the hope that beyond our time there will be no lack of those who
will *find* bright and honored models of worthiness in the present Court of
Urbino, even as we are now *finding* them in that of the past" (S, 287; my
italics). This chimes with the hope expressed in 3.1 that the "nobili cavalieri
e valorose donne" will suppose and take it for certain ("presumano e per
fermo tengano"—compare Hoby's "cast in their minde and thinke for a
suretie") that the court "was more excellent and adorned with singular men"
than the author is able to express.[41]

My account of the moves in these prefatory chapters begins with the observation that in the above passage cited from Singleton the two italicized
verbs, "find" and "finding," are such loose and bland translations of their
equivalents that they obscure the sense of the Italian: what Castiglione
writes is that there will be no lack of those "che *piglino* chiari ed onorati
esempi di virtù dalla corte presente d'Urbino, così come or noi *facciamo* dalla
passata" (C, 275). Hoby's translation of "che piglino . . . dalla corte presente"
and "facciamo dalla passata" is more precise: "such as shall take . . . at the
present Court" and "[as now] wee . . . doe at the former."[42] The aggressiveness of "piglino"—"take, seize, catch hold of"—infiltrates and takes hold of
the malleable "facciamo," and even squeezes "dalla" into the more predatory
shape of "from": "take these examples from the present court of the new
duchess as now we are taking them from the past." "Or noi facciamo"
stresses the present act as the locus of inventive predation, and "facciamo,"
modified by "piglino," returns the favor by offering the authorial act as a
model for the *inventio* of future readers. Immediately before this passage the
author shows them how to go about it with an exemplary sentence of praise
for the new duchess, compressing and echoing the earlier praises of the former duchess in an idealized cameo: "for if ever there were joined in a single
person wisdom, grace, beauty, intelligence, discreet manners, humanity, and
every other gentle quality—they are so joined in her that they form a chain
that comprises and adorns her every movement, uniting all these qualities at
once" (4.2; S, 287). Readers who model their interpretive appropriations on
his Michelangelesque seizure of exemplary forms from the (perhaps recal-
citrant?) Urbino material will help ensure that "la felicità della casa e dello
stato" not only may not fail ("non sia per mancare") but may be more rapidly increased ("per accrescersi") from day to day (C, 274). The meaning of
the dissociation of "lo stato" from "la casa" is established, as I noted, by the
list of successful courtiers that precedes this statement, and the two passages
together help unpack the contents of the Trojan horse analogy.

I find the analogy strange and confusing in spite of the claim that in Castiglione's time the ancient episode was generally not viewed as the example of a deceitful and destructive stratagem.[43] Even if it were true, it doesn't preclude the possibility that Castiglione didn't dutifully view it through the period lens, and at any rate our ability to narrow the focus of its meaning depends on our parallel ability to narrow the focus of intertextual allusion. J. R. Woodhouse flatly asserts that the source the analogy picks out is "a simile in the *De oratore* of Cicero, referring to the school of Isocrates," from which " 'as from the Trojan Horse, came out innumerable men of the first rank,' " and his next sentence explains this choice: "Castiglione evidently regarded the court (and particularly the Urbino court) as his *school*, an institution with a record of practical successes proved by its distinguished 'graduates.' "[44] Woodhouse's understanding of the passage leads him to light on a source that suppresses the negative features of the analogy. This is unsatisfactory for two reasons. The first is that Castiglione mentions the Trojan "caval" just after referring to the "nobili cavalieri . . . che . . . creati si sono" in Urbino; the natal figure recalls Virgil's references in *Aeneid* II (20, 52, 243) to the horse's belly as a womb, making this the preferred source, as well as an obvious one.[45] Whoever makes this fairly accessible connection would not be likely to ignore the prominent role played in the episode by Sinon's insidious misrepresentations. The second reason is supplied by Carla Freccero's important comments on the network of indirect or "censored" references to troubled relations between Urbino and the papacy, which, "as the centralized and distant authority most closely resembling the new statist government, . . . constituted the principal threat to the court of Urbino in 1516 and became, as well, the principal employer for most of the prominent courtiers in the text." The employees include not only five of the courtiers listed just after the analogy but also "Castiglione himself," who "suffered under Clement VII as a result of the sack of Rome."[46]

Together, these two considerations suggest a more complex interpretation of the Trojan horse, and also one that is more obvious in its relevance than the benign interpretation because it makes the analogy prefigure the central topic of Book 4 in an acerb epitome: the propagation of courtiers from Urbino to other courts where they will reform the prince (including the papal prince) and "lo stato" is depicted as an act of infiltration and conquest. The courtly skills developed in Urbino will be the wiles enabling courtiers to ingratiate themselves with princes so that they can (to borrow T. E. Shaw's pun) des-Troy evil and build a new imperium through moral reform. This end justifies directing the art of dissimulation into a practice that brings it closer to the level of Sinon's guile. So, for example, Daniel Javitch argues that "very subtly, and under pretense of lauding absolute monarchy, Ottaviano promotes a constitutional form of monarchy in which final authority lies not in the king but in the laws," and that he does this "by ostensibly denying the virtues of republican government and by seeming to have overcome any argument against monarchic rule." Javitch proposes "that such oblique tactics are offered as an example of the cautious and deceptive instruction indispensable in winning the sovereign's assent," but also, I add, in trying to limit his sovereignty.[47]

The message of Book 4, however, is that this agenda of princely reform is quixotic and not likely to succeed. Its failure is inscribed in the pastoral structure of attitudes that dominates the book: intense idealism, verging on idyllicism, combined with skepticism, distrust, and pessimism, causing Ottaviano's discourse of reform to lose its momentum and give way to Bembo's inward/upward withdrawal. It is as if the defeated warriors of Urbino returned to the Trojan horse and climbed back in—perhaps (recalling Virgil's metaphor) to be reborn. But such a fantasy of rebirth or resurrection no sooner suggests itself than it opens up a new interpretation of the Trojan horse, and once again Rebhorn's commentary provides the insight that illuminates it. In his view the analogy consummates the author's "gradual elevation of Urbino's image to the heights of heroic grandeur": "Urbino becomes an epic realm in his imagination and metamorphoses into the Trojan horse, a gigantic receptacle for the greatest heroes of ancient Greece."[48] What this rhetoric clearly suggests is that the Trojan horse refers not to Urbino but to the New Urbino created and commemorated by the author's book. The Trojan horse is *Il libro del cortegiano*. It is the book that gestates the noble cavaliers and disseminates the portrait of their manners and discourse throughout the courts of Europe, the book that will cause Urbino "still to produce the same effects" at home and abroad, if, that is, the author is right in predicting that there should be no lack ("non debbano mancare") of noble cavaliers who will take from it "bright and honored models of worthiness." For such readers, "la corte presente d'Urbino" will not simply be the one in Umbria at the time of writing, it will be a copy of the author's model of the past Urbino projected into Umbria as from a simulacrum.[49]

For such readers, but not for all readers; not for those who question the nostalgic author's repeated claim to be preserving a probable, authentic, and reliable image of the splendor of Urbino. Taking up the textual invitation to occupy the site of metapastoral agency, they scan the pastoral prospect that gradually rises through four books to improbable "heights of heroic

grandeur" for clues to the anxieties of a disempowered elite seeking to justify their political emasculation. When they read about the "gradual elevation of Urbino's image" and the "increasing insistence on its moral excellence and its value for posterity" (Rebhorn, 96), they might suspect that
these claims are the targets picked out by the author's metapastoral signpost-
ing of "the improbability of his fiction" (55), and that the claims have the
same function as Sinon's lies: they are strategies intended to persuade readers
to welcome this verbal receptacle full of heroes into their own little cities so
that its exemplary discourses will infiltrate, conquer, and elevate the minds
of potential courtiers. The noble portrait will induce them to desire, and enable them to acquire, the power, autonomy, and authority lacking in their
fictive counterparts.

Should this happen, the literary model will become a social reality, and
the author's pastoral readers may then achieve the goal that escapes him. For
he appears to be trying to do something the text won't let him get away
with. If what is finally most probable, authentic, and reliable about the *Cortegiano* is the underportrait of courtiership as disempowerment, and the nostalgic courtier is disempowered by their disempowerment, his pastoral readers become his salvation. He is helpless without them, and so throughout
the parerga he presses, cajoles, beseeches, and beguiles them into accepting
his portrait and "proposito." To them he directs his smartly executed performance of the inability topos that tells them he is incapable of saying how
good his subjects are. But translated into the metapastoral register, inability
becomes his basic condition, for, in the way of truth, he is incapable of saying they are good, or at least as good as he says they are. The inability topos
thus functions as a lightning rod. The sign of the rhetorician mastering his
craft and audience, trying to realize his fantasy by persuading them it is real,
it conspicuously diverts attention from his powerlessness to realize it without
their help.

In the conclusion of my account of Book 3 I suggested the possibility
that the representations men inscribe, and the self-representations they induce, in women may give rise to bad conscience and to something I called
representation anxiety. Now, in concluding my study of the parerga, I revive
that suggestion in the context of the author's portrait not only of Urbino
but also of himself. The metapastoral representation of representation anxiety is what I have been trying to track down in the text of the parerga. There
are two major clues to this effect. One, which I have already mentioned,
consists of the various moments of conspicuous evasion by interlocutors
who reveal their troubled awareness of their political emasculation but slide

quickly away from it in unpersuasive demurrals or displacements into more manageable topics. At such points the author represents their own bad-faith drive toward self-idealization and thus establishes in Urbino the model of idyllic escape that he, as nostalgic courtier, imitates and offers to the "nobili cavalieri" of the future. The second clue is one I mentioned at the beginning of this chapter and the interpretation of which I have reserved for the end: the abrupt and surprising statement in 1.1 that the author was absent from the discussions. Noting that the record shows this to be a fabrication, a "slight distortion of history," since Castiglione had left England and was back in Urbino at the time of the discussions, Rebhorn explains it as a device that allows the author "to avoid the indiscretion of participating in his own dialogue."[50] I would like to venture a different explanation based on what I take to be an allusion to another famous absence.

When, in the *Phaedo*, the narrator of the dialogue declares that Plato was absent from the discussions he, Phaedo, reports, it is one of several devices by which the author signifies his distance from, his critical reading of, the narrative he assigns to Phaedo. Phaedo enthusiastically endorses, and Socrates reluctantly succumbs to, the idyllic desire of his interlocutors to have him persuade them that, if they are good, they will live forever in a state of unchanging happy consciousness. Plato shows, in the equivalent of a metapastoral critique, that Socrates' attempt to convey a more difficult and painful conception of moral self-reform was blocked by the intensity of the interlocutors' desire, and thus that Socrates died in more ways than one. I suggest that whatever Castiglione may have thought about the *Phaedo*, which is mentioned in the *Cortegiano*, his use of the reference to authorial absence makes it function in the same way. The authorial performance is divided between the perspective of the enchanted courtier/author whose narrative is the product and epitome of the Urbino it praises and the perspective of the disenchanted author/courtier whose text characterizes the narrative *as* enchanted and internally distantiates itself from it. The view from within Urbino is countered by a view from abroad.

Reference to Castiglione's absence is made once again, by Ottaviano in 4.38. It follows the chapter in which he depicts Hercules as a slayer of tyrants and admires the peripatetic Alexander not merely for all the good things he did as a conqueror but also for spending so much time abroad doing them. The author's absence is mentioned during the course of a bizarre proposal that modern Christian heroes—the youthful heirs to the thrones of France, England, and the Empire—should in effect emulate Alexander by going on crusade: they should join together and "direct their efforts to subjugating the infidels" and saving them from themselves. The outlandishness and apparent irrelevance of the proposal betrays the desperation underlying the courtiers' superficially sanguine conduct of their agenda for the moral reform of princes. But its implications are not really irrelevant. Sending princes abroad to do good things is a panacea: it is morally commendable, and it gets them out of the country for a while, no doubt to their own relief as well as that of their subjects. Castiglione's absence is interpreted by this context: to be away from Urbino is to be able to do good, useful, and possibly heroic work, the kind of work that one does not in "la casa," where people only talk about it, but in "lo stato." Perhaps in England Castiglione engages in some of the activities courtiers are praised for in Book 4: his remarks on the prince of Wales's promise, as reported by Ottaviano, reflect the pedagogical viewpoint of the wise old counselor of young princes.

The author pretends he was in England; he did not participate; someone else, perhaps Gasparo Pallavicino, told him about it. All this serves to clear him of responsibility for the origin and quality of "questa chiara memoria" he feels obliged to preserve from oblivion and bequeath to posterity (3.1). This may suggest that the brightness and clarity of the memory owes as much to his desire as to his source (if indeed there was a source). The desire was whetted by the intervening years during which he suffered the outrages of fortune. Two distances, of time and of space, separate him from the events he describes, even though he describes them as if he were present. Let the temporal distance be that of the storm-tossed victim of the virago, hoping to revive or at least commemorate the past.[51] Let the spatial distance stand for the metapastoral resistance to the idyllic portrait he nevertheless yearns for from afar. Such a resistance is, as we have seen, present in the text but conspicuously excluded from the idyllic portrait. While the nostalgic author commemorates Urbino's games and golden age, the worldly diplomat commemorates the figure of loss they are an escape from, namely, the figure of Duke Guidobaldo and what the author makes it mean.

Two constitutive absences frame the *Cortegiano* and send their vectors of meaning toward each other through the broad expanse of the text: the absence of the bedridden duke who instituted Urbino's games and the absence of the worldly diplomat who writes about them. Like the sacrificial victim buried under the cornerstone, the courageous loser represented at the games by his grass widow upholds the ludic foundation so that his courtiers may safely fashion themselves and their ideals in the mirrors of their conversation. Conspicuously excluded under the basis of the foundation is the career of failures the courtiers hope to avoid and the moral stamina they replace with sprezzatura. At the beginning of the Proem the author associates himself primarily with the duke: he was moved to write his book by the memory of the lately departed Guidobaldo, who, like him, had been fortune's victim and who, like him, had been unable to participate in the games. The sentiments expressed in the Proem, we remember, represent his recent reaction to rereading the draft of many years ago preparatory to revising it for publication. In the fictive chronology of composition, it appears that his self-portrait in the Proem is partially modeled on his portrait of the duke in 1.3. The publication of his nostalgic memoir will resolve and compensate him for his troubles, as did the duke's withdrawal into the ludic words and deeds of the "very noble and worthy gentlemen" with whom he surrounded himself. The author, who, according to Rebhorn, heroizes himself as fortune's courageous victim, has, "like the heroic lords and ladies of Urbino, . . . finally triumphed over fortune; in finishing his book, he pays his debt and erects a monument so that the image of Urbino may live again in the minds of posterity."[52] But is it heroic to triumph over fortune by being memorialized in a book? The expression of hope that the heroic image may live again seems rather to serve the pastoral objective of persuading readers to believe that its referent "lived" before and was the original of this copy. But what if the image conceals or compensates for a lack—the gap marked by the missing Hercules and the absent duke, and constructed by the idyllic representation as *the unrepresented*? To write such a "life" of Urbino is to write its death. It is an act of thanatography. And I have been arguing that the *Cortegiano* offers the reader a metapastoral pathway through the textual traces of thanatography, among them the glimpses of a form of heroism alien to the values of courtiership—the heroism of the impotent duke, which is conspicuously excluded from the idyllic enclosure to which the duke withdrew, an exclusion as conspicuous as that of the impotence the reference to his nightly absence commemorates.

Metapastoral resistance to the enclosure—the resistance that discloses the impulse to thanatography—is discernible not only in the parerga and in local clues but also in larger interlocutory and diegetic patterns, specifically, in the interventions of Gasparo Pallavicino and in the shape given the narrative sequence of discussions. I shall consider each in turn.

Gasparo stands out from the other courtiers in several respects. Unlike Ludovico di Canossa, Federico and Ottaviano Fregoso, Cesare Gonzaga, Bernardo Bibbiena, Giuliano de' Medici, and Pietro Bembo, he is not a featured speaker with a positive agenda. Unlike the minor figures, he intervenes more than occasionally. He plays the devil's advocate, the most insistent house misogynist,[53] the counterpuncher—he tends in general, as Thomas Greene notes, "to play the role of the demystifier."[54] He is the first to be asked to propose a game, he kicks off the discussion of sprezzatura by voicing skepticism about the importance of noble birth, he motivates and resists the profeminist argument from 2.90 through the third book, he offers Ottaviano important thematic targets at 4.11 and 29, and his comment on the old courtier provides the spur to Bembo's Pegasusian ascent. His is the first and the last name to be mentioned in Book 4, and, as I suggested, 4.3 opens with a phrase that implies he may be the author's source. Several of his interventions in Books 2, 3, and 4 are expressly demystifying. At 2.23 and 28 he asks hard questions about real vs. apparent good and internal vs. external criteria of judgment, at 2.24 he poses a hard question about the limits of the courtier's obedience to the prince, at 2.40 he glances at the ethics of sprezzatura by stating that it is wrong for a man of honor to deceive anyone, at 3.17 he strikes at the heart of the profeminist argument when he remarks that Giuliano, "in giving false praises to women, shows that no true praises can be found for them" (S, 218), at 3.33 he strikes at the heart of the author's argument in 3.1 as well as Giuliano's praise of strong women in stating that "many lies can be told" about things that happened long ago, and twice in Book 4 (14 and 35) he pithily states realistic objections to Ottaviano's idealistic proposals for educating the prince. He thus provides a series of metapastoral glimpses of problems the courtiers persistently ignore or evade. Woodhouse remarks that the game he proposes in 1.6–7 "gives the theme which underlies most of the rest of the treatise"—"the important notion . . . that our natural affection for object or person may deceive our judgment" is, he argues, restated "several times in the course of the book," most notably by Giuliano in Book 3 and Bembo in Book 4.[55] But more important than any of these occurrences is its application to the nostalgic courtier's affection for the court of Urbino. Finally, as Rebhorn shows, Gasparo twice uses the metaphor of resurrection (1.15 and 18) that structures the idyllic art of thanatography.[56]

It makes sense, therefore, that the *Cortegiano* ends with Emilia threatening to hale Gasparo into court should he wish to continue his habit of slandering ("dar . . . falsa calunnia") women. That slander, we recall, crested near the end of Book 3 (S, 74–75) in a passage that registers as much pleasure in the rhetorical performance of paranoid exaggeration as in the paranoia itself. Gasparo's diatribe is no less citational than Bembo's ecstasy. It generates a speaker who revels in the mimicry of irrational shrillness, and whose vam-

pirish images are drawn from the male hysteria section of the Petrarchan archive. Reading of the on-again-off-again games with which "these wild animals who have a greater thirst for blood than tigers have" torment their
lovers (3.74; S, 280), one thinks of such familiar moments in the courtly discourse of Petrarchism as Thomas Wyatt's

> They fle from me that sometyme did me seke
>   With naked fote stalking in my chambre.
> I have sene theim gentill tame and meke
>   That nowe are wyld and do not remembre
>   That sometyme they put theimself in daunger
> To take bred at my hand; and now they raunge
> Besely seking with a continuell chaunge.

In Gasparo's bravura display of hate talk the effects of citation and caricature indicate that his is not a spontaneous outburst but a representation of
discursive excess in what was rapidly becoming a pan-European inscription
of gynephobic fantasy, and one in which erotic victimization was often used
to encode a more pervasive sense of social or political disempowerment. At
1.15, for example, Gasparo attributes the same cruel sports to "la fortuna,"
whom we see "hold sway over all things of this world and, as it seems, amuse
herself often in uplifting to the skies whom she pleases and in burying in the
depths those most worthy of being exalted" (S, 30). Early in Book 4, after
Ottaviano criticizes the effeminate character of the previously described
courtly accomplishments, his account of the difficulty involved in winning
the prince's favor, and especially the favor of today's despotic princes, for
whom "reason or justice . . . would be a kind of bridle" (4.7; S, 291; see also
4.8–10), abounds in echoes of the problematic erotic relations discussed in 3:
the despot's arbitrary and domineering behavior resembles that of Gasparo's
Cruel Fair, and the art the courtier is enjoined to cultivate in order to entice
("adescar") his prince to justice and virtue (4.9) resembles the art of tempt-
resses and seducers. By this time the fickleness and power of fortune, wicked
princes, and cruel objects of desire are interchangeable. Gasparo's antifeminism thus converges with Ottaviano's.[57] In laying bare the gynephobic basis
of Giuliano's profeminism, Ottaviano prepares the schema he will apply to
the threat of political effeminization. Gasparo's interventions and Ottaviano's
discourse combine to make explicit the sands of vulnerability on which the
fortress/palace and courtly games of Urbino are built. So also does the larger
shape the *Cortegiano* gives to the narrative sequence of discussions, which I
now turn to consider.

Allusions to the difficulty of life in the courtiers' political and social ambiance and to the political impotence of the Italian upper class appear fleetingly in Book 1 and more directly in Book 2. José Guidi lists a series of such allusions and cites them as evidence for his thesis that Castiglione willfully denied history and evaded its "too painful realities" in his nostalgic and utopian drive to perpetuate an idealized portrait of Urbino's aristocracy.[58] But Guidi's list itself indicates that the denial and evasion are conspicuous— that the author clearly displays what is being denied and evaded, and thus represents himself denying and evading; such a performance calls for a meta-pastoral modification of Guidi's thesis. The first three books describe a pastoral trajectory, enact withdrawal from politics, but they do so against this background of conspicuous allusion and exclusion. Though the shift to the woman question in Book 3 is political to the core, the background makes it appear to protract the withdrawal as the discussion moves inward from relations with the world to relations within the court. Book 4 retrospectively reinterprets courtly self-fashioning as preparation for the more serious return to politics, but in fact the irrelevance of much of the preparation produces an even stronger impression that the preceding books portrayed the deferral and diversion of aesthetic *paideia* rather than the propaedeutic for political engagement.

When Book 4 finally reverses the movement of withdrawal, it does so only to enact the failure of the reversal. The failure is inscribed in the counterfactual framing of Ottaviano's fantasy of political instruction and in the subtly shaded skepticism that marks the representation of Bembo's speech. Each is an aggressive and expansive manifestation of the paradise principle, as Wayne Rebhorn suggests when he describes them as "attempts both to escape time and history and to raise man to a position beyond the power of fortune to touch his individual life." He adds that "such visionary solutions" are diversions from "Castiglione's immediate problem" of commemorating a glory that has "already started slipping away irrecoverably into the past."[59] But since they are *represented* as visionary solutions and are part of what the author commemorates, doesn't the text portray his own effort "to vindicate [vendicar] the brilliant memory" (3.1) as another visionary solution?

When the discussion slides from the courtier's difficulties with princes to the old lover's difficulties with women, Bembo's high-minded response to erotic inadequacy executes a double escape: not only from politics and the power of princes but also from erotics and the power of women. Ottaviano's argument that the courtier should try to make his prince more virtuous is shifted by Bembo to an injunction to the "Platonic" lover, who is urged to "obey, please, and honor his Lady with all reverence, and hold her dearer than himself," and also "to lead her to modesty, temperance, and true chastity" (4.62; S, 348); lurking behind both injunctions are the twinned specters of the despot and the virago. We should note that this return to the problematic figure of "il vecchio" caricatured in 2.1–3 narrows the focus from the general sense of decrepitude to specifically erotic performance. As Marina Beer argues, the link to 2.1–3 is effected by passing through the old courtier, Morello da Ortona, to Bembo's appeal to the positive Platonic/Ciceronian tradition.[60] But this is once again a conspicuous displacement of the "figure della castrazione" (Beer, 215) inscribed in the gynephobia that haunts and motivates the political, social, and sexual self-representation of the courtiers. We should also note that Bembo's "non giovane" lover isn't represented as less susceptible than his youthful counterpart to the desire and suffering induced by contemplation of beauty in the (female) body; he is only—if he adopts Bembo's method—more adept at escaping them, and the remedy prescribed by Bembo recalls Giuliano's Ovidian no less than Ficino's Neoplatonic procedure because it consists in cleaving Pygmalion-like to the product of one's own fantasy (4.66).

Although Bembo's account of the lover's pangs glances primarily toward passages in Plato and Ficino (the *Phaedrus/Symposium/De Amore* medley), the problems and pleasures it addresses are not those of pederasty or Platonic love but those that confront the (*a*) sensual and (*b*) heterosexual lover who "considers beauty only in the [female] body" (4.66). Platonic furors modulate into Petrarchan furors as we read of "le lacrime, i sospiri, gli affanni e i tormenti" (C, 327) that afflict this lover when he is denied the presence of his beloved. Comparison with the previous account of male miseries this passage recalls—Gasparo's diatribe in 3.74–75—shows that Bembo is careful to blame the miseries not on women but on misdirected desire. Yet as the second half of 4.66 clearly discloses, that is only a more courtly and devious way to put women down, since the argument is that what causes trouble is not beauty but its female embodiment.[61] The deviousness is economically if unwittingly underlined in the following passage by Woodhouse: "There are constant allegorical hints for men to seek the true love; deceived . . . by an appearance of love, the sensualist experiences only unhappy passion (cp. lii); the senses are deceiving . . . (liii); reason must correct the wickedness . . . of the senses, etc." (185). By drawing only on the earlier and more general sections of Bembo's argument, Woodhouse obscures the fact that the negatives

are eventually attracted to the pole of female embodiment. Even more in-
structive is his qualified endorsement of the thesis that Bembo's discourse is
more than "fashionable Platonism" because it points out "the need for truthful vision" and allows "the courtier continuing and higher ambitions of self-
improvement" (185, 182). The attainment of these goods is expressly contingent on the lover's ability to transcend heterosexual entanglements.

No less than Gasparo, Bembo focuses on the problem of male disempowerment. His distinction between "giovane" and "non giovane" slides through
sensual vs. spiritual to self-disempowering vs. self-empowering and these
polarities frame a continuum that leads upward from the heterosexual body
through its autoerotic idea to theosocial union. But "theosocial" may not be
entirely accurate: at the climax of the experience the lover embracing God
assumes the power of the penetrator who finds beauty hidden in the "secreti
penetrali" of God (4.69). This figure of subl(im)ated sexuality marks its heterosexual original as the distortion of a homosexual climax and thus, in its
own way, supports the traditional misogynist view of woman as a badly
flawed version of man. This is not a view the text of the *Cortegiano* leaves
unchallenged and tacitly endorses. Its affinity to Gasparo's position is indicated by his first comment after Bembo's speech. Cesare Gonzaga has just
stated that the road leading to "questa felicità" seems so steep it would be
difficult to travel; difficult for men, Gasparo adds, but impossible for women.
Chided by Emilia, he bumptiously amplifies the claim, insisting that wom-
en's souls "are neither so purged of the passions as those of men nor so
skilled in contemplation," and that one doesn't read of any woman experi-
encing the divine love, only of such patriarchal greats as Plato, Socrates,
Plotinus, and select holy fathers (4.72). This brings Giuliano galloping in to
the ladies' rescue, wielding a clutch of counter-examples, which, at the beginning of the book's final chapter, Gasparo predictably prepares to challenge. The duchess, however, cuts him off, proposing that Bembo be "giudice," that they "accept his verdict [stiasi alla sua sentenzia] as to whether or
not women are as capable of divine love as men," and that they postpone
debate until the next session.

What does it mean for the *Cortegiano* to end on this note?—for the
duchess to reschedule the unresolved debate of the third night, and to
choose Bembo as its arbiter? But first, how is the interpretation of these
choices affected by the famous topographia that fills the center of 4.73?:
when the courtiers, beguiled ("ingannato") by their delightful conversation,
realized they had talked through the night, the casements were opened

on the side of the palace that looks toward the lofty peak of Mount Catria, where they saw that a beautiful rosy dawn had already come into the east, and that all the stars had disappeared except the sweet mistress of the heaven of Venus that holds the border between night and day; from which a soft breeze seemed to come that filled the air with a brisk coolness and began to awaken sweet concerts of joyous birds in the murmuring forests of the nearby hills. (4.73; S, 359)

The references to Catria and Venus combine in a fast flicker of allusion that blurs together Bembo's erotics of contemplation with the moment in *Paradiso* xxi when the contemplative St. Peter Damian mentions his lofty hermitage on Mount Catria, his haven high above the thunders of a worsening world. Influenced by that flicker, "la dolce governatrice" glances back through Bembo's speech to the twin Venuses in the Platonic/Ficinian text, from which he borrows their functions if not their names, modifying the difference between the earthly and heavenly Venuses to conform with his sharper focus on the transcendence of heterosexual love.[62] At the same time, the epithet personifying the planet that marks the turning of the third heaven suggests the expanded reach of what Thomas Greene has characterized as "the feminine enclosing power" represented by Emilia and the duchess.[63] But that planet, the last star, the Venerean border patrol, is about to disappear: the sweet mistresses of Urbino and heaven can only temporarily stave off the forces of despotic male power and its product, "la fortuna."

The sequence of auroral images that follows the naming of Catria softens and melts into an Arcadian prospect the literary power of which lies not in a picturesque evocation of "nature" but in the poignant tension between generic or intertextual indicators. On the one hand, the sequence signifies pastoral; it connotes the literary source and convention, the idyllic conditions and desires, that control the author's portrait of Urbino. The courtly conversations are, as Rebhorn notes, enclosed within inaugural and valedictory scenes of generic allusion, the former at 1.2 and the latter at 4.73.[64] Those scenes are metapastoral brackets marking the containment of the portrait within the field of desire organized by the paradise principle. But on the other hand, in this closing moment the author returns the portrait to its generic source and bids it farewell. The pastoral thus modulates into the alba or aubade, the lover's good-bye at "the border between night and day." Guidi calls it an "aube trop sereine" because it "announces, in fact, new disasters for a class that knows itself condemned."[65] The bird ubiquitous in dawn songs appears in the phrase "risveglier dolci concerti dei vaghi augelli" (C, 334), but the phrase also fleetingly suggests a kind of literary dream vision in which the courtiers are metamorphosed into happy hurtless creatures filled with the Venerean grazia that translates their waking desire into immediate melodious expression. At 2.22 Vincenzo Calmeta complains of the courtier's lot that "countless considerations" constrain him "not to leave a patron once he has begun to serve him," and, princes being what they are, "courtiers are like those unfortunate birds born in a dismal valley" (S, 116). Calmeta expresses the sense of powerlessness that runs through the *Cortegiano* and haunts the paradisal scene of birdsong from which it is conspicuously excluded.

The point I want to make about this diffuse richness of implication is that the language of the topographia sows traces of Bembo's lofty Catrian ideal into the auroral pleasance. Even the birds are traces, for at 4.67 Bembo says of lovers who have transcended and learned to disesteem "the particular beauty of one woman" but whose vision of abstract beauty "is not wholly purged of material darkness" that they "are like little birds beginning to put on feathers" and that "although with their weak wings they can lift themselves a little in flight, . . . [they] dare not go far from their nest or trust themselves to the winds and open sky" (S, 352–53).[66] The next step is to practice the autocontemplation ("let him turn within himself in order to contemplate that beauty which is seen by the eyes of the mind," 4.68; S, 353) that will enable the soul to fly upward toward union with the angelic nature (4.68). I borrow the term "autocontemplation" from the description of Castiglione's Urbino by Thomas Greene: "a community itself turned inward, flawless in the perfection of its withdrawal, *protected momentarily* by its mountains, its palace, its style, its harmony, from the violence and vulgarity beyond it. A chrysalis of a culture seems to exist in its own static circumscribed self-sufficiency and proposes to mirror its contentment by a game of autocontemplation."[67] This characterizes Bembo's Neoplatonic game no less than the game of imagining the ideal courtier, and Valeria Finucci's reminder that the autocontemplation of the latter is gender-specific obviously applies to the former.[68]

I have been arguing that the *Cortegiano* represents Greene's "chrysalis" only as the nostalgic author's dream vision, not as the portrait that saturates the text. It is the target of a metapastoral critique that discloses as improbable the claim of the portrait to be historically authentic in its idealization. The scene of birdsong contributes to the disclosure, fading the vision out in a reductive caricature. This is why I place the emphasis of Greene's description on the italicized words, for the dream passes within the night, and in the next moment daylight inaugurates the new regime: "as they were about to leave the room, the Prefect turned to the Duchess and said: 'To terminate [terminar] the dispute between signor Gasparo and the Magnifico, we shall come with the judge this evening earlier than was done yesterday'" (4.73; C, 334; S, 360, altered). Although it seems that he is only picking up the duchess's proposal to appoint Bembo the judge, his use of "veniremo," whether the plural is royal or collective, has quasi-imperative force. The prefect makes a bid to take over the authority hitherto ceded to Guidobaldo's "locotenente" and to her "locotenente," Emilia—as if to replace their justice with his and to reestablish the prerogatives of male principality on the more aggressive model of Federico's regime. But Francesco Maria della Rovere, whose military character and career are commemorated in Titian's famous portrait, would return Urbino to a less benign and more unstable version of that regime.[69] Its fortunes would be dominated by increasingly hostile forces in the Rome of which he was prefect, an office that (at least nominally) carries disciplinary, judicial, and peacekeeping responsibilities.

This mention of the prefect, which appears superficially to be no more than a passing tone, takes on resonance when the full orchestration of his role in the *Cortegiano* is considered. Though an insider at court, he is not part of the original conversational circle. Breaking in near the end of Book 1, he interrupts and in effect terminates that evening's discussion. The abruptness, the sudden force, of his entry contrasts sharply with the *raffiné* quality of the conversation he intrudes on, an argument between the count and Cesare concerning the pleasure men take in looking at beautiful women. Cesare was about to defend his exquisite taste and connoisseurship when

a great trampling of feet was heard, and the clamor of loud voices, upon which everyone turned and saw the glare of torches appear at the door of the room, and immediately after there arrived, with a large and noble company, the prefect, who was returning from having accompanied the Pope on part of his journey; and on entering the palace and asking at once what the duchess was doing, he learned of what sort the game was that evening . . . and he came as fast as he could in order to be on time to hear something. (1.54; my translation)

s'udì un gran calpestare di piedi con strepito di parlar alto; e così rivolgendosi ognuno, si vice alla porta della stanza comparire un splendor di torchi e sùbito drieto giunse con molta e nobil compagnia il signor Prefetto, il qual ritornava, avendo accompagnato il Papa una parte del camino; e già allo entrar del palazzo, dimandando ciò

che facesse la signora Duchessa, aveve inteso di che sorte era il gioco di quella sera . . . ;
però quanto più gli era possibile studiava il passo, per giungere a tempo d'udir qualche
cosa. (C, 112–13)

The energy this description conveys is violent, headlong, imperious, virile—though of course if we figure in the archival *donnée* of the historical
della Rovere's age, roughly seventeen, Guidobaldo's appointed heir comes
across as an eager, precocious, self-assured, and probably spoiled familiar of
the company. He is, nevertheless, the terminator, Urbino's future, and the
day that dawns in 4.73 is the day of the prefect. In that final moment the
duchess and Emilia express the desire to reopen the postponed debate, but
the prefect's emphasis is on closing it: "per terminar la lite . . . veniremo col
giudice." It is as if to stave off the future, defer the day of the prefect, that
Guidobaldo's "locotenenti" turn back the clock from Book 4 to Book 3.
They hope to reinstate the past discussion so they can continue facing inward in the idealized circle and cling to their fragile paradise of autocontemplation. But the circle had been broken at 1.54.

To repeat the question I asked earlier, what does it mean for the duchess
to choose Bembo as arbiter? This is a question not about the psychology and
motivation of the speaker but about the interests and conflicts at work in the
discursive position the speaker embodies: the position of a woman who
marries into patriarchal authority and gets the opportunity to exercise it
within the confines—ludic but culturally functional and significant—of
courtly entertainments. It would seem to be in her interest to pick a judge
she could count on to decide in favor of the profeminist argument. From
the end of Book 2 on, the women have been shown to want Gasparo's argument defeated, and their comments in the final chapter imply that they
don't consider Giuliano to have defeated it in Book 3; for them it remains
unfinished business. Yet as we have seen, the discursive situation is more complicated than the participants appear to recognize. Bembo's strategy of abjecting the male's sensual weakness to the "material darkness" of embodied
female beauty reveals an underlying affinity with Gasparo's position. The
arguments of Gasparo, Bembo, and Giuliano intersect and reinforce each
other. They produce a profeminist discourse that betrays but disowns its basis in—and thus perpetuates the hegemony of—the gynephobic fantasy to
which it responds by striving to safeguard both man's sexual autonomy and
his constitutive power over the representation of gender. Thus Guidobaldo's
placeholders are shown to endorse the authorized or profeminist version of

an antifeminist discourse, which is why the hero they choose to uphold that version is powerless to defeat the discourse.

The *Cortegiano* represents its interlocutors as unaware of the discursive kinship that unites the opposing positions. Whether one interprets their unawareness as ignorance or as some degree of the strategic self-blinding Stanley Cavell calls "disowning knowledge," that contradictory singleness of discourse is conspicuously excluded from the ludic surface of debate carried on by self-assured and friendly performers. The exclusion and its cost are registered at the end of the book when, in the dawning of the day of the prefect, Emilia insists that Gasparo "star a ragione" if he wishes to continue accusing and falsely calumniating women. Perhaps because she picks up the judicial metaphor introduced by the duchess and appropriated by the prefect, Singleton follows Hoby in translating "star a ragione" as "to stand trial," and Leonard Opdycke renders it "to sustain his charge."[70] Since in her final words Emilia declares Gasparo to be "suspetto fuggitivo," I take the sense of her statement to be that she wants him not to sneak off but to stand the test of refutation, which is to say she wants more than the occasional intervention that allows him to counterpunch and then step aside, and more than the irrational barrage of the epideictic explosion that went unanswered at the end of Book 3. She wants the antifeminist to commit himself to laying out the position—as Giuliano and Ottaviano have laid out theirs—so that it may be inspected, interrogated, dissected, and defeated.

But what would it mean to defeat Gasparo's argument? The question is only half answered by imagining that the women who hear the argument would be pleased to have the slander against their sex refuted. The other side of the thesis that women are raging, powerful, and lethal monsters, weak only in rational control and virtue, is that men are pathetic, helpless victims. Insofar as the antifeminist argument is not merely misogynistic but also, and more deeply, gynephobic, its very expression is a sign of male weakness, a sign compounded by the anamorphic displacement of the cause of weakness from despotic princes to despotic women. It isn't only that women resent misogynist slander; they resent being scapegoated by men who, in doing so, parade their own fear and inability. The ladies at court want their men to be strong. Therefore their position agrees with Gasparo's in at least one respect: men should be strong enough to maintain the orderly operation of those institutions—marriage, family, inheritance, the court—that preserve the social and political values of the society they cherish; strong enough to be able to contain whatever threatens to disrupt the order, whether it be bad princes or bad women. At the same time Gasparo's diatribe makes explicit the bad-faith interpretive practice in which men avail themselves of their interlocutory prerogative, their power of speech, to proclaim themselves emasculated and to vilify the embodiments of what they define or imagine as woman.

The strategic value of the antifeminist attack is twofold. First, it motivates the profeminist defense, creates the opportunity for refutation. Second, by doing so, it generates the spurious separation of a single complex, self-divided discourse into two one-dimensional arguments and thereby makes it easier for the debaters to remain unaware that, as Linda Woodbridge puts it, their respective "definitions of female goodness and badness are identical."[71] My argument is that the *Cortegiano* makes both these moves visible to the reader. It does so primarily through the figure and treatment of Gasparo, and the moves are never more visible than at the end of the book when the duchess recruits Gasparo and Giuliano for the fifth-night discussion and Emilia insists that Gasparo give bond "star a ragione." For this shows that the women of Urbino do not want to let Gasparo and his discourse slip away, that they want to keep him in tow; not, however, so that his argument may be defeated once and for all but so that it may be continually restated and redefeated in the varied repetitions of ludic play that protract the night of the duchess well into the day of the prefect and beyond the confines of the *Cortegiano*.

Gasparo offers himself and his argument as the target, the lightning rod that draws critical animus away from a deceptively "clean" profeminism and enables the gallantry of the defender of ladies. Readers who have tracked the working of the discourse of profeminism through Giuliano's performance of it, and who have watched it subvert itself and give way to the antifeminism it is based on, have an ironic advantage over the participants. They see the self-professed demystifier Gasparo as a collaborator in the process of remystification whereby the participants cheer on a profeminist discourse that ultimately expresses and reinforces the courtier's sense of powerlessness. In the convergence of gynephobia with tyrannophobia, and in the passage through Ottaviano's performance to Bembo's, they mark the increasing force of pastoral escapism and the increasing counterforce of the drive toward idealization that both legitimizes and conceals the escapism. From this meta-pastoral viewpoint, Emilia's final demand is in the service of the nostalgic author's project of thanatography, the self-blinding project of protracting the night of the duchess, deferring the day of the prefect, by burying the mimesis of powerlessness under the cornerstone of an enduring art of idealization. Emilia's statement is as quick and witty as all her previous rejoinders.

But in continuing the judicial metaphor introduced by the duchess and appropriated by the prefect it validates the latter's appropriation and seals the death of Guidobaldo's Urbino.

That death, however, is written into the *Cortegiano* in the form of the violence implicit in the act of resurrection, the violence that makes the portrait of Urbino a thanatography. It may be that Castiglione takes the metaphor of resurrection seriously because "the worst crime . . . [he] can conceive is to *bury beneath the ground* something good and humanly significant that deserves to live" and that may be resurrected by art, to which "he repeatedly ascribes . . . a particularly memorialistic . . . function."[72] But for this to happen something else must be buried, whatever in "nature" or in the object of mimesis doesn't conform to the criteria determining the "good and humanly significant." Such a burial is presupposed by the idyllic desire to glorify the body, and it is, as I have tried to show, the traces of inhumation that keep the portrait of the glorified body from saturating the text. Thus in commemorating Urbino's games the *Cortegiano* commemorates what they—ever more intensively, from Book 1 through Book 4—are an escape from: not merely time, history, death, and fortune, but the ducal specter of impotence and courage that is the cornerstone of the idyllic enclosure. That specter, to change the metaphor, is slashed across the portrait of Urbino like the skull in Holbein's courtly painting *The French Ambassadors* (1534); the skull of which Lacan writes that it is the figure of the subject annihilated in castration; the figure of the gap filled by the missing Hercules.[73] In the act of representing itself or being represented, the courtly subject discovers its own destruction, the Narcissan victim buried under the specular image of the ego ideal the cavaliers artfully fashion "ridendo" in their courtly conversations. "The effect of representation is . . . the suspicion that some reality is being camouflaged, that we are being deceived as to the exact nature of some thing-in-itself that lies behind representation."[74]

The reality behind representation is the gap engendered by genetic aporia. The ambiguity the author builds up as to whether he invented the discussions and how he received them elicits alternative genetic hypotheses and prevents them from being resolved. The result is that the reader is encouraged—or at least entitled—to keep all the possibilities in play, which makes it impossible to determine whether one is more "real" than the others. All are equally fictive and, if so, none can be taken as a reference to, an indexical sign of, the actual genetic process, the process worked out by Ghino Ghinassi.[75] Rather, they are pseudo-references, indexical fictions, that have the value of meaning effects. That is, a specific genetic account encodes a specific interpretation of the author's motive for giving that account. Behind all the accounts, however, is a gap, a cipher, an absence, a missing Hercules.

Rebhorn's judicious and carefully balanced description of the dilemma supports and illuminates this reading, as does Guidi's earlier essay on the politics of the *Cortegiano*.[76] They focus not merely on the author's idealization of Urbino but on the *display of idealization*; correspondingly, they focus not merely on the selectivity of the account but on the *conspicuous exclusion* of problematic data in the historical record, data with which many of Castiglione's contemporaries may be presumed to have been familiar.[77] They make it possible for us to see that unless the author had expressed the desire to paint an accurate and true portrait of Urbino, we could not measure the force of the counterdesire to gild Urbino's lily. This conflict and the failure of the pastoral desire for an idealized reality come into view when we occupy the standpoint of the absent author in England. From there we see that—and why—the putative history veers toward fantasy under the pressure of elegiac and eulogistic desire even as the author in Urbino strives vainly to preserve historical truth. We see that—and how—the tricks of memory and desire undo themselves, betraying idealization as a form of courtly evasion, dissimulating as exemplary and noble the courtly practices of a politically dependent elite. For this elite the author displays his fondness as well as his admiration. But his own commitment to the paradise principle is not so firm as to prevent him from *displaying* idealization and, beneath it, the complacencies of what his harsher critics have depicted as a self-aestheticizing, smooth-talking, thumb-twiddling community.

Raphael understood this. My fantasy of the author finds its material body in his portrait of Castiglione. I see sadness, resignation, softness protectively swathed in velvet, linen, and fur—with black, of course, for nostalgia. And I see something more complex in the exotropic relation of the eyes than, say, the direct refusal of the sitter to acknowledge observers by returning their glance. The sitter's look and the panoply of the turning shoulder compose into a quiet, stately, patient vulnerability. But that isn't all. There is a trace of blankness in the look, the faintest shadow of amusement about the mouth. I think of the sitter not only as holding the pose for the painter and getting it ready for me, but also as eyeing himself in the mirror. For to some extent every portrait is a self-portrait and, to vary an old Florentine saying, every patron paints himself. That is not the nostalgic courtier who studies himself. It is the metapastoral diplomat modeling, and interrogating, the nostalgic pose.

7.   Narratorial Sour Grapes: Reading *Galateo*

In his brisk little entry on Giovanni della Casa in *The Concise Encyclopedia of the Italian Renaissance*, J. R. Hale makes short work of *Galateo*: "It was, after Castiglione's *The courtier*, which it trivializes, the most influential of Italian books on behavior. It is more attractive in style than in tone, of which a fair sample is: 'We must subscribe not necessarily to the best customs but to those which prevail in our day.'"[1] As Hale's well-chosen "fair sample" makes clear, he doesn't mean that *Galateo* exposes the triviality of the *Cortegiano*. He means that in its shortcomings della Casa's conduct book trivializes material that was better handled in the *Cortegiano*, and the fair sample picks out a significant shortcoming: *Galateo*'s unattractively cynical commitment to expediency. My aim in what follows is to rehabilitate a version of the first alternative based on a defense of the tone Hale finds unattractive. The argument will be that *Galateo* presents a critique or exposé of the ideology of courtly conduct it imputes to the *Cortegiano*, and that it does so by showcasing the unattractiveness and ambivalence of its own narrator's performance as a spokesman for the ideology. In other words, far from being identifiable with the sites of enunciation called "della Casa" or his "text," "narrator" in the *Galateo* is a targeted, a conspicuously unattractive position. "Unattractiveness" is of course so general an attribute as to be little more than a blank check that has to be filled in with more specific values before it is cashable. "Cynicism" may be one such value. "Misanthropy" may be another. "Paranoia" may be a third.

The narrator begins by conceding the value of the moral virtues but dismissing their practical importance:

> [One ought to be] polite, pleasant, and well mannered. If this is not a virtue, it is at least something very similar. And although liberality, courage, and

generosity are without doubt far greater and more praiseworthy things than charm and manners, none the less, pleasant habits and decorous manners and words are perhaps no less useful to those who have them than a noble spirit and self-assurance are to others. This is so because . . . good manners must . . . be practised many times daily, whereas justice, fortitude and the other greater and nobler virtues are called into service much more seldom. Generous and magnanimous persons are not called upon to put such virtues into practice on a daily basis; rather, no one could behave this way very often. . . . Thus, while these virtues easily surpass [vincono] the others in greatness and weightiness, the others surpass [avanzano] these in number and frequency [ispessezza].[2]

The different connotations of "vincono" and "avanzano" in the last sentence are worth noting. The nobler virtues vanquish the others "di ['in' or 'by'] grandezza e quasi di peso" but are outnumbered and overtaken as the others move forward and advance themselves. The lineaments of the conflict between older nobility and the "nuovi ricchi" begin to materialize in the narrator's prose.

As the argument proceeds, the relation between the greater and lesser virtues shifts from resemblance to surrogation, and the conflict becomes more visible. In the above passage, manners "forse . . . giovano non meno"— "perhaps are of no less use"—to their possessors than virtues. What follows indicates that they will in fact be of more use:

I could very easily, if it were appropriate, mention to you many men who, though not worthy of praise in other things, nevertheless are or have been highly esteemed only by reason of their pleasant manner. Thus helped and sustained, they have attained high rank, leaving far behind those who were gifted with those nobler and more outstanding virtues which I mentioned earlier. (D, 4)

Is the second sentence uttered in admiration or in bitterness? What is the speaker's stake in the claim that the lesser virtues are useful not only because they resemble the greater ones but also because they can displace them? And in the related claim that more than virtues are displaced?—the claim expressed in the concluding clause that "coloro che erano *dotati* di quelle più nobili e più chiare virtù" (*Op.*, 369; my italics) are also left behind? Here the difference between virtue and manners corresponds with that between ascriptive and performative criteria—in the lexicon of the *Cortegiano*, the difference between grazia, which is inborn or *dotata*, and sprezzatura, which is not.[3] The rhetoric hints at an ideological struggle in which the older nobility lay claim to traditional moral virtues as their birthright.

To take up this hint is to add a wrinkle of disenchantment to the theme Frank Whigham proposes for the *Galateo*: "Moral categories are dominated by stylistic ones."[4] The examples of virtue selected by the narrator may lead one to suspect that "moral categories" is itself a stylistic category deployed by the older nobility to euphemize despotic power: "l'esser liberale o constante o magnanimo . . . la grandezza dell'animo e la sicurezza . . . la giustizia, la fortezza . . . il largo e il magnanimo . . . gli animosi uomini e sicuri . . . il valore e la virtù" (*Op.*, 368). "Magnanimo" condenses "generous" with "great-spirited," the former accentuated by "liberale" and the latter shaded by "constante" toward manly self-sufficiency. The term bears the mark of its Nichomachean legacy, and the quality of disdain embedded in Aristotle's conception of the *megalopsyche* as one confident in one's own superiority glimmers through its literal Latin and Italian translations. That disdain together with the aggressiveness lurking in "-animo" become more explicit when "magnanimo" is in effect rewritten as "la grandezza dell'animo e la sicurezza." The phrase influences the coupling of "giustizia" and "fortezza," the only cardinal virtues mentioned here: the sense of justice is narrowed and modified by a term that in turn tends to equate "fortitudo" with the force and fortification on which "sicurezza" depends.[5] The doublet "il largo e il magnanimo" connects liberality and largesse to the largeness, the amplitude, of the extensive (and fortified) holdings owned and defended by "animosi uomini." Finally, "fortezza" reappears in the more domesticated and generalized form of "il valore e la virtù," which has the feel of a hendiadys.

The terms in this series thus tend to identify virtue with the two traditional forms of aristocratic advantage, the forms characteristic of the agrarian and warrior nobility in feudal Europe: superior control over the resources and strategies of donation/prestation and over those of force.[6] Whether or not the narrator recognizes this as a legitimate style of self-representation, he acknowledges its ineffectiveness in the face of a more mobile and, so to speak, liquid culture of despotism based on the currency of manners. But the "whether or not" is itself a crucial issue in the interpretation of *Galateo*. What *does* the narrator recognize as legitimate? If, as I put it above, the examples of virtue he selects "may lead one to suspect that 'moral categories' is . . . a stylistic category," and one "deployed by the older nobility to euphemize despotic power," which of the two despotisms does the narrator prefer? Does he defend the prerogatives of the new aristocracy or of the old? Or of neither? Or of both? Is his dilemma that of the courtiers in the *Cortegiano*? Or does it beg the question to speak of the narrator as a single-minded "he"? For we have already seen enough to suspect that the expositor of the new manners may not be fully committed to its values.

Our suspicion is kept alive at the end of the chapter when the narrator praises "il sapere essere . . . grazioso e piacevole" in terms that glance at its socially as well as ethically disruptive effects:

> The other virtues require greater resources, lacking which they amount
> to little or nothing, while this is rich and powerful without any such
> patrimony precisely because it consists solely of words and gestures. (My
> translation)
>
> *Le altre virtù hanno mestiero di più arredi, i quali mancando, esse nulla o poco
> adoperano; dove questa senza altro patrimonio è ricca e possente, sì come quella
> che consiste in parole e in atti solamente.* (*Op.*, 369; emphasis mine)

The figures of displacement that stud this passage convey both an admonition and an invitation: the unadorned practice of the greater virtues can be afforded only by those who are already safely ensconced in their "arredi," the furnishings that metonymically imply real property and the real breeding it underwrites, whereas any arriviste, even a vicious one, can make it to the top—and many have already done so—merely by mastering the requisite rhetorical and theatrical skills of self-representation.

This being the way of the world, the narrator opens the second chapter by warning his pupil (so that he "may learn this lesson more easily") that

> it will be to your advantage to temper and adapt your manners not according to your own choices but according to the pleasure of those with whom
> you are dealing, and act accordingly. . . . Therefore—seeing that our manners
> are considered pleasant when we take into consideration other people's
> pleasures and not our own—if we try to distinguish between the things that
> generally please the majority of men and those that displease them we can
> easily discover what manners are to be shunned and what manners are to be
> selected for living in society. (D, 4–5, altered)

The speaker's flow of worldly wisdom is bland and self-assured, but let's look more closely at the substance of his teaching: not merely how to get along by practicing moderation, discerning what pleases others, and acting accordingly; not merely how to represent oneself to others. He also teaches an art of rationalization and self-persuasion; his precepts are wrapped in advice about reflexive self-representation. The sentences that actualize his "sentenzia" are themselves demonstrations of how one may persuade oneself that self-serving behavior is altruistic and that in toadying to others one is motivated by moral sensitivity and concern for their welfare. "We are being considerate of others and putting their pleasure before ours" is what we should tell ourselves we are doing as we go about pleasing them in order to get what we want.[7]

Such advice, though silky smooth, is lined with cynicism, and the narrator's discourse is frequently slashed to let the lining show through. In a relatively early example (chap. 8) the tone is dry and cool and the cynicism epigrammatically contained in another comment on the liquidity of the culture of manners.

> Everybody wishes to be respected even if he does not deserve it. . . . It is proper to accept . . . [people] readily not for what they are truly worth but rather, as with money, for their stated value. (D, 14)

> *Ciascuno appetisce di essere stimato ancora che egli no 'l vaglia. . . . [È] convenevol cosa lo esser presto di accettarli non per quello che essi veramente vagliono, ma, come si fa delle monete, per quello che corrono. (Op., 380–81)*

The implication is that people are worth less than their stated value. The cynicism, glibness, and shiftiness of this maneuver are noticeable enough, but in the early chapters the sense of moral duplicity is diminished by the narrator's circumscribed perspective. Just as he explicitly dissociates manners from virtue, so the ethical questionability of his teaching is fended off by its presumptive goal: through Chapter 11 he concentrates his precepts and examples on the importance of not giving offense, the importance of respecting and learning how to gratify other people's desire to be respected.

We are allowed a glimpse of the apprehensiveness that fuels this desire in the tenth chapter. Its subject is hypersensitivity, which is handled in the standard misogynist manner as a mark of effeminacy:

> It is . . . not appropriate, especially for men, to be overly sensitive and fastidious, for to deal in this way with other people is called not companionship but servitude. There certainly are some who are so sensitive and easily hurt that to live or to be with them is nothing more than finding oneself

surrounded by many fine glass objects, for they fear every blow, and so they must be treated and respected like fine crystal. . . . Such sensitivity and such fastidiousness are best left to women. (D, 16–17)

These men are described as exceptional in their touchiness. And yet the code of manners the narrator unpacks is basically a practice of continuous surveillance and minute scrutiny, one that—as the anecdote of Count Ricciardo shows—demands unflagging vigilance in self-representation. It is therefore guaranteed to heighten everyone's sensitivity to the insults and rebukes one suspects everyone else is poised to deliver. The paranoid exceptions may be only caricatures, but caricatures are signifiers of the state of affairs they caricature. In that respect the mannerly interactions delineated in *Galateo* conform to the picture drawn by Joan Kelly and others—and more than hinted at in the *Cortegiano*—of an apprehensive, effeminized courtier class.

Chapter 10 may act as a lightning rod by shunting such bolts of anxiety off to one side, but by Chapter 13 the rod has become less effective. A new topic is introduced, one that more directly impinges on the ethics of manners and the problem of *self*-respect: lying. This chapter is the gateway to the *Galateo's* central and tonally most complex section, the four chapters in which good manners are identified with appropriate ceremonial behavior (chaps. 14–17), and I want to pause over a pair of minor mistranslations in the Dovehouse English version of Chapter 13 because they point revealingly if inadvertently toward the moral problematic that will make it hard for the narrator to maintain the distinction between lies and ceremonies.

The forms of lying he picks out for discussion are extremes of ostentation and diffidence in dress, speech, and public behavior. Though he predictably urges the *via media* between these extremes, he emphasizes the need for controlled understatement: "Non dee adunque l'uomo avvilirsi né fuori di modo essaltarsi, ma più tosto è da sottrarre alcuna cosa de' suoi meriti che punto arrogervi con parole: perciocché ancora *il bene*, quando sia soverchio, spiace" (*Op.*, 390; my italics). In the Dovehouse translation, this becomes "One should neither humble nor unduly exalt oneself. Instead, one should rather subtract something from one's merits than add something to them with words, for even *the truth*, if flaunted, is displeasing" (D, 21; my italics). Rendering "il bene" as "the truth" rather than "the good" seems harmless enough, but since "il bene" stands in a pronominal relation to "suoi meriti," and since the context is a discussion of lying, that choice sharpens the assumptive edge of the translation it produces: the assumption is that the merit one attributes to oneself is the truth about oneself—that it is possible not to deceive oneself about the truth of "il [suo] bene" even as one develops the habit of salutary lying. Interrogating the free translation turns the spotlight toward a risk that is marginalized by the focus of the discussion but falls like a shadow across its perimeter: the risk of lying to oneself. If, for example, the courtly performer supposes that his merit is egregious enough to require him to tone down his self-descriptions, isn't he in danger of unduly exalting himself *to himself*?

On second thought, the translators' equation of "il bene" with "il vero" may be dramatically appropriate if the narrator's sentence is given the force of a confidence-building demonstration or stage direction: "This is what you should think about yourself, how you should value yourself, what you should say to yourself, as you prepare the little white lies of understatement by which you can most effectively, because least offensively, convey the truth of your superior merit." Admittedly, "confidence-building" may be a euphemistic way to characterize a paraphrase in which the speaker seems mainly to offer an incentive to self-deception. The paraphrase is intended to convey my sense of the mordancy that laces the text's voicing of the narrator, an effect also produced by noting and correcting the second instance of questionable translation. After he has cited further examples of aggressive diffidence, he reaffirms the need for understatement with increased emphasis on its function as a calculated defensive maneuver: "Dee di sé ciascuno quanto può tacere o, se *la opportunità* ci sforza a pur dir di noi alcuna cosa, piacevol costume è di dirne il vero rimessamente, come io ti dissi di sopra" (*Op.*, 390–91; my italics). "As far as possible, one should keep quiet about oneself, and if *the situation* forces us to speak of ourselves, then it is a pleasant habit to speak truthfully and modestly, as I have already said" (D, 22; my italics). To translate "la opportunità" as "the situation" is to buffer the happy shock of a skewed idiom, since opportunity is proverbially something we seize rather than something we are forced by. "If opportunity forces us . . ." perfectly mimes and exposes the *pretense* of reluctance that conceals one's pleasure in displaying not only how much better one is than one admits but also how deft one is at understating one's superiority.

The discussion of lies in Chapter 11 makes it hard to know where lies end and truth begins. It seems to be merely a selective survey that reduces strategies of self-presentation to more and less effective strategies of lying. But tonal insinuations like those mentioned above arouse the reader's curiosity about the effect of the cult of manners on self-esteem. They render conspicuous the narrator's inattention to the necessity and moral cost of lying to oneself. It is as if he glances at but turns quickly away from the lesions of distrust and bad faith he knows are chafing under the cloak of politesse. That knowledge peeps out periodically in references to the lack of substance common to mendacious, mannerly, and ceremonious speech. It is first presented only in the light of practical advantage in the assertion, quoted above, that concludes Chapter 1: manners are acquired more easily than virtues because they consist solely in words and gestures (D, 4). Early in Chapter 13, after acknowledging that "lies are sometimes accepted as the truth," he asserts that in the long run no one believes or even listens to liars; their words "have no substance in themselves but are more or less like those of people who aren't talking but sending out puffs of air" ("come s'eglino non favellassino ma soffiassino," *Op.*, 389). Similarly, in Chapter 14 he speaks of a custom that, "so beautiful and becoming on the outside, is totally empty [vana] within, and consists in shadows without substance [sembianti senza effetto] and words without meaning" (*Op.*, 394). But this comment is not about lies; it is about the permissible and even necessary form of ceremony. The echoic resonance that links these three statements suggests the difficulty the narrator faces when he turns to discuss—and ultimately to justify—what he describes as ceremonial observances. They also suggest the difficulty faced by any self-respecting observant who has a hard time distinguishing his ceremonial practice from a practice of continuous lying.

In Chapter 14 the discussion of ceremonies begins with the flat assertion that they are a foreign import, unknown to our ancestors and, "because of their emptiness [vanità], very little removed from lies and dreams" (D, 24–25). This denunciation of an "usanza ... forestieri e barbara" that has invaded and victimized Italy continues almost to the end of the chapter. Italy's humiliation is redescribed as the plight of each person forced "to honor those whom we hold in no special reverence and those whom we sometimes hold in contempt" (D, 23). But after all this he concludes the chapter—in a passage containing the third of the three statements quoted above—by insisting that ceremonies must nevertheless be observed:

> In the past titles used to be determined and distinguished by papal or imperial privileges ... [but] nowadays, one must grant much more liberally these titles and other similar indications of honor because custom—far too powerful a lord [troppo possente signore]—has greatly privileged the men of our times with them. This habit, then, so beautiful and becoming on the outside, is totally empty within, and consists in shadows without substance

and words without meaning. Nevertheless, we are not permitted to change it; on the contrary, we are constrained—since it is not our fault but [that] of the times—to countenance it; but one should [or would wish to] do this discreetly. (D, 24, seriously altered)[8]

The personification of custom as despot serves up a tactfully skewed reference to self-legitimizing despots who impose their will and rewrite their desires as customary privilege. This figure prepares the way for the classic victim's disclaimer of responsibility, which in turn is fortified by another transformation of "possenti signori" when "uomini del nostro tempo privilegiati" returns in the generalized form of "peccato . . . del secolo." The final clause then registers the victims' grudging acquiescence, their forced compliance, by means of an impersonal construction ("ma vuolsi ciò fare discretamente") the sense of which oscillates between what one is constrained or ought to do and what one wishes one could wish to do since one has to do it.

There is nothing subtle about this disingenuous little appeal to the victim's discourse. It rides on the surface of the rhetoric, and its strenuous adversative tacking testifies—in conspicuously unembarrassed embarrassment—to the tricky crosswinds of an argument that calls for tact precisely because it jeopardizes self-respect. The argument is more than a persuasion; it is a demonstration. Not merely "These are the reasons why you must resign yourself to ceremonies and learn how to perform them," but "This is how you should persuade yourself that—so long as you don't overdo it—it is all right to do what you can't avoid doing." In other words, the argument for discreet acquiescence should be read as if it were in quotation marks. Whether these should be interpreted as scare quotes remains to be seen.

In the brief paragraph that constitutes the fifteenth chapter, the narrator begins to rehabilitate ceremony and continues to rationalize the necessity of submitting to it. He does so by distinguishing three motives for observance, two bad (profit and vanity) and one good (duty), and this sets the stage for his defense of ceremonies observed out of duty, which occupies the next and by far the longest of the chapters devoted to ceremony. Chapter 16 begins on a positive note: the project of distinguishing the good from the bad is introduced with the confidence of one who anticipates no trouble in concluding his argument: "Restami a dire di quelle che si fanno per debito e di quelle che si fanno per vanità" (*Op.*, 394); "It remains for me to speak of those [ceremonies] that are performed out of duty and those that are performed out of vanity." But the confidence is premature, for we soon find him laboring to put the best face on the modern predicament and to justify submission to what he has clearly depicted as a bad-faith morality:

> The strength of custom is very great and in such matters should be considered a law. . . . It is advisable for us to obey not what is the best but what is the modern custom, just as we obey even those laws which are less than good until *the state or whoever has the power* to do so changes them. Thus, in the land where we dwell we must diligently assume the gestures and the words that usage and modern custom normally employ in welcoming, greeting, and addressing each man in his own station; and when dealing with society we must abide by these practices. . . . These I call obligatory formalities, for they do not originate from our own desire or from our own free will, but are imposed on us by law, that is, *by general custom*. In matters that do not have anything evil about them but on the contrary seem to have a semblance of courtesy, it is desirable or rather necessary to obey general customs and not to dispute or disagree with them. (D, 25–26; my italics)

At two points in this passage questions of translation implicate questions of interpretation. (1) In the first sentence, the translation attenuates the hint of coerciveness by depluralizing the noun phrase, thereby rendering it more abstract. Here is the text followed by an alternate rendering: "le forze della usanza sono grandissime . . . e voglionsi avere per legge in simili affari" (*Op.*, 395); "the forces of custom are very great . . . and are required to be taken for laws in such matters." What such matters are, and who controls the forces, had been illustrated by the preceding sentence: "It has happened many times that swords have been drawn merely because one citizen, meeting another on the street, did not show him due honor" (D, 25). The impersonal "voglionsi" thinly veils a hidden collective subject possessed of "le forze . . . grandissime."[9]

(2) The first two words of the first italicized phrase, "the state or whoever has the power," translate not "lo stato" but "il Comune," the republican form of government. The tonal change this produces is small but distinct and important: "the commune or whoever (else) has the power" ("il Comune o chi ha podestà," *Op.*, 395)—the power to change laws and customs for the better, but also to enforce the ones in play—becomes an archly indirect but pointed reference to the "whoever else," that is, the possessors of "forze grandissime." Note how the despotizing reference to "le forze della usanza . . . grandissime" is then countered in the second italicized phrase by modifying "l'usanza" with the adjectival form ("comune"), which once again

evokes a thought of the republican constitution. That such constitutional discrimination—or irony, or even, perhaps, sarcasm—is in play is suggested by the reappearance of "Comune" later in the same chapter in a passage critical of those who defend informal salutations because they were used in addressing letters to the ancient "Comune . . . di Roma" (*Op.*, 396). Noting that this is a gaffe because the narrator is referring to the senate, a chorus of editors sound their disapproval of this inappropriate reference to a patrician institution. But they explain it as one of the moments in which della Casa has the narrator display or betray the character, assigned to him in the *Galateo*'s subtitle, of an unlearned "idiota." To this persona they also attribute occasional moments of unsightly rhetorical tumescence. Yet this is a formal rather than a motivational explanation, and it doesn't engage the issues of ethical self-portrayal raised by the odd tonal variations in the narrator's performance.

Consider, for example, the penultimate sentence, with its harrumph of official authority ("nomino io") rendered a little flatulent by another occurrence of "conciossiaché": "E queste nomino io cirimonie debite, conciossiaché elle non procedono dal nostro volere né dal nostro arbitrio liberamente, ma ci sono imposte dalla legge, cioè dall'usanza comune . . ." (*Op.*, 395). When he softens "ci sono imposto dalla legge" by equating legal imposition with "l'usanza comune," does he merely engage in the fishy tactic of justifying what can't be opposed or does he demonstrate its fishiness by mimicry? If we associate these plays on "comune" with the reference to the despotism of custom in the preceding quotation from Chapter 14—"l'usanza, troppo possente signore"—we see it as a continuation of that motif: the personification of despotic custom is now extended to the pressure of despots who would wish to hurtle down the tracks of mystification from force to custom, custom to law, and law to nature. But to flag despotic desire in the mode of discursive mimicry is to throw it off course. The rhetorical semaphorics by which the narrator makes these passages intercommunicate has the effect of derailing the ideological train before it reaches its destination in nature. Does this mean that he resists or that he resents the political culture of the very "usanza" he claims to be teaching? Then why is he teaching it—or what is the project behind his claim, or pretense, to be teaching it?

Such questions lead us back to the tactics of his initial proposal. In Chapter 1 he himself suggests that obeying custom is tantamount to obeying nature. After stating that pleasant manners alone have enabled less virtuous men to attain high rank, and that clownish and rough manners cause us to be disdained, he concludes that even though displeasing behavior isn't considered serious enough to punish by law,

> and is not in fact serious, we see nonetheless that nature herself punishes us severely for it, depriving us for this reason of the company and benevolence of others. (D, 4, altered)

> *e certo egli non è grave, noi veggiamo nondimeno che la natura istessa ce ne castiga con aspra disciplina, privandoci per questa cagione del consorzio e della benivolenza degli uomini. . . .* (Op., 369)

The informal but powerful *arbitrium elegantiae* wielded by mannerly trend-setters of questionable virtue is mystified by displacement to nature.

This is clearly how the trend-setters would like us to see it. Does the narrator then make himself their mouthpiece? In resignation? In resentment? Is he among those of "us" who—as he says in Chapter 14—"sometimes present ourselves as most devoted servants to those to whom we would rather do a disservice than a service"?[10] If so, he still voices a reservation before he drives home his (and their) finger-wagging moral: "e certo egli non è grave" seconds the judgment of the law that ethical breaches are worse than bad manners, and thus implies that "nature's" values leave something to be desired. Yet, with another "e certo," he immediately changes tack and goes on to urge submission to "nature's" dominance in terms borrowed from the so-called natural order:

> And certainly, just as serious sins are more harmful, so these lighter faults are more annoying, or at least annoy us more often; and just as people fear wild beasts and have no fear of some very small animals like mosquitoes and flies, so, because the latter are a continual nuisance, people complain more about them than they do about the others, and so it happens that they hate unpleasant or bothersome people as much as, if not more than, evil ones. (D, 4, much altered)

"As flies to wanton boys": since this is the nature of culture's labile hierarchy of manners, whoever "decides to live in cities and among men rather than in desert wastes or hermit's cells" (D, 4) has to take precautions to avoid getting swatted. In the jungle of civil society, manners are preventive medicine or (to change the metaphor) camouflage. The narrator presents his course in conduct as a course in survival and sweetens the medicine with the promise that since the material to be learned consists "in parole e in atti solamente," it will be easier to acquire the "ricca e possente" resources of this art than those of the virtues (*Op.*, 369).

Considering this passage together with all those previously discussed, I find it difficult to evade the conclusion that the varied collection of dissonant notes—of cynicism, resistance, resentment, resignation, and irony or sarcasm—produces a strong effect of narratorial distance, an effect of continuous mimicry, of free indirect discourse or quotation rather than direct statement, and of quotation that frequently veers toward the function of scare quotes. The speaker seems at once to ventriloquate and to dissociate himself from the prescriptive rationalizations he represents as the discourse of despots. He *represents* in two senses, for in addition to giving a representation of the discourse, he appears to speak as its representative or advocate. Such an appearance is the sine qua non, the necessary if not sufficient cause of the effect of ironic impersonation.

In defending obligatory or dutiful ceremony as a golden mean between boorishness and sycophancy, the narrator projects the nervous equilibrium of a tightrope walker. Viewed academically, this performance displays some of the characteristics of the method of arguing *utramque parte*, but the following sequence from Chapter 16 suggests that method has less to do with it than the precarious teeter-totter of acrobatic rationalization: on the one hand, "men of great virtue and excellence do not use many formalities; nor do they appreciate or expect that many be used toward them, for they will not waste their thoughts on such vain matters"; on the other, "these kinds of formalities should be freely performed, for what one person does out of obligation is received as due and is of little merit to the one who does it. But he who offers much more than is his duty seems to be offering something of his own and is loved and considered generous" (D, 28). The speaker shifts his weight from an emphasis on ceremonial restraint to an emphasis on precautionary excess. A few sentences later he counters the latter move as if to avert a fall into the sin of overpraising overpraise: "But the person who is over-lavish and extravagant with formalities will be accused of being vain and frivolous, and, what is worse, it may happen that he will be considered a wicked man and a flatterer." Thus teetering back and forth, he abandons his dutiful defense of dutiful ceremony and heads, almost as if with relief, toward "the third kind of ceremony which arises from our own will and not from custom," and from vanity rather than from duty (D, 28). The remainder of the chapter is a diatribe against flattery.

The introduction of this third kind triggers a skeptical recoil from the effort to cordon off or quarantine obligatory ceremony, and a return to the original position staked out at the beginning of Chapter 14, where the narrator had commented on the foreign origin of ceremonies and equated them with lies and dreams. Now he urges his addressee to "remember that ceremonies were not necessary by nature, as I said at the beginning. Rather, one could do perfectly well without them, as our people [nazione] did until not so very long ago. But someone else's ills have made us ill with this and many other infirmities" (D, 28–29, altered). The threatened collapse of his attempt to isolate and defend obligatory ceremony—defend it from his own arguments—produces a new tone of exasperation, expressed in another hint at Italian susceptibility to the bad Spanish influence he has railed against in Chapter 14 and will expressly indict in Chapter 17.[11] This leads to a loss of balance the Dovehouse translation seems reluctant to acknowledge. Here is the Italian text followed first by the Dovehouse version and then by my own:

> *Per la quale cosa, ubbidito che noi abbiamo all'usanza, tutto il rimanente in ciò è superfluità e una cotal bugia lecita; anzi pure da quello innanzi non lecita ma vietata, e perciò spiacevole cosa e tediosa agli animi nobili che non si pascono di frasche e di apparenza.* (Op., 399)

For this reason, once we have obeyed custom and used such permissible lies, anything more is superfluous; however, it is impermissible and forbidden to go further than custom allows, because formalities then become an unpleasant and boring thing for men of noble spirit who do not indulge in such games and pretences. (D, 29)

For this reason, once we have obeyed custom, all the rest of this [practice] is excess and thus a permissible lie; or indeed, better still, from that point on [it is] on the contrary not permissible but forbidden, and therefore an unpleasant and tedious thing to the noble spirits who don't nourish themselves on trifles and pretenses.[12]

The Dovehouse translators rearrange clauses, shifting "una cotal bugia lecita" (which they pluralize) into a compound predicate dominated by "ubbidito . . . abbiamo" and changing the adversative force of a disjunction, "non lecita ma vietata," into the supportive redundancy of a pleonastic conjunction ("impermissible and forbidden"). In an obvious effort to straighten out an unruly swerve in the argument, they sharply dissociate permissible lies committed while one obeys custom from the proscribed behavior that exceeds those limits. The extremes to which the translators go is in fact symptomatic of the narrator's failure to make just this distinction. The argument *does* swerve, and not for the first time: that he changes his opinion in mid-sentence—"the excess is permissible; no, it is not permissible but forbidden"—simply registers and continues his uncertain progress along the tightrope he has been on since he undertook to defend obligatory ceremonial observances at the beginning of this long chapter.

What is most notable about the set of chapters on ceremony is that they cause the narrator to turn up the volume of the ground bass of misanthropic sentiment that pulses beneath his high-wire act. As he inventories the types of ceremonial venality in Chapter 17, the rhetoric of faultfinding increases in virulence while the amplified waves of his contempt wash over broader sectors of humankind:

> Those who take pleasure in using formalities more than is suitable do so out of fickleness and shallowness, like men of little worth. . . . They cannot learn weightier matters because they are too weak for such a burden. . . . They have no solid muscle beneath their thin, glossy skin; and if you touch them they are withered and mouldy. . . .
>
> There are others who exceed in courtly words and deeds in order to make up for the faults of their own wickedness and their uncouth, limited natures, for they are aware that if they were as deficient and rough in words as they are in accomplishments, no one would be able to put up with them.
>
> In truth . . . the majority of people abound in the superfluous formalities which generally bother most men. (D, 30)

This passage registers more than the speaker's loathing for the way the majority of men conduct themselves. It also implies that something like self-loathing motivates their acts of self-representation and inwardly corrodes the performers. Having thus unloaded on humankind, the narrator begins the eighteenth chapter with a hilarious admonition, "One should not speak ill either of other people or of their affairs"—hilarious whether we take it as the utterance of an earnest moralizer unaware that he has just described himself, or as blank-eyed mimicry of such wide-eyed pedagogical obtuseness, or as a straightforward slap on the wrist that is no sooner administered than it is forgotten, since his next words continue the diatribe: "even though it is clear that, because of the envy we generally have for other people's wealth and honor, ears will gladly stoop to hear it" (D, 30–31). He shoots off a few more little barbs of wholesale condemnation in this chapter[13] and periodically repeats the practice during the next six.

The sense of misanthropy strongly colors this performance, and in the last section of Chapter 18 it is complicated by a reflexive swerve, a boomerang effect, as the narrator's criticism verges on self-description when he angrily finds fault with faultfinders

> who take it upon themselves to correct other men's failings and reprimand them, and want to pass final judgment upon everything and lay down the law to everyone. "Such a thing should not be done." Or, "What a word you have said!" Or, "Stop doing and saying such things." . . . [Such men] never cease reprimanding or correcting. . . . But it is too much to bother to listen to them. Just as there are few or no men who could stand to live with their doctor or with their confessor, or even less with a criminal court judge, similarly there are few men to be found who will risk becoming familiar with this type of person because everyone loves freedom and by appearing to be our teachers they deprive us of it. (D, 32–33)

"For this reason," he adds, "it is not a pleasant habit to be eager to correct and teach others"; "non è dilettevol costume lo esser così voglioso di correggere e di ammaestrare altrui" (D, 33; *Op.*, 404).

The *costume* is presumably unpleasant to those forced to suffer correction and instruction. But the clauses that follow and conclude the chapter spin this meaning around so that the unpleasantness of the false teacher makes the task of instructing and correcting unpleasant to the true teacher: "This [task] must be left to teachers and fathers. Even from these will sons and students eagerly distance themselves, as you well know" (D, 33); "e deesi lasciare che ciò si faccia da' maestri e da' padri, da' quali pure perciò i figliuoli e i discepoli si scantonano tanto volentieri quanto tu sai che e' fanno" (*Op.*, 404). As the narrator dissociates himself from the false teachers he resembles, he acknowledges the bad effect of that resemblance with an ironic glance at the resistant object—"tu"—of his own captious and misanthropic pedagogy. The question posed by his performance in this and the surrounding chapters is whether the misanthropy is all-inclusive—whether, that is, it targets the narratorial first person along with everyone else. This question calls for a closer look at the narrator's self-representation.

Galateo is a fiction of pedagogical discourse that presents instruction in manners as the advice given by an older man to a young noble. It follows the general model of advice to (young) princes or aristocrats. More specifically, it recalls a discussion in the *Cortegiano* in which Ottaviano tries to rebut Giuliano's argument that the courtier when old would not be able to instruct the prince in those courtly activities he is no longer capable of performing himself. Ottaviano responds that although the courtier may be too old "to engage in music, festivals, games, arms, and bodily exercises," if he has done these things in youth, the "increase of knowledge" that accompanies age and experience will make it possible for him to know "more perfectly how to teach them to his prince." He then goes on to agree with Giuliano that it may be better to think of the older courtier as a philosopher, an Aristotle to the prince's Alexander (4.45–47).

The opening sentence of *Galateo* places the speaker in a similar position. He addresses his young charge affectionately but deferentially even as he assumes the authoritative mantle of seniority, and he does so, as everyone has noticed, by beginning with a hypercourtly flourish and some resonantly literary phrasing in which editors have variously detected echoes of Dante, Petrarch, and Bembo:

> Inasmuch as you are now just starting that journey that is this earthly life which I, as you can see, have for the most part completed, and because I love you as much as I do, I have taken it upon myself to show you (as someone who has had experience) those places in which I fear you may easily fail or fall, as you proceed through them, so that, if you follow my advice, you may stay on the right path towards the salvation of your soul as well as for the praise and honor of your distinguished and noble family. (D, 3)

> *Conciossiacosaché tu incominci pur ora quel viaggio del quale io ho la maggiore parte, sì come tu vedi, fornito [finito], cioè questa vita mortale; amandoti io assai, come io fo, ho proposto meco medesimo di venirti mostrando quando un luogo e quando altro, dove io, come colui che gli ho sperimentati, temo che tu, camminando per essa, possi agevolmente o cadere o come che sia errare; acciochè tu, ammaestrato da me, possi tenere la diritta via con salute dell'anima tua e con laude e onore della tua orrevole e nobile famiglia. (Op., 367)*

The force of this prefatory piece of self-credentation is complicated by features of its context that precede and follow it. To take the latter first, the concluding distinction between "salute dell' anima" and family honor anticipates the split between morality and manners that the narrator's next sentence introduces:

And since your tender age would not be capable of grasping more important or subtle teachings, I will save them for a more suitable time and start
with what many others might perhaps consider frivolous, that is, how I
believe one ought to behave when speaking or dealing with other people
so as to be polite, pleasant, and well mannered. If this is not a virtue, it is at
least something very similar. (D, 3)

E, perciocché la tua tenera età non sarebbe sufficiente a ricevere più principali e più
sottili ammaestramenti, riserbandogli a più convenevol tempo, io incomincerò da
quello che per avventura potrebbe a molti parer frivolo; cioè quello che io stimo che si
convenga di fare per potere, in communicando ed in usando con le genti, essere costu-
mato e piacevole e di bella maniera; il che nondimeno è o virtù o cosa molto a virtù
somigliante. . . . (Op., 367–68)

He enacts the subject of his discourse, how one ought to behave, by his own
courteous solicitude and sense of decorum—in a word, his *convenevolezza*—
but at the same time he anticipates and defends against the disapproval of
those whose standards may be more rigorous and in whose eyes his strategically lax approach may "per avventura" seem frivolous.

This preemptive move gives us a suspicious narrator who performs as if
before a virtual audience or readership that keeps him under surveillance. It
registers his uneasy awareness that the constraints imposed on him by his
mannerly desire to accommodate (*convenire*) his discourse to the youth of his
addressee put him at a double disadvantage: an apology for his decision to
teach manners rather than something "più principali" is also an apology for
manners per se. It is an apology for the values, the customs, the modes of
performance and self-representation he expressly commits himself to promote. Thus invidiously construed, instruction in manners seems more likely
to help his tutee preserve the honor of his family than to contribute to the
salvation of his soul. The faint odor of queasiness these opening moves give
off lingers throughout the remainder of the narrator's performance.

The other factor that complicates the narratorial position is introduced
in the book's titular heading. Up to now I have personified this position
merely as a "narrator" and have, except for one mention, generally ignored a
vital piece of information contained in this heading: the young noble's in-
structor is called "un vecchio idiota"—an untutored or illiterate or uncul-
tured person, a noncourtier, an outsider who looks up at the beautiful people from below. But the instruction is not simply given *by* this figure: it is
given "*sotto la persona d'*un vecchio idiota" (my italics), a phrase that conspic-

uously theatricalizes—or fictionalizes—and distances the idiota as a site of enunciation. The equivalent of an establishing shot, it encourages the reader to look at rather than through the idiota, and, more specifically, to entertain the possibility that the persona may itself be performed or ventriloquated by another "voice"—that the site of narratorial enunciation may be compound. The interpretive evidence I have adduced so far suggests pretty clearly that the sentiments of the performer or ventriloquator may be those of a courtier or noble.

A courtier playing a noncourtier or a noble a commoner: there is an ancient precedent for this in Plato's *Phaedrus*, Lysias's speech purporting to be by a nonlover who pretends to be a lover followed by Socrates' counter-speech purporting to be by a lover who pretends he is a nonlover. Closer to hand is a suggestion in *Cortegiano* 2.11: among the ways to show "una certa sprezzatura circa quello che non importa" is "for a youth to dress like an old man, yet in a loose attire so as to be able to show his vigor."[14] The *Galateo* narrator wears his persona loosely enough so that constellations of learned allusions—to Petrarch, Boccaccio, Dante, and classical authors—glimmering through its coarse-grained texture divulge his not unvigorous erudition. This intensifies the suspiciously strained effect of rudeness produced when the idiota either flaunts his lack of culture or clumsily puts on airs. Thus on the one hand, he periodically parades his unfitness: "in my youth I did not progress very far with my schooling" (D, 34); "there are other treatises on this [the elegance of witticisms], written by far better writers and experts than I" (D, 36); "when I was planning this treatise, not trusting in my little knowledge, I consulted with several worthier men of learning" (D, 29). Many of the familiar classical references he drops are marked as hearsay by locutions expressing unfamiliarity (he was told of "a king, whose name was Oedipus," of "a good man of that time by the name of Socrates," and of "a worthy man whose name was Pindar"), as if he is being careful to stay in role.[15]

On the other hand, the way he parades his contacts with learned men combines with his occasional weakness for fancy locutions to present a speaker who "strives for a learned effect but achieves, instead, pedantic academic affectation."[16] These are parodic imitations of failed sprezzatura. They mark the idiota's performance as a sustained effort to keep in play the ethical trope that dramatizes sprezzatura at the rhetorical level, the modesty or inability topos. In so doing, they raise a question about the actual class or rank of a speaker who performs the persona of idiota conspicuously enough to encourage readers to suspect that neither his culture nor his perspective is reducible to that figure. Another question is raised by the way the speaker time and again seems to dissociate himself from a behavioral code the idiota has made it his project to explicate and advocate. What motivates the odd mixture of impersonation and dissociation depicted in this strangely convoluted mode of narrativity? Some light on these questions is thrown by two passages—in Chapters 12 and 25–26—that directly or indirectly focus attention on the narrator.

The first is the strange episode of Tomarozzo's dream in Chapter 12, an episode in which failed sprezzatura and its misanthropic basis irradiate the idiota's self-representation. He begins with a predictable sneer at people who inconsiderately bore others and waste everybody's time with detailed accounts of their dreams, most of which are silly nonsense. Of course, he continues a little too deferentially, he often hears tell ("io sento dire assai") that "the ancient sages [gli antichi savi] included a great many dreams in their books, written with deep knowledge and in fine style"—"con alto intendimento e con molta vaghezza." Nevertheless, "it is not suitable for us unlearned men [noi idioti] and for the common folk to do this in our conversation. Indeed, of all the dreams I have been told—but I pay attention to few of these—I have never heard any that was worth the noise" (D, 19; *Op.*, 386–87), except one, which he immediately proceeds to relate "con molta vaghezza."

In this dream, the shop of "a very rich apothecary" gets vandalized by the mob, who consume all his pharmaceuticals except one flask of "chiarissimo liquore." After the looters leave, a majestic elderly figure enters and drinks off the liquid they spurned. The "alto intendimento" of the dream is clear enough. It is an allegory of social anxiety. "Levatosi il popolo": their upward mobility is perceived as rapacious desire, an eruption of bad manners, from the standpoint of those who rightfully possess the honeyed medicine of good manners the looters wrongfully want in their vain desire to improve their lot. The "chiarissimo liquore" that the old man drank and "everyone else . . . despised and refused was good judgment [la discrezione], which, as you may have understood, no man is willing to taste by any means" (D, 19–20). It's obvious that the egregious hero of the story is a rhetorically burnished version of the idiota: not "vecchio" but "antico," "un uomo grande di statura, antico e con venerabile aspetto" ("a man of great stature, old, and with a venerable appearance"). And it comes as no surprise that this self-romanticizing *figura narratoria* turns out to be a *figura dei*, "Domeneddio" Himself, who, being the supreme embodiment and source of grazia, must be presumed already to possess the virtù of the liquid he consumes. The "vecchio idiota" is linked to this figure as if to the illustrious source of the true nature he travesties.

Tomarozzo's dream is a veiled diatribe against the learning and consumption of manners via the method advocated at the beginning of the *Galateo*, a method that "benefits many men who, though not worthy of high praise in other things, nevertheless are or have been highly esteemed only by reason of their pleasant manner." These men have succeeded in "leaving far behind those . . . gifted with . . . nobler and more outstanding virtues" (D, 4). The implied equation of those men with looters suggests that in the dream episode there is not even an ironic or a parodic trace of the sycophantic booster of the new order. The bitterness that produced those traces surfaces here in its true form as the narrator runs up the flag of misanthropy and self-sanctification from the position of the older aristocracy, the nobility of the sword and of grazia. And he shows his good "discrezione" by planting the flag in the dream of another, a "gentiluomo Romano" who was "non mica idiota" (*Op.*, 387), not at all what the narrator impersonates, and whose fear of the have-nots, peasants, and upstarts he expressed and displaced by dreaming that the victim was his very rich neighbor.[17] Dreams like this, the narrator concludes, should be heeded because they are those of good and learned men who, even when sleeping, are better and wiser than criminals and "gl'idioti" (*Op.*, 388). Dreams like this are also a little paranoid.

The looters sneak into the next chapter, the chapter on lies, when the narrator warns against those "of middle or lower rank" who know how "to keep silent and lie [puossi . . . mentire tacendo]" by bearing themselves "with great solemnity . . . and arrogance . . . , usurping the prerogatives of judges and peacocking about so much that it is a deadly nuisance just to watch them" (D, 20–21, altered).[18] The last clause casually alludes to such judgmental watchers as the narrator himself, and later in the same chapter his scornful mimicry of the rhetoric of obsequiousness veers very close at one point to a self-description of the idiota "persona," a term I leave untranslated in the following passage in order to bring out the speaker's emphasis on the mere theatricality (or conspicuous mendacity) of self-deprecation:

> *Signor, Vostra Signoria mi perdoni se io no 'l saprò così dire: io parlerò da persona materiale come io sono, e secondo il mio poco sapere grossa-mente. . . .*
> (*Op.*, 391)

> My lord, I beg your lordship's pardon if I don't know how to express [my opinion]. . . . I shall speak like the simple persona I am, and in rough terms, according to the little I know. (D, 22, altered)

Although the prime target of mockery is the sycophant's shameless groveling, the backlash stings the idiota—and perhaps also the narrator, who may be expressing impatience with his performance of an idiota trying to ingratiate himself with his betters. If the persona is embarrassingly hyperdeferential, do we conclude that it is performed to supply a negative standard, a model of the bad manners one should eschew?

The question of the negative standard is expressly considered in the most complex moment in the narrator's performance of faux naiveté, in Chapters 25 and 26. As he had done in the Tomarozzo episode, the idiota couples himself to a lofty double, this time the Greek sculptor Polykleitos, and he quietly recalls that episode when he uses the Italian equivalent of Polykleitos, *Chiarissimo*, which was the epithet applied to the clear "liquore" of "discrezione" drunk by the "antico e . . . venerabile" Domeneddio: "As a very antico chronicle reports, there once lived in Morea a good man, a sculptor, who—for his illustrious reputation, as I believe—was nicknamed Maestro Chiarissimo."[19] Here again, the narrator mischievously drops names and plays dumb; the effect of "sì come io credo" is quite smashing. He goes on to tell us that when Chiarissimo was advanced in years—unlike the idiota (and more like Domeneddio), the sculptor is described not as "vecchio" but as "di anni pieno"—he "wrote a treatise in which he gathered up all the rules of his art with the authority of someone who had known them very well." He "called this volume *Il regolo* [The Canon], meaning that from then on the statues that would be made by other masters should be corrected and regulated according to it, just as beams, stones, and walls are measured with a standard ruler."[20] But Chiarissimo didn't stop there. Because he recognized that "most men, and especially laymen and uneducated persons like me, are always readier with the senses than with the intellect," he commandeered "a fine block of marble" and from it "carved a statue . . . that was as regular in each of its limbs and in each of its parts as his treatise proposed in its rules. And he called the statue 'Rule,' just like the book" (D, 48).

A glance at two of the classical pre-texts this passage indexes will suggest the kind of spin the narrator imparts to the old story:

Beauty . . . inheres . . . in the commensurability of the parts . . . and of everything to everything else, just as it is written in the "Canon" of Polykleitos. For having taught us in that treatise all the commensurate proportions of the body, Polykleitos made a work to support his account . . . and called it, like the treatise, the "Canon."[21]

Polyclitus . . . made a statue that artists call the "Canon," and from which they derive the principles of their art, as if from a law of some kind, and he alone of men is deemed to have rendered art itself in a work of art.[22]

My response to the function of Chiarissimo is guided by one of the emphases Andrew Stewart finds in these and other *testamenta*: an emphasis on Polykleitos's polemical and hegemonic desire to live up to his name by overgoing Pythagoras and setting up "a new standard (*kanon* = 'rule'), a work of absolute perfection created on unshakable principles arrived at by a priori reasoning, which others should—and did—follow 'like a law.'"[23] Similarly, what the *Galateo* narrator describes in classicizing, perhaps Platonizing, terms is Chiarissimo's bid to become the Domeneddio of statuaries—the creator of the Model Body and the ruler of all future *demiourgoi* who will piously and obediently turn out copies according to its specifications. And another, more proximate and familiar, creation is never far from the surface of this anecdote: that of the model courtier (and court lady) in *Cortegiano*. The idiota gives Chiarissimo's polemical and imperialistic project a more profoundly disturbing edge: the hegemonic desire to overgo not only other systems and practices of artistic construction and representation but also those discursively relegated to the realm of "la natura," which in the *Cortegiano* takes the specific form of "la grazia" that distinguishes the absolute courtier from the perfect courtier.

The narrator puts Chiarissimo and his two canons into play to provide a contrastive analogy that lets the idiota feature his own shortcomings. In the most prolonged and plaintive reference to his deprived condition, he confesses that although he can "put together in this volume the proper measures, so to speak," of the art of manners, he can't play the statue's role by offering himself as a visible example of the art:

> It is too late for me to . . . illustrate in my habits the above-mentioned rules, making of them a visible example, like the actual statue. . . . If in my youth, when I was pliable and impressionable, those who cared about me had known how to bend my habits—which were perhaps somewhat hard and rough by nature—and had softened and polished them, I could perhaps have become a man such as I am now trying to make of you. . . . Since, for the reasons I have told you, I cannot suit my deeds to my words . . . , let it suffice for me to have said at least in part what one should do; for I am unfit to put any part of it into practice. But . . . you will be able to perceive, in looking at my poor and uncouth manners, what the light of pleasant and praiseworthy manners may be. (D, 48–49, 51)

In this remarkable passage the narrator most fully subjects the sophistical self-presentation of the idiota he ventriloquates to the raking light of parody. The ventriloquator's wry mimicry makes it clear that for the idiota to entertain, even counterfactually, the idea that he might have offered himself as "il secondo Regolo"—his own model—is to exceed Chiarissimo in chutzpah. And the relatively lengthy passage in which he is made to proclaim his unfitness to be a model of good manners registers his effrontery in another form. It is no less than an autobiographical memoir, the profile of one who was victimized in youth by the negligence of his elders but who turned his misfortune to others' advantage. He borrows terms from the art of modeling to suggest that he could have become an exemplary statue had they taken more trouble to suppress "le forze della natura" within him and, like sculptors, labored to shape him from the outside in. If only they had bothered to soften and polish ("ammollirgli e polirgli") his "costumi" while his "animi," the inner forces of his nature, were still pliable and impressionable ("teneri e arrendevoli"), he would not have taken the wrong turn and lost his way.[24] Nevertheless, he has overcome adversity by learning to use it to help others avoid his mistakes. Indeed, he claims, he may be both a better teacher of good manners and a better model of bad manners than those who keep to the straight-and-narrow and lack firsthand experience of what is to be shunned. In the course of rejecting his fitness to model his discursive regolo, the idiota steps forward as a statuesque antimodel, an antihero, who has in his own way transcended his origins to become a true defender of the Galatean faith—who has, in a word, *arrived*, and whose rhetoric demonstrates what it takes to succeed as an arriviste.

At the heart of this sophistical argument, lurking in the text of the Chiarissimo/idiota analogy, the narrator exposes the apparition of the idiota's real hero, which a harder look at the structure of the analogy will uncover. Its basis lies in the resemblance between sculpture and manners, two *technai* devoted to the *poiesis* of perfect form—of beautiful (male) bodies in art and of beautiful (mostly male) behavior in life. If we make these analogues couple, they androgenetically breed a sinister offspring in which the end of manners is to construct a living mannequin who (or that) fully, effortlessly, automatically embodies the rules. The idea of a living statue prompted the Dovehouse editors to an enticing if problematic speculation about the relevance of Ovid's version of the Pygmalion myth (*Metamorphoses*, 10.242–97) to *Galateo*: "Galateo is . . . the masculine form of Galatea, the name given to the statue sculpted and loved by Pygmalion. . . . This allusion . . . represents the purpose of the book—the search for human ideals and the means of animating those ideals through fulfilling the potential in all men" (D, 63). Once we clear away the two difficulties posed by this reading, we may realize its value. The first is that Ovid's version has much less to do with a positive search for and animation of human ideals than with the pathological animation of a misogynist, androgenetic, homoerotic, and indeed autoerotic fantasy. This has often been pointed out.[25] The second difficulty is that, so far as I have been able to determine, the name Galatea seems not to have been bestowed on Pygmalion's ivory love by anyone before Rousseau; since it doesn't appear either in Ovid's version or in translations or commentaries through the sixteenth century, it wouldn't have been available to della Casa or his contemporary readership.[26]

Granting the insurmountability of the second obstacle, we may use the first to rehabilitate and revise the Dovehouse reading. For surely the figure of Messer Galateo, the perfect courtier briefly delineated in Chapter 4, may stand as an equivalent to Chiarissimo's statue. In a metamorphosis that actually reverses the Pygmalion process, Bishop Galeazzo Florimonte has been reduced from his living complexity to an exemplary artifact, a marmoreal measure of good manners—"an easy tool, / Deferential, glad to be of use," one who, as we saw, accommodates his *modi* to the wishes and pleasures of his betters.[27] The figure who briefly materializes in Chapter 4 is as integral as marble or ivory statues, which are constructed from the outside in, and within which there is only more of the same—marble or ivory matter. Unlike Count Ricciardo and Bishop Giberti, whose encounter was discussed above in Chapter 2, the Galateo displayed by the narrator exhibits no signs of interiority or unrevealed motivation. We are shown nothing more than meets and greets the eye. He is all appearance, all accommodation, all impression; appearance and accommodation and impression right down to the core. His "nature" is to embody the canon of conduct developed in the discourse to which he gives his name, and to embody it so fully, so perfectly, as to be spared any trace of the inwardness that hollows out and complicates and bifurcates and in general makes life difficult for the more fallible nature classified as "human." This is the nature the idiota laments he was unable to transcend because those responsible for his nurture didn't bother to do the work of "dirizzare e regolare" that would turn him into a statue.

If the narrator has the idiota present himself as a model of human nature's fallibility, the complexity of that nature is adumbrated in Chapter 4 by the charged but puzzlingly opaque interaction between the bishop and Count Ricciardo. The bishop's voyeuristic *curiositas*, his concern for his guest's feelings, his mastery of the art of humiliation, his considerate and tendentious deployment of the discourse of the gift: these, together with the illegibility of the count's response, compose into a complex scenario that leaves conspicuously unanswered the doubts it raises about motive and affect. In contrast, the picture of Galateo the ideal courtier is not so much understated as transparent, chiarissimo, unstained by any such doubts. Yet while the narrator's discourse makes it obvious that the impression of the statuesque integrity of surface and core, body and soul, is the ideal condition the Galatean canon of conduct is intended to produce, the same discourse makes it equally obvious that in anyone who isn't Galateo this integrity is nothing more than an impression, an appearance, on and of a signifying surface behind which may be concealed the darker purposes and more persistent anxieties of the apprehensive society of manners.

Messer Galateo thus models a canon of conduct that simultaneously constitutes and destroys its ideal. Galatean integrity is an ideal offered as the dreamlike goal of a pedagogy guaranteed to prevent any student from believing in its realization; the more one learns, the less one believes. This is a recipe for cynicism, for suspicion, for paranoia. The production of a vanishing ideal leaves in its wake the misanthropic vision of a society dominated by the Hobbesian war of every peer against every peer, a society in which the weaponry of new manners supplants and displaces that of old virtues. In this warfare Galateo may be the emblem, the colors, of the new army but the narrator presents the persona of the old idiota in the anomalous pose of the standard-bearer who marches in its vanguard and waves its rationalizations bravely aloft. At times those rationalizations are shamelessly bland and evasive, as when they elide the question of *the ethics of manners* on the grounds of a purely procedural decision: "since I undertook to show you men's errors and not their sins, my present care must be to deal not with the nature of vice and virtue, but only with the proper and improper manners we use toward each other" (D, 54). A perverse hierarchy of values is thus presented as a merely arbitrary—and expedient—choice of perspectives.

If the Pygmalion myth can illuminate Galatean discourse, it is in turn modified by that discourse: when we blend Chiarissimo's fantasy of idealization with the idiota's and then compress both into that of Pygmalion, we transform the misogynist basis of the latter's desire into misanthropy and, even more broadly, into *misophysis*, that is, art's contempt and slander of nature, art's desire to suppress, transcend, and replace nature. This slander and desire intertwine to provide one of the central themes in Chapters 25 and 26. The theme is introduced early in Chapter 25 when the idiota explains that

Chiarissimo added the statue to the book because "most men (and especially we *laici e idioti*) are always readier with the senses than with the intellect" (D, 48, altered).

For a moment the glibness of the idiota's parenthetical self-reference may dull the misanthropic edge of his cliché about "la maggior parte degli uomini" (*Op.*, 425). But the tone sharpens after he mentions his own pathetic misfortunes and turns to consider the defects of the majority at greater length. He begins this consideration, however, with an optimistic forecast and a concise statement of the thesis he is about to develop: "Although the forces of nature are great, nevertheless they are often overcome and corrected by custom [l'usanza]." By cultivating "l'usanza" one can overcome the unruly natural forces within oneself. But the happy ending depends on one's willingness to resist those forces "early, and to control them before they become too powerful and bold." And unfortunately this seldom happens. "The majority of people, however, do not do this and instead are misled by their instincts, following them without resistance wherever they may lead. Thus they believe they are obeying nature as if reason were not a natural thing in them" (D, 49, altered).

So far this is straightforward. But something odd occurs at the beginning of the very next clause, which I give in both the Italian and the Dovehouse versions: "*anzi ha ella, sì come donna e maestra*, potere di mutar le corrotte uzanze e di sovvenire e di sollevare la natura, ove che ella inchini o caggia alcuna volta"; "*On the contrary, reason is lord and master: she* has the power to change corrupt habits and assist and raise up nature whenever, from time to time, it slips or falls" (*Op.*, 426; D, 49; my italics). We might have expected "la ragione" to be a male figure in spite of its grammatical marking and I agree with Kristen Brookes, who argues that the semantical marking of reason as female ("donna e maestra"), which is consistently maintained in this chapter, is both surprising and significant.[28] Perhaps this confused the Dovehouse translators; they change and vary the italicized terms as if the semantic gender doesn't matter. We'll see in a moment why it does.

Although we should obey reason, the idiota continues, we don't because "the senses love and lust for immediate pleasures . . . and they abhor bothersome things and put them off." As a result, reason "seems bitter to us" and we "excuse our faintheartedness by saying that nature knows no spur or rein that can drive her on or hold her back." Against this opinion he insists that reason "has power over the senses and the instincts, and it is our wickedness, not her fault, if we go amiss in our lives and our habits" (D, 50). Nevertheless, the idiota makes it clear that not everyone—indeed, hardly anyone—is as enlightened as he is. "The majority of people [le più persone] . . . are misled by their senses" (D, 49). Throughout this passage he leans on the trope of the self-excepting first-person plural in which the moralist implies that "everybody's doing it, even—but not really—I": "For the most part [per lo più], however, we do not listen to our reason"; "we . . . excuse our faintheartedness"; but "it is our wickedness, not her fault."[29] The message is that most of us "still live according to the senses" and are thus too easily swayed by "love and lust for immediate pleasures" (D, 49–50).

In other words, "la ragione" may be our "donna e maestra" but she doesn't have much real power. She is for the most part an ineffective sovereign. And why should this surprise anyone who recognizes her sex and who also knows that—as the idiota reminds us at one point—she is affiliated with "la natura"?[30] This deficiency sets up the conclusion to the argument. The idiota restates his original thesis—"the forces of nature . . . are often overcome and corrected by custom [l'usanza]"—in a stronger and more complex form:

> It is . . . not true that against nature there is neither rein nor master
> [maestro]. On the contrary, there are two of them: one is good manners
> [il costume] and the other is reason. But as I told you a little earlier, she
> [ella, i.e., "la ragione"] cannot make the unmannerly mannerly without
> custom [l'usanza], which is the child and offspring of time. (D, 50, much
> altered; *Op.*, 427)[31]

"La ragione" is helpless without the intervention of "maestro costume," who incorporates "l'usanza" and differs from reason because he is not an essential faculty of the soul and not, therefore, as timeless as (human) nature but is rather—like his sister, Truth—the child of the times. The consequences and relevance of this argument are clear: since reason is part of human nature but human beings for the most part allow themselves to be dominated by the senses they share with animals, they can be saved only by cultural forces external to *le donne* Natura and Ragione. They must submit to "il regolo," the rule of art—to the pedagogy, artifices, and behavioral technology of self-representation laid out in the currently dominant canon of manners.

Even if the reference to Father Time seems innocent enough in this passage, the shadow of bad faith falls over it when we consider that l'usanza and maestro costume are identical with "the proper measures of the art" about which the idiota discourses.[32] For, according to the argument I teased from the earlier chapters, these measures could be determined by a different source of power. We saw that in one set of assertions "l'usanza" itself is the tyrant—

"troppo possente signore"—whose forces "are very great . . . and are required to be taken for laws" (*Op.*, 394–95). But we also saw that in another set of assertions what dominates behavioral negotiations and controls the course of custom is the desire to please and be pleased—more specifically, the desire of the less powerful to accommodate themselves to (or to become) the more powerful.[33] Tyranny in this view is wielded by whoever has the power ("chi ha podestà," *Op.*, 395) to change customs or enforce those currently in play. In other words, custom may often be the child not of time or nature but of the men I referred to above as mannerly trend-setters of questionable virtue—the men who, in the narrator's words, "though not worthy of praise in other things, nevertheless are or have been highly esteemed only by reason of their pleasant manner," and who, through this facility alone, "have attained the highest rank, leaving far behind those . . . gifted with . . . nobler and more outstanding virtues" (D, 4). In such a regime one must expect manners to take precedence over virtue because custom reinforces the senses against reason, the worse desire against the better. Thus in Chapter 16, in the midst of the discussion on ceremony, the narrator concedes that "it is advisable for us to obey not what is the best [la buona] but what is the modern custom" and, a little later, that "when leaving or writing you must greet and take your leave according to what not reason but custom dictates" (D, 25–26).

Let's pause over these concessions. Consider the equation of "the best" with "what reason . . . dictates" and of "la ragione" with the better part of nature. Doesn't this suggest that "la ragione" may be the source of the "più nobili e più chiare virtù" with which those who have been left behind are "dotati" (*Op.*, 369)? Doesn't it also suggest that in such sensibilities the senses obey reason and do not need to be policed by "l'usanza"? In brief, doesn't it suggest that "la natura" + "la ragione" = "la grazia," the absence of which is itself signified by sprezzatura and ensured by "maestro costume," that is, by "l'usanza" of the Galatean code? The concessions, then, rub against the idiota's endorsement of the code. They raise questions about the view of human nature presupposed and reinforced by a manual of conduct that thrives on the absence of grace, the failure of reason, and the revolt of the senses; a code that produces and is sustained by misanthropic suspicion and distrust. Thus I find it difficult to read this manual without imagining that the site of enunciation it constructs is the source of a double-edged discourse: on the one hand, the Galatean code of conduct is articulated by a pragmatic, earnest, even enthusiastic—if morally neutral—technician of manners intent on telling his tutee How to Make It in high society, and on the other hand, the picture of the apprehensive society that code produces is conveyed through a satiric portrayal of the idiota/technician, an impersonation lined with bitterness and moral outrage. The idiota shows his respect and admiration for the code by parading his inability, thereby appropriating one of the most overworked tropes of courtiership. Viewed from the standpoint of the narrator who performs the idiota, this imitation is recast as a parody, a comic hyperbole; a trope not of modesty but of sycophancy.

But what does it mean to speak of a narrator who "performs the idiota" and who has a "standpoint"? And if the performance is parodic, does this make the idiota an unreliable speaker? Performed by a reliable narrator?— that is, a narratorial standpoint identical with the one the reader ascribes to the author? Or is this performer as unreliable as the idiota, and does the text encourage its readers to find still another viewpoint from which to scrutinize and resist the narratorial viewpoint that scrutinizes and resists the idiota's viewpoint? It is time to face up to the methodological potholes I have been creating for myself by driving my interpretation through *Galateo* in so unwieldy a narratorial vehicle, an exegetical rig forced to haul a series of trailers each loaded with a different viewpoint. I'm sensitive to the dangers of ignoring "Leicester's razor," the caveat laid down by H. Marshall Leicester on the model of the principle of parsimony attributed to William of Ockham. Leicester took Ockham's razor, "Entities must not be multiplied without necessity," and redirected its cutting edge from entities in general to narrators: "Narratores non sunt multiplicandi sine absolute necessitate."[34] But just what constitutes interpretive necessity? Can the same rig travel to its destination and deliver its load with fewer trailers? Wouldn't it be safer to fall back to a more skeptical position that consolidates the viewpoints, packs them together, lets them shift about and bump and even blend into each other—a position that allows for, even celebrates, inconsistency and discontinuity in the author's representation of his narrator(s)?

For several decades we've been repeatedly told that the term "author" may be nothing more than a validating synonym or signifier the signified of which is "the reader's interpretation of the text." Depending on their interpretive affiliations, prejudices, and protocols, readers may characterize the text in different ways, but even their disagreements are possible only because most of them—all but the most rabid deconstructors—have already pledged allegiance to the metaprinciple that founds interpretive practice and its "communities" (or empires): the principle that any text has affiliations, prejudices, protocols, and character of its own—that it imposes constraints on interpreters and therefore that within the textual body produced by interpretation there beats a core of autonomous discursive agency. It's entirely possible to *characterize* this agency—ascribe character to it—without personifying, animating, humanizing, or subjectifying it; without situating it in the figure of an author, a narrator, or a speaker.

The sheer "itness" of the agency of discourse can be affirmed even as we probe it for "attitude," for interests and commitments, for complexity (contradiction, incompatibility) in "tone" and "point of view." But of course to affirm this is apologetically to acknowledge the stubbornness of the anthropomorphic investment that makes the ascription of itness so alien, so awkward to maintain with consistency for all but the most rabid structuralists. Nevertheless, it's a mistake to assume that itness is the reality of discursive agency and "person(ific)ation" only an appearance, a fantasy, or an allegorization. The "purest" structuralist construal is no less a construction than any other that competes in the marketplace of interpretive opportunities; no less a fiction, a convenience, a strategic choice, than any version of anthropomorphic construal, including the one I have put into play in this study.

Since the text of *Galateo* is an instruction manual and is voiced in the conventional rhetorical form of a pedagogical monologue, it constructs for itself a speech prefix as its site of enunciation. Furthermore, it confers on that speech prefix a complex but describable set of interests, values, and motivations. The text, that is, impersonates and interprets or characterizes its site of enunciation as a narrator. And in my interpretive fantasy, this impersonation transgresses the narrow boundaries of the site expressly delineated by the speech prefix "la persona d'un vecchio idiota." Very early in this chapter I suggested that the expositor of the Galatean code of conduct may not be fully committed to its values even though he promotes the code and expresses his enthusiasm for it. Since making this suggestion I have repeatedly picked out effects of tonal dissonance that trouble this exposition, effects that hint at resistance to the code and mimicry of its expositor. In such moments the narrator's advocacy of the code is oddly skewed by undertones of cynicism and misanthropy that render the nominal site of enunciation opaque rather than transparent and thus encourage the reader to look suspiciously at rather than innocently through the idiota.

To underline the commitments of this interpretive fantasy, I contrast it with the account given in the Dovehouse introduction:

> The presence of the idiota narrator leads to two important considerations. First, it suggests that the subject matter of the *Galateo* is to be seen not as

the exclusive right of the learned but as the common property of all men: the manners and style reflected in the book can be acquired and practised by anyone, though a gentleman born of a good family and with access to leisure time and the necessary amount of wealth would of course find the regimen more useful and easier to follow. Second, the matter discussed can be learned from experience and from daily life much more easily and far better than from books. The implied reference to Castiglione's elegant and learned coterie assembled in Urbino and described in *The Book of the Courtier* is self-evident.

The narrator figure, then, is not an image of Della Casa, the humanist with a complete classical education. Nevertheless, Della Casa's refined culture, extensive learning, and consummate experience in the world of high society are built into the structure and meaning of the text. (D3, 22–23)

These two considerations flow from the dual premise that the narrator figure is identical with the idiota and that the idiota's views and values are those of *Galateo*. On this reading, the exclusive/inclusive opposition is narrowed to one between learned vs. unlearned or humanist book-learning vs. quotidian experience, and the text fully endorses the idiota's program of inclusivity. The choice of a speaker "who relies on his own experience rather than on books" (22) suggests to the Dovehouse editors that the text proposes opening the ranks of the elite to anyone who can acquire and practice the manners and style the idiota recommends. This suggested proposal is innocuous so long as it concerns only the books-vs.-experience contrast. It becomes less innocuous when it concerns an interrelated pair of oppositions the editors tend to overlook: one between old and new aristocrats and the other between ethics and manners.

The Dovehouse interpretation depends on the dual premise: the idiota is the sole narrator constructed by the text, and he is reliable. The present interpretation challenges both the hypothesis that he is reliable and the hypothesis that he is the sole narrator. Although I have depicted him as unreliable, the scope of unreliability is unclear. It isn't clear, for example, whether he is or only pretends to be unlearned, since he seems at times self-deprecatingly to mock the pretense, making it conspicuous and a little silly. It isn't even clear who or what "he" designates in the preceding sentence, which describes the idiota as if he were an independent agent and performer. The description reductively falsifies the effects produced by a complex and contradictory discourse that (as I just noted) transcends its putative source in the site of enunciation marked out as "idiota." To treat this site as a consistent "point of view" is to commit the fallacy of simple location.[35] Perhaps it isn't less fallacious to resort to the heuristic device of a compound speaker, one in which the idiota exists only as a persona performed by another narrator, and not merely performed but parodied. This performer would still be a site of agency and motivation, a personification of the discourse we attribute to the site, an exemplary someone, a "he," and we would still have to decide about "his" status and reliability.[36] But let's bracket the problems such a construction raises until we try experimentally to characterize our performer.

Someone, then, "speaks" the idiota in a manner that makes fun of his pretensions to learnedness, as in the occasional sesquipedalian flourish and the coy moments of conspicuous faux naiveté discussed above. Someone also caricatures the ingenuous stance of a speaker who looks up in admiration at a scene of high society he has long observed, closely studied, and never been part of, who shows himself impressed by a behavioral code advantageous to upstarts and other social intriguers, and who instructs his tutee in the fine points of that code. With bitterness but with obvious rhetorical pleasure and wit, someone expansively parodies the absence of grace, the coarsening of sprezzatura, and the consequences of the desire to extend membership from the few to the many. The chief target of caricature is the effort to justify and extenuate a code the negative effects of which *Galateo's* discourse of manners keeps turning up and repeatedly exposes—a code that places manners before ethics and that produces a version of the apprehensive society dominated by the desire to take and the fear of being taken. The caricaturist enjoys his performance but pulls no punches: the code endorsed by the idiota is represented as a factious and fractious social practice guaranteed to arouse anxiety, defensiveness, surveillance, and hypocrisy, and to demand that the actor sacrifice self-esteem to expediency and subordinate ethical considerations to the main chance.

In short, someone impersonates an idiota who endorses a practice and a social ethic that would not be unfamiliar to Machiavelli's *principe nuovo*. The society he portrays is one in which each actor pursues strategies of covert force and theatrical deception analogous not only to those embedded in the superficially benign recommendations of Castiglione's interlocutors but also to those Machiavelli recommends in *The Prince*.[37] I'm reminded, in fact, of the figure Machiavelli uses in his dedication of *The Prince* to Lorenzo de' Medici when he refers to observers who "place themselves in a low position on the plain in order to study the nature of the mountains and highlands," and goes on to add a sentiment the savagery of which is only thinly veiled:

"in order to know well the nature of princes one must be a common citizen." In the *Cortegiano*, it is not the common citizen who is enjoined by Ottaviano to adopt "a low position" in order to study and influence that nature; it is the sprezzata courtier.

How should we characterize the someone who plays and bitterly parodies the idiota as a lowly outsider? My reading of *Galateo* has produced a narrator whose sympathies are less with an aristocracy predicated in terms of humanist book-learning than with the older aristocracy of noble birth and the privileges that flow from it. It is the resentment of an old aristocrat, a disaffected courtier, that vibrates through the caustic impersonation of the idiota. The impersonation dramatizes his antipathy toward a discourse aimed at alienating what was once rightfully the special property of nobles like himself and making it—in the words of the Dovehouse editors—"the common property of all men." He resents the idea that anyone can, by learning some behavioral skills, succeed in appropriating the power, authority, and status that rightfully belongs to those whose possession of the paradisal fortezza of grazia should entitle them to stockpile their privileges and safeguard their prerogatives.

The Dovehouse editors suggest that the idiota's emphasis on learning from experience rather than from books amounts to a critique of *Galateo*'s most important precursor, for it is an "implied reference to Castiglione's elegant and learned coterie" (D3, 22). But according to my hypothesis the critique of *Cortegiano* is focused neither on learning per se nor on elegance per se. Rather it is focused on the thesis, which I develop in Chapter 1 above, that in the *Cortegiano* the presence of sprezzatura is coupled with—and denotes—the absence of grazia. From this it follows that if indeed the narrator who performs the idiota expresses the values and fears of a believer in the power and virtue of grazia, his relation to the society depicted in the *Cortegiano*, his attitude toward it, should be legible: an old aristocrat, a member of or visitor at Urbino's court, a witness to its games and inventions, and, finally, a refugee from it because the virtù praised there is already nuovo rather than naturale, is sprezzatura rather than grazia. I suggested above that he bitterly impersonates the lowly outsider who looks up in admiration at Machiavellian princes, upstarts, and other social intriguers. The relation between Machiavelli's *principe nuovo* and his *principe naturale* or *ereditario* is parallel to that between the perfect or ideal courtier (master of sprezzatura) and the absolute courtier (inheritor of grazia) in the *Cortegiano*. The principe nuovo comes into play in the absence or failure of a principe naturale.[38]

This Machiavellian schema condenses and caricatures but doesn't misstate the implications of the sociopolitical problematic Burckhardt identified as the condition and the price of individualism: the general cultural failure I describe in Chapters 1 and 3 above as a failure of ascriptive norms of blood and lineage—norms developed under feudal and early mercantile conditions—to sustain their moral authority and sometimes their political efficacy. As I note in those discussions, in the face of redistributions of power exploited or endured by self-made princely regimes and mercantile oligarchies, ascriptive norms remain necessary but it is no longer sufficient merely to invoke them. They have to be enacted—supplemented by skills of self-representation that respond to the new legal, political, and ideological pressures on aristocratic status. An increasing emphasis on the need of all principi, whether nuovi or naturali, to take Machiavellian precautions and learn to *perform* status means that factitious "court genealogies" with their "masquerade of distinguished origins" more openly conceal "sheer political domination."[39] This is the need the *Cortegiano* thematizes and dramatizes, and the *Galateo* narrator uses the idiota's elaboration of the Galatean code to expose this truth about the *Cortegiano*, expose the competitive and anxiety-ridden practices it promotes under the silky elegance of the courtly ideal.

Of course, it's easy to object that this elaborate linkage of *Galateo* to *Cortegiano* is gratuitous because, although the two works have much in common, there isn't a single direct reference to the latter in the former.[40] At one moment, however, we encounter an odd lexical slip, a parapraxis, that may function as a pseudo-reference. In Chapter 13, during a diatribe against the lies people tell "for their own aggrandizement," the idiota singles out those who, "although they have no greater wealth than others," pretend that they do by overdressing: "they . . . have so many gold chains around their necks and rings on their fingers and so many broaches on their hats and here and there on their clothing that it would not befit the Seigneur of Castiglione himself" (D, 20–21).

This reference to "[il] sire di Castiglione" (*Op.*, 389) is the subject of an illuminating gloss by the Dovehouse editors, who remind us that the referent is not the author of the *Cortegiano* but a figure mentioned in Boccaccio's *Decameron* 6.10, "the rich and powerful Seigneur de Châtillon-sur-Marne." They suggest that since the name of the original Châtillon is "italianized by Boccaccio as Ciastiglione," it is the "similarity of title [that] . . . causes our uneducated narrator to confuse the original Châtillon . . . with the contemporary writer and the town of Castiglione" (D3, 51n). The idiota makes a tiny spelling error, dropping the first *i* and hardening the initial consonant. But is the sole purpose—or, at least, the sole effect—of this mistake to characterize him by adding another gaffe to the series that keeps readers aware he is idiota? A glance at the context of the mistake will shift our attention to a more broadly intertextual effect produced by the fact that this is the text's one and only mention of the author of *Galateo*'s most important precursor and its major target of allusion.

Boccaccio's anecdote concerns Brother Cipolla's hoggish servant, Guccio Imbratta (i.e, the Slob). In order to impress Nuta, an innkeeper's maid, Guccio "gives himself the airs of a very rich foreigner by claiming to be the 'Siri di Ciastiglione' "—this is the Dovehouse paraphrase (D3, 51n), and it is misleading because the *Decameron*'s Guccio doesn't "claim" to be Ciastiglione. It is the storyteller, Dioneo, who mockingly compares him to that great lord: Guccio, he says, "speaks as if he were" Ciastiglione when he promises to buy Nuta "new clothes and take her away from all this drudgery and . . . give her the hope for a better life"—all of which "amounted to nothing but hot air."[41] The comic force of Dioneo's analogy comes from the imagined contrast between Guccio's fine words and his gross appearance. But this contrast is conspicuously irrelevant to the "lie" the idiota uses the Boccaccio allusion to illustrate—the mendacious practice of sartorial overkill. Therefore a reader well enough informed to recall this moment in *Decameron* 6.10 may find the applicability of the contrast to its context in *Galateo* questionable, for an allusion to Guccio the Slob is conspicuously irrelevant to the idiota's point about overdressing.

Such a reader might then wonder whether the signifier "Castiglione" doesn't glance more directly at the *Cortegiano* than at the *Decameron*. If this is a mistake, it is a classic instance, even a parody, of a meaningful parapraxis. For "Castiglione" pops up in *Galateo* precisely during a listing of examples of the *Cortegiano*'s cardinal sin, *affettazione*, the sin against the principle of efficacious hypocrisy Castiglione's courtiers legitimize as sprezzatura. The narrator has the idiota name "Castiglione" while explaining what the aspirant to good manners should avoid in order successfully to model his appearances on the behavioral norm enshrined in the *Cortegiano*. So complex and sophisticated a set of moves borne so lightly on the wings of a casual mention is itself a display of sprezzatura, and one that the sprezzata courtier would appreciate and be flattered by. Any narrator capable of this display flags his knowledge and mastery of courtly practices. But not necessarily his approval of them.

I began my reflections on the narrator by suggesting that *Galateo* encourages its readers not to "look *through*" the narratorial site of enunciation as if it were a transparent and fully reliable mediator of the "author's" meaning, but to "look *at*" the narrator and view his performance with enough suspicion to question his motives and values. This is the weaker and more innocuous form of my proposal. Its stronger and more dubious form stakes a claim that *Galateo* is primarily *about* that performance. My doubts center on the complexity of a proposal that requires a compound narrator, and possibly—to make it more bizarre—a compound unreliable narrator. Nevertheless, I can live with these doubts so long as the proposal allows readers to fix their attention on what I referred to above as a double-edged discourse in which the Galatean code is simultaneously promoted by the idiota persona and pilloried by his impersonator. Is the impersonator represented as unreliable? This is not the same as asking whether the representation is unsympathetic. I find myself caught up by the energy, the astringency, the savage exuberance, the high-spirited irony with which the critical edge of his discourse slices through its three-headed target: the idiota, the Galatean code, and the *Cortegiano*. I admire the impersonator's subtle analysis of the contradictions that beset the code, the bad faith that structures it, the ethical dilemmas that embarrass it. I would have no trouble identifying that analysis with the message of the text or positing full convergence between the author's and the impersonator's views of the target.

At the same time, however, I can't ignore the strong impression of special pleading that saturates the impersonator's performance, the critical edge of whose discourse is sharpened by the *ressentiment* born of privilege lost and power expropriated. His is the argument from grazia, the argument against sprezzatura, the argument—as I shall now call it—of *the old aristocrat*. The misanthropy he represents as a consequence of the Galatean code leaks into the representing medium of his own discourse. This makes him simultaneously more interesting and less sympathetic as an object of interpretive concern. The *ressentiment* is often vented on the object of his savage ventriloquation, and it comes to a head near the end of the treatise (chap. 29), in the single passage devoted to a sustained critique of "gli uomini letterati" who "praise some man by the name of Socrates" for his ability to hold his liquor.

The idiota ridicules these pundits because they misuse the *Symposium* episode to justify the moral benefits of bibulous intemperance, though he doesn't seem to notice that in their report they wrongly interpolate into the episode the geometry lesson that occurs in the *Meno*. He concludes that "through their grandiose talk" they "very often manage to have the wrong side win and reason lose." Their praise of drinking, he asserts, was motivated by a desire "to excuse and cover over the sin of their city [loro terra] corrupted by this vice. For it could have appeared dangerous to reprimand their fellows and perhaps they feared that they should suffer the same fate as Socrates," who, because he "used to go about pointing out everybody's faults . . . was accused out of envy of many heresies and . . . was condemned to death, even though the charges were false and he was in fact, according to their false idolatries, a good man and a Catholic" (D, 59; *Op.*, 437).

This meandering, inaccurate, and anachronistic outburst is obviously constructed to ventriloquate not merely the idiota's illiteracy but also his desire to extricate himself from the contradictions of an argument that produces misanthropy as the by-product of flattery. The passage, that is, targets his desire to assimilate his faultfinding to that of the courageous Athenian truth-sayer (*parrhesiastes* in Greek) and to dissociate himself from the learned flatterers who justify the corrupt beliefs and habits—and manners—of those in power. Of course the thrust of the old aristocrat's ventriloquation is to expose the futility of that desire by representing the idiota as a flatterer: one who promotes a code of manners in which ethics and Socratic *parrhesia* are subordinated to the practice of pleasing one's betters and overgoing one's peers; one who, like the "uomini letterati" or "scienzati" he criticizes, periodically tries to excuse and obscure the naked expediency of the code. The old aristocrat thus shows how the idiota, in finding fault with learned flatterers, finds fault with himself and his own practice, how his exposition of the code betrays its basis in misanthropic distrust of human nature, and how he enacts the paranoia the system breeds and is bred from.

This passage is one of those that most clearly distinguish the satirist, the old aristocrat, from the object of his satire, the idiota. And yet even during so mordant a portrayal of the idiota's attempt to assimilate himself to Socrates and play the truth-saying outsider, doesn't the narrator reflect his own stance as a truth-saying outsider?—as a traditional aristocrat displaced by the emergent culture of sprezzatura he satirizes in the idiota's manual for social climbers? Does the text of *Galateo* invite us to look at rather than through this narrator, to view his motivation with critical detachment, to "see around" him and search out the textual indications that separate him from full reliability? Or does his bitterness leak into the text? I don't feel confident enough to hazard a clear judgment on this issue. That is, I'm not prepared to decide whether I am withholding sympathy only from the old aristocrat's discourse at the prompting of the text I ascribe to della Casa or whether the leakage also permeates the latter. Is the present essay engaged in a critique of *Galateo* or an analysis of *Galateo*'s critique of the double-edged discourse of impersonation? And if this discourse is indeed a two-edged sword, does one edge accidentally strike the text that wields it?

It is at any rate in the terms of such a double-edged discourse that the final section of *Galateo*, beginning with Chapter 25, assumes its critical importance. For the idiota is shown attempting to revise the basic model of behavioral relations he has depicted in the preceding chapters. In the basic model good manners conspire with the senses against reason and virtue in an alliance that favors temporizers and trimmers over honorable men. He tries to revise that model in Chapter 25, as we saw above, by realigning "maestro costume" with "la ragione" and against the senses. But the effort of realignment is represented as a struggle, one that continues in the succeeding chapters, and one that I want to review for two reasons: first, because the passage shows how the old aristocrat severely tests—and dramatizes—the resources of the idiota's bad faith; second, because even while doing so it often obscures the clear distinction between the motives of the aristocratic satirist and his idiota object.

Near the end of Chapter 25, when our Chiarissimo manqué repeats his offer to serve as a counter-example, he does so in analogies drawn from sense perception: "just as in seeing darkness one learns what light is, and in hearing silence one learns what sound is, so also, in looking at my not very pleasing [poco aggradevoli] and, so to speak, dark [oscure] manners, you will be able to catch a glimpse of what the light of pleasant and praiseworthy manners may be" (D, 51, altered; *Op.*, 428). The idiota then ignores the distinction he has just made between the basic and revised models; he closes the chapter with a summary formulation that reinstates the basic model: "Returning to the discussion of these manners, which will shortly come to an end, let us say that pleasant manners are those that give delight or at least do not give offense to any of the senses, or to the desire or the imagination of those with whom we are dealing [coloro co' quali noi usiamo]. It is about these things that we have talked till now" (D, 51, altered; *Op.*, 428).[42]

Till now, however, most of those with whom we have been dealing were flatterers and trend-setters. But as if catching himself in a momentary backslide the idiota begins the next chapter with an adversative that brings the revised model to the fore. He redefines the object of desire in intellectual terms: "But you must also realize that men [uomini] are very desirous of beauty and measure and proportion [bellezza ... misura ... convenevolezza], and, conversely, they abhor ugly, monstrous, and misshapen things."[43] The next statement indicates that "uomini" is generic rather than gender-specific because it picks up the uomini/animali contrast introduced in Chapter 25: "this is our special privilege, for the other animals don't know how to recognize any degree of beauty or proportion" (D, 51, altered). Here the idiota's discourse borrows wings and soars aloft bearing the justification of good manners into the sphere of purely intelligible and aesthetic value. He turns to mainstream—classical and humanist—ideas of Beauty, recalling a piece of philosophy he has learned from one of his many "erudite and knowledgeable" ("dotto e scienziato") sources: beauty wishes to be One ("to be as unified as it can") and ugliness is Many (*Op.*, 429).

This is fine talk, but it doesn't last. Another classical memory sends our Icarian idiota tumbling headlong back into the realm of the watery senses. He illustrates the One and the Many with a meditation on prettiness and homeliness in girls obviously inspired by the story of Zeuxis: each of the different "membri" of an ugly woman, he muses, may be beautiful by itself "but put together they are displeasing and dirty [spiacevole e sozzi]" because they belong to "more beautiful women and not to this one, so that it seems she borrowed them from this or that [more beautiful] other." At this point Zeuxis himself barges in: "And perhaps that painter who had the Calabrian girls set nude before him did nothing more than recognize in many the body parts [membri] they had, so to speak, borrowed—some one and some another—from a single [beautiful woman], whom, after he had made everyone give her back her part, he started to paint, imagining that such, and so harmonious, should be the beauty of Venus."[44] The narrator is starting up a small gallery of ideal forms: Chiarissimo's statue, Zeuxis's painting, and perhaps, lurking in the background, Pygmalion's ivory beloved. What all three have in common is the desire to construct, exhibit, and possess a rigorously controlled fantasy of idealization that puts nature to shame. And the linkage also suggests that the resulting misophysis (contempt or disdain of nature) is tightly intertwined with misanthropy and misogyny.

The significance of the Zeuxis anecdote is the light it throws on a casual or instrumental use of misogyny coupled with misophysis, a use made all the more glaring by the inattentiveness of the user, who is preoccupied with grander affairs of the Art and Standards of Beauty. In this connection, the genealogical fortunes of the Zeuxis story are interesting. As it moves from Pliny (or Cicero) through Alberti to *Galateo*, the misogyny gets more aggressive. In Pliny's and Cicero's versions, Zeuxis modeled his statue (of Helen, not Venus) on the best body parts of five virgins because he didn't "believe that it was possible to find in one body all the things he looked for in beauty, since nature has not refined to perfection any single object in all its parts."[45] Alberti gives the story a sharper rhetorical edge in his treatise on painting (1435–36). Arguing that although it is necessary to imitate nature, it isn't sufficient because nature is defective with respect to the criteria of beauty, he urges painters not only to follow but also to surpass nature as Zeuxis did by taking, or robbing, or seizing ("pilliare," "torre") "from every beautiful body . . . whatever beauty is praised" so as to combine into one figure these choice body parts that in nature are always "dispersed in many bodies."[46] Thus "to take from nature" involves not only careful study and observation, not only the mimetic skill of reproduction, but also the discriminative rapacity expressed as the desire to rob or pillage or despoil nature of her best parts (and, by implication, to discard the remainder). The Zeuxian fantasy of idealization mediated through Alberti's rhetoric becomes a fantasy of amputation and proto-cyborgian reconstruction.[47]

The passage in *Galateo* adds still another misogynist twist by shifting the blame for ugliness from nature's ineptitude to the covetousness and tastelessness of the women who stripped a beautiful body of its parts and were forced by Zeuxis to restore them. Having fallen so precipitously from the sphere of intelligible beauty, the idiota seems unable to level off. Although he transfers the anecdote's message about the beautiful and the ugly from bodily appearances to manners, he can't stop complaining about the follies of the weaker sex. In the chapter's concluding example, his eyes, his ears, his imagination remain thoroughly engrossed by woman's behavioral blemishes:

> Nor do I wish you to think that this happens only with faces and limbs or bodies, on the contrary it happens just as much with words and actions. If you saw a well-dressed noblewoman washing her dirty dishes in the gutter at the roadside, *her failure to show self-consistency would displease you* even if you did not otherwise care for her. Her appearance would be that of an elegant noble lady, but her behavior would be that of a low serving woman. Even if there were no harsh odor or taste from her, or any irritating sound or color, or anything else about her that should trouble your senses, you would still be displeased by that inelegant and unseemly manner and discordant act [diviso atto]. (D, 52, seriously altered; my italics)[48]

"You would be displeased by her indecorous behavior even if she did not offend your senses"—a sneaky disjunction; it has the force of a conjunction because the misogynous reference to sensory disgust leaks into and intensifies the criticism of behavioral dissonance. An indecorous woman can disgust the mind as well as the senses. "That inelegant and unseemly manner" may indeed be more offensive because it oozes forth not merely from her face, limbs, or body but from her words and deeds ("nel favellare e nell'operare"). The misogynist faultfinding continues when the disunity previously blamed on ugly women is recalled in the chapter's penultimate word, "diviso," and transferred to the noblewoman's disorderly "atto."

The effect of leakage lingers on in the next sentence, the first in Chapter 27, and is confirmed by the repetition of the word "unseemly" ("sconvenevoli"). For, without breaking his stride, the idiota turns to warn his male tutee against such lapses of decorum and redirects his misogynously toned admonition to the general forms of misbehavior that up to now have been almost exclusively attributed to males: "It therefore behooves you [Convienti adunque] to guard against this disordered and unseemly behavior as carefully as—no, more carefully than—against those things of which I have spoken so far; for it is harder to know when one errs in these matters than in those, inasmuch as perceiving is seen to be easier than understanding" (*Op.*, 430). Presumably the reason the "disordinate e sconvenevoli maniere" exemplified by the noblewoman are harder to avoid is that, since they involve words and actions rather than mere physical appearances, they presuppose some mastery of the intelligible principle of decorum.

Once again the idiota tries to rise above the region of bodies and senses that he associated in the preceding two chapters with unruly feminized nature. But as he continues explaining the difference between rational and sensory criteria, the burden imposed on him by his attention to intelligible decorum challenges his sense of narrative decorum:

> Nevertheless, it can often happen that whatever displeases the senses
> displeases the intellect as well, but not for the same reasons, as I explained
> earlier when I said that a man should dress according to the custom of
> others so as not to show that he is reprimanding them or correcting them,
> for this frustrates the desire [noia allo appetito] of the majority of people,
> who like to be praised. But this is also offensive to the judgment of dis-
> cerning men, for the clothes of another age do not go well with a man [la
> persona] of our times. (D, 53, altered)

Here "whatever displeases the senses" ("che spiace a' sensi") turns out to be an evasively imprecise *pars pro toto* reference to the displeasure of the majority, dominated by their insecurity and suspicion—their fear of being insulted—and by their vanity. The introduction of the intelligible principle al-

lows the idiota to have it both ways. He can now look down on this majority—a majority effectively created and empowered by the Galatean code—
and contrast their appetitive caviling to the more disinterested judgment of
an elite who are motivated by the principle of decorum rather than by vanity; but he nevertheless reminds us that the "uomini intendenti" (*Op.*, 430)
endorse the majority view. The Galatean code, with all its flaws and dangers,
is supported, validated, by an appeal to a higher standard that could not have
been made earlier in the treatise.[49] The question posed by this move is
whether it is presented as a stronger argument or as another example of the
idiota's bad faith.

But presented by whom? To pose the question is once again to inquire
into the double-voiced structure of the site of enunciation—into the relation between the impersonator and the persona, the old aristocrat and the
old idiota. And I'm reluctantly forced to acknowledge that in these closing
chapters of *Galateo* I often find it difficult to dissociate the persona from the
impersonator. This is especially true where attitudes toward gender are concerned, and in the comments that follow I flag such moments by referring
simply to "the narrator." But what about the passages in which the idiota,
however apologetically, puts classical and humanist topoi into play and seems
(as I phrased it above) to be starting up a small gallery of ideal forms? Is this
to be interpreted merely as a tactic by which the literate satirist exposes the
pretentious pseudo-intellectualism thinly veiled behind the idiota's faux
naiveté? And what about the revisionary move, situated almost immediately
after the passage quoted above, in which the narrator changes course and
pauses to reconsider his analysis? He confesses that many and perhaps all of
the bad manners discussed in the preceding chapters were bad because they
violated the intelligible principle of unity and decorum he is now discussing
but has refrained from introducing until Chapter 26. They reveal their performers' failure to keep measure or to bring into accord "the time and the
place and the deed and the person, as they should have done." "The mind of
men," he continues, approves of and delights in this principle. "La mente
degli uomini": note that he doesn't say "the mind of man" or "the minds of
men"; he designates a generic mind, and the context of idealism and misogyny in which the principle of decorum was introduced suggests that "gli
uomini" in question are once again—or still—males. As we'll see in a moment, the suggestion is forcefully confirmed at the end of the chapter, after
he makes his next, and perhaps his most peculiar, move: he apologizes for
not having brought the principle into play until so late in the game.

The reason for this delay, he explains, is that he wished to organize ("accozzare e divisare") his earlier discussions of bad manners under the "insegna" of the senses and desire—rather than assign them to the intellect—so that "everyone might recognize them more easily. Everyone experiences feelings and desires quite easily, but in general not everyone can do the same with understanding, especially [the understanding of] what we call beauty and charm or attractiveness [bellezza e leggiadria o avvenentezza]" (D, 53, altered; *Op.*, 431).[50] This is less an apology than an aggressively condescending put-down of his potential readers, and also of the majority of arrivistes and trend-setters, who march or fight under the same banner in their efforts to reach or stay at the top. Is this, then, the elitism of the idiota or of his aristocratic impersonator? And what about the elitism of the sentiment that this majority has trouble achieving understanding, especially when they confront manifestations of the august principle of measure, harmony, proportion, unity, and so on, manifestations that may themselves be too abstract for those who spend their lives pursuing more worldly goals? Isn't this a sentiment that sets off the snobbery of an old aristocrat from the idiota's more worldly orientation?

There is, however, another kind of elitism that unites the noble impersonator with the persona he satirically ventriloquates: gender elitism. It surfaces when we recognize that "bellezza e leggiadria o avvenentezza" together connote the specifically female and Venerean ("av*venen*tezza") beauty previously introduced in the reference to Zeuxis. The terms that suggest a trio of Graces both echo and displace the trio mentioned at the beginning of Chapter 26, "bellezza e . . . misura e . . . convenevolezza." Even the august principle of beauty-as-proportion, the paradigm of good manners, can be subversively infiltrated, hollowed out, by the ghostly lineaments of Venerean desire and fantasy. Not every—that is, hardly any—man can stay focused when the goal, the good, of higher understanding is itself invested in the seductive attributes of female beauty, which bring the senses and the desires back into play. Thus in spite of the idiota's effort to transcend the senses by bracing up the code of manners with intelligible criteria, he repeats the movement of Chapter 26 when, as we recall, he plummeted down from those criteria to beauty and ugliness in women. Are these *lapsus* to be attributed to the satiric pressure exerted on the idiota by the old aristocrat who impersonates him or is theirs a mutual fall?

Whatever we decide about narratorial responsibility, one thing is clear: such repeated lapses convey the message that whether she is figured as a negative or positive model, as a scapegoat or an ideal,[51] woman is man's curse. But as the Zeuxis story suggests, the woman who is man's curse is the woman man rescues Pygmalion-like from her "natural" state: the woman inside man; the woman inside male discourse. "She" infiltrates with her allure the behavioral ideal constructed by male desire, and "she" represents its danger: when the principle of male decorum is rhetorically shadowed under the image of ideal female beauty, the danger of being overcome by the desire to embrace the ideal and make it one's own is the danger of becoming effeminized. To be seduced by the desire to make oneself seductive to the men whose favor one curries or whose power one fears is to risk both ethical and political disempowerment. This is a danger analogous to the one that, as we saw, confronted the courtly elite in the *Cortegiano*, the anxiety of disempowerment associated with the political dilemmas of courtiership in a Machiavellian world dominated by principi nuovi, an anxiety reflected in the portrayal of the courtier who, perfected and protected only by sprezzatura, is a figure—in Constance Jordan's words—"without authority of his own and effectively powerless."[52] Of this danger and anxiety no one would be more bitterly cognizant than a believer in the aristocracy of grazia.

The narrator doesn't have very much to say about actual women, good or bad, and this is itself a function of cultural misogyny. After Chapter 25 (in addition to the passages discussed above) there is a cluster of warnings—all in Chapter 28—against behaviors unbecoming to un uomo "gentile" or "nobile." Here solecisms of gender are conflated with those of class: a gentleman shouldn't coif, perfume, dress, or comport himself like a woman—or like a beggar or a bravo or a groom. Before Chapter 25 there is only one clearly marked reference to the danger of effeminacy, but it has considerable resonance. It occurs in Chapter 10—I cite it above—where it is set up in the opening clause and driven home, after several examples, in the conclusion: "It is . . . not appropriate, especially for men, to be overly sensitive and fastidious. . . . Such sensitivity and such fastidiousness are best left to women" (D, 16–17). Although this touchiness is described as morbid and something to be avoided, it is precisely the form taken by the paranoia that the idiota's code of manners, with its emphasis on continuous surveillance and scrutiny, encourages.

My claim, then, is that in Chapters 25–28 woman expressly assumes the function of a signifier in the semiotics of male self-subversion. It's important to distinguish this from the more strident misogynous assertion that *because* of woman's allure, the senses and desires overwhelm "la mente degli uomini." The claim is rather that in these chapters woman as a male signifier intervenes in the discursive interaction between a behavioral code and a gender code. The behavioral code privileges the criteria of sense and desire over those of ethical judgment, and it privileges manners over virtue—where "manners" includes the artful performance of sprezzatura and "virtue" may include not only ethical judgment but also the virtù, the preeminent power and authority, that rightfully flows from the possession of grazia. The gender code is put into play either to dramatize bad habits manly men should avoid or else to show how even the intelligible criterion of beautiful behavior may be contaminated by the promptings of sense and desire, and thus distorted into a Venerean fantasy that registers a key danger of the behavioral code: it is reducible to an effeminizing, perhaps homoerotic, art and desire of social seduction—or of prostitution.

The narrator holds men's vulnerability to such lures and criteria responsible for his conduct of the argument. It is only out of respect for these shortcomings, he insists, that throughout this book he has discussed good and bad customs under the heading of senses and desire, pleasure and delight, rather than under the heading of the intellect. Here, once again, the question of narratorial responsibility arises. And this time I think we can state with confidence that the argument I just outlined reflects a deeply critical view of the idiota's project and its effeminizing effect. The fundamental bad faith of the project surfaces in Chapter 28, where the idiota begins by repeating the move he made in Chapter 27. That is, he transfers qualities associated with graceful female behavior to the general principle of decorum that governs the behavior of men:

> Therefore a man must not be content with doing what is good, but he must also seek to do it gracefully [leggiadre]. Grace [leggiadria] is nothing else but something akin to a light that shines from the appropriateness [convenevolezza] of things that are suitably ordered and arranged one with the other, and in relation to the whole. Without this measure, even that which is good will not be beautiful, and beauty will not be pleasing. (D, 53)

This has the conventional Neoplatonico-humanist ring. But the idiota immediately transforms it into another bad-faith assertion of the principle of expediency that governs the code of manners: it is less important that men be good than that they make themselves seductive to others, male or female, young or old. Since, as he suggested at the end of Chapter 27, intelligible desire of the good easily yields to sensory desire of the beautiful, men should more energetically cultivate the latter than the former.

What is offensive about vices, he continues, is that they are ugly and improper. "Therefore it is most advisable for those who aspire to be well liked in dealing with other people to flee vices, especially those that are foul [sozzi] such as lust, avarice, cruelty, and the like," along with those that are despicable ("vili"), filthy, and evil ("scellerati") (D, 54, altered; *Op.*, 431). The justifying climax of this argument occurs in a passage I have already cited, one in which—as I noted—the principle that manners should supersede ethics is evasively voiced as a purely procedural decision. Significantly, it is in this passage that we revisit Count Ricciardo and, by association, Messer Galateo:

> Since I undertook to show you men's errors and not their sins, my present care must be to deal not with the nature of vice and virtue, but only with the proper and improper manners we use toward each other. One of these improper manners was the one used by Count Ricciardo, of whom I told you above. It was so different from and discordant with his other beautiful and fitting manners that the worthy [valoroso] bishop immediately noticed it, as a good and well-trained singer notices wrong notes. (D, 54)[53]

"Our concern is not with the good but with the beautiful," not with ethical judgments but with the formal or aesthetic discriminations of the behavioral technician. Vices are to be avoided not because they are evil but because they "render a man unpleasant in the company of others."

These sentiments carry a disturbing resonance, in part because they evoke and pervert a traditional understanding of the relation between the good and the beautiful. Here, for example, is the Neoplatonic formula articulated by Ficino in the preceding century:

> There is both an interior and an exterior perfection: the interior we call goodness, and the exterior, beauty. . . . Virtue of the soul . . . manifests itself in a most noble kind of beauty in words, actions, and deeds. . . . In all these cases, it is an internal perfection that produces the external. . . . For just this reason, we say that beauty is the blossom, so to speak, of goodness. By the allurement of this blossom, as though by a kind of bait, the latent interior goodness attracts all who see it.

> *Est autem perfectio interior quaedam, est et exterior. Interiorem, bonitatem; exteriorem, pulchritudinem dicimus. . . . Virtus . . . animi decorem quendam prae se ferre videtur in verbis, gestibus, operibus honestissimum. . . . In his omnibus interna perfectio producit externam. . . . Quocirca bonitatis florem quendam esse pulchritudinem volumus, cuius floris illecebris, quasi esca, quadam, latens interius bonitas allicit intuentes.*[54]

Ficino translates—but doesn't fully sublimate—terms and symbols of heterosexual desire ("flora," "esca," "illecebris," "allicit") into the higher seductiveness of the good that manifests itself ("gives itself to be seen"—"prae se
ferre videtur") in the beautiful behavior of male coequals. *Galateo* retains the
seductiveness of the beautiful but hollows out the core of "bonitas."

To link this perverse sentiment so sneakily but recognizably to the episode from which *Galateo* takes its name, the episode in which its version of
the cortegiano perfetto makes his only appearance, is a devastating move. It
concentrates the whole force of the old aristocrat's ethical and social critique on the idiota and the Galatean code. And this effect is driven home
immediately after the reference to Ricciardo with another admonition
against a man's embellishing himself as a woman, since "his adornments will
then contradict his person," as is the case with men who curl their hair and
beards and cake themselves with an amount of makeup that "would be un-
suitable for any young wench, even for a harlot who is more anxious to
hawk her wares and sell them for a price" (D, 54). This proscription may be
seen as a caricature that produces the lightning-rod effect, safely shunting off
the fantasy of effeminization from the Galatean ideal to which it has been
affixed. But it may also have the contrary effect, serving as reductive comment on the basic orientation of the Galatean code of conduct.

Coda

In my chapters on *Cortegiano* I argue that the discussion of sprezzatura opens
onto a culture of surveillance, that it conveys a general sense of apprehensiveness in its performers, and that it ascribes this sense to two different but
interrelated specters of castration, one of which I associate with the day of
the Prefect and the other with the night of the Duchess, the first hovering
in the political background and the other in the performative foreground of
courtly interactions. Readers are never allowed to ignore the manifest practical consequence of the courtier's pursuing a career in the service and under the surveillance of a prince: the weakness of his position. This weakness,
the signs of which glimmer through the palisade of discussion, is shown to
infiltrate—and, indeed, to motivate—the panache of aggressively polite re-
partee. Nor are readers allowed to ignore the latent ethical consequence suffered by those who master the technology of sprezzatura and submit to its
normative demand: the very discipline by which the performer learns to
embody and display an exemplary inwardness forces him to discover or create within himself an "original" private self as a kind of rejected remainder

or residue of the process. Rooted in the myth of the absence of grace, the normative demand for exemplary inwardness activates a regime of self-surveillance that brings this less exemplary inwardness into being and sustains it as the target of repression or suppression.

Sprezzatura is obviously meant to be more than an art of behaving as if one were always under surveillance. But by its very nature it can arouse suspicion no less than admiration, the suspicion that in fact motivates increased surveillance and justifies the performer's caution. The misanthropic undertones that are subordinated in *The Book of the Courtier* to its portrayal of misogyny are more explicitly brought out in *Galateo*, which performs an ironic critique of the culture of courtesy books, representing it as a paranoid system of pornographic surveillance and containment. This demystification goes on at two levels.

On the first, the idiota represents the unruly body and its effluvia as the source of trouble and target of repression. Good manners are founded on—and help intensify—fear and loathing of the body. The idiota depicts a world in which everyone—including himself—has a dirty mind and assumes everyone else has a dirty mind. He dwells on and rhetorically embroiders the examples of disgusting behavior he so indignantly denounces. In his allusions to what goes on beneath clothing, the potentially incontinent body becomes a figure that condenses and displaces orthopsychic anxiety about *homo clausus*, the unrepresented (suppressed or repressed) because unideal self constructed in the backwash of new models of exemplarity. Fear of the body's unruliness and irruptiveness is fear of the hidden self and its intentions. This fear is thus linked to the second level of demystification. Here the focus shifts from disgust to distrust. *Galateo*'s opening argument is that charm and good manners resemble and can therefore replace virtue; if you have the former, you can fake the latter or get by without it. So if you could persuade everyone (or everyone who counts) to act on this principle, and master the requisite techniques of self-representation, you would produce a behavioral utopia, a virtual reality of beautiful people all of whom know themselves to be, and suspect others of being, hypocrites.

In the narratorial perspective I have assigned to the old aristocrat, then, the consequence of the program in which sprezzatura replaces grazia is that the successful courtier makes other people's desires his desires as he evacuates—or represses or disowns—and devalues whatever desires don't conform. Destroying what he perceives as the natural in order to reconstruct and resurrect it on the model of the idea, he aspires to enstatue himself in the hopes that the hard classical shell of his courtly second nature will both protect and conceal him from the world—and from himself. *Galateo* takes the logic of sprezzatura to its misanthropic and perhaps paranoid conclusion: "suspicion of misconduct is just as disturbing . . . as the certainty of it" (D, 10). Given this suspicion, it doesn't help to insist, as the idiota does, on transparency of language and behavior, or on the properly restricted denotation of verbal and behavioral signs, as he does in Chapters 21 and 22.[55] His insistence only betrays the fascinated awareness of one who listens for the rustle of the unruly connotations, the dubious motives, that must be proliferating like a jungle behind the urbanity of good manners.

REFERENCE MATTER

Notes

Preface

1. Linton, *The Study of Man*, 115. For a more qualified and detailed account of ascription, see my "From Body to Cosmos."

2. Ibid. As we'll see in Chapter 1, the use of "grazia" by the author and his interlocutors is actually more complex, varying between ascriptive and performative orientations, but the basic opposition between grazia in its ascriptive sense and sprezzatura as its performative simulation is established in 1.24, when the latter term is introduced.

Introduction

1. Berger, *Fictions of the Pose*.

2. Maus, *Inwardness and Theater*.

3. Independently of Maus, Claire McEachern makes the same point about literary and discursive representations in the English Reformation in *Poetics of English Nationhood*. Both show how the representation of inwardness makes it an object of suspicion in the English Renaissance.

4. See Berger, *Making Trifles of Terrors*, 297–301 and passim; *Imaginary Audition*; and "Prince's Dog."

Chapter 1. Sprezzatura and the Absence of Grace

1. Castiglione, *Libro del cortegiano*, 81 (abbreviated as C followed by page number in future references); *Book of the Courtier*, trans. Singleton, 43 (abbreviated as S followed by page number in future references). Frequently when citing passages or phrases in which the particular context or translation is not at issue, I give only book and chapter numbers (in this case, 1.26). At times, where it seems helpful, these may be accompanied by references to C or S.

2. Rebhorn, *Courtly Performances*, 38. See C, 83–84; S, 46–47.

3. Whigham, *Ambition and Privilege*, 99.

4. Saccone, *"Grazia, Sprezzatura, Affettazione,"* 59–64; Javitch, *"Cortegiano* and the Constraints of Despotism," 24–25.

5. Different facets of sprezzatura are nicely turned and ambiguated by George Puttenham in discussions that fuse social with rhetorical tropes, court-liness with allegory: (1) *"allegoria,* which . . . not impertinently we call the Courtier or figure of faire semblant," and (2) "the courtly figure Allegoria, which is when we speake one thing and thinke another," and "which for his duplicitie we call the figure of [*false semblant* or dissimulation]": Puttenham, *Arte of English Poesie,* 299, 186.

6. See the wonderfully apt allusion in 2.19–20 to the passage of Scripture (Luke 14:8–11) in which Christ explains to the wedding guest the advantages of strategic self-abasement: those who sneakily try to exalt themselves risk being humbled, but those who make a big show of humbling themselves stand a good chance of getting their host to raise them to a higher place. The inter-change at this point between Federico and Cesare dramatizes a wry version of the moral, one that brings out the competitive motive that drives even Chris-tian sprezzatura. Federico lets Cesare identify the allusion and accuse him of theft, and then confesses in effect that he committed a terrible crime but didn't think Cesare was up to catching him out: "It would be too great a sacrilege to steal from the Gospel; but you are more learned in Holy Writ than I thought" (S, 114).

7. Whigham, *Ambition and Privilege,* 116.

8. Rebhorn, *Courtly Performances,* 38. Though I find Whigham's articulation and elaboration of social tropes enormously helpful, I choose here to depart from his scheme, in which sprezzatura is merely one in a set of eight "tropes of personal promotion" all on the same level. My narrower focus on Castiglione leads me to treat sprezzatura as a master trope of which deceit and cosmesis are variant inflections responding to different motives and pressures.

9. See the excellent discussion of this and other features in the *Cortegiano* by Jonas Barish in *Antitheatrical Prejudice,* 167–83.

10. Why must it be stolen? Is it because the notion of explicit pedagogical transactions between teacher and student contradicts the basic premise of sprezzatura? Robert Hanning associates this advice with the model of Zeuxis and Alberti's use of it to emphasize "the painter's duty to create an idealized yet mimetic art by imitating only the most nearly perfect models. . . . The courtier is both Zeuxis and Zeuxis's portrait, forming one ideal from many fine parts": "Castiglione's Verbal Portrait," 134–35. Yet behind the blandness of the Zeuxis anecdote is a fantasy of imaginary dismemberment. This aspect of the Zeuxis anecdote is discussed further in Chapter 7.

11. Saccone, *"Grazia, Sprezzatura, Affettazione,"* 59–64.

12. Ibid., 49.

13. Ibid., 52.

14. To translate "aggraziati" as "acquiring grace" is to make Gonzaga's request more arch and perhaps aggressive than it actually is, and to miss the slight but interesting fluctuation in his request. The passive construction "esser aggraziati" places the emphasis on reception (as of a gift) rather than acquisition, and the crescive implication of "ag-graziati" also works to soften the acquisitive force. Sandwiched between two instances of "acquistare," it helps mark a subtle difference between the implication of the first statement, which is that we can't acquire heavenly gifts by our own power, and that of the second, which is that we can.

15. Saccone, *"Grazia, Sprezzatura, Affettazione,"* 50. Saccone somewhat tortuously rationalizes grazia as "a modality, an ability," "a virtue . . . become in itself a habit" (51–52). The point is that what the courtier performs is not grazia in its defined character as a gift of nature or the heavens but its dissimulated specter or eidolon. The ability is at the same time the manifestation of the absence of grace.

16. Flynn, "Defoe's Idea of Conduct," 73.

17. Javitch, *"Cortegiano* and the Constraints of Despotism," 27.

18. Greenblatt, *Renaissance Self-Fashioning,* 140–41, 13.

19. Shearman, *Mannerism,* 17–18.

20. See, for example, Grendler, *Schooling in Renaissance Italy.*

21. Bourdieu, *Outline of a Theory of Practice,* 94.

22. On primary and secondary socialization as modes of implicit and explicit pedagogy, respectively, see P. L. Berger and Luckmann, *Social Construction of Reality,* 129–47.

23. In a later study he briefly touches on them with a reference to Plato's account of the rift between "the kaloi kagathoi" (aristocrats or oligarchs) and the "new masters" (the self-styled Sophists) on "the question of the relationship between the habitus and the 'rule' [that] is brought to light with the historical appearance of a specialized, explicit action of inculcation": Bourdieu, *Logic of Practice,* 103. For an extended account of the sociology, ideology, and politics of higher education in his own time and milieu, see Bourdieu, *Homo Academicus,* especially the distinctions developed in pts. 1 and 2.

24. This is of course more explicit in the nomenclature of religious training, with its sisters, brothers, fathers, and mother superiors.

25. See Grendler, *Schooling in Renaissance Italy,* 3–41 and passim.

26. Stone, *Crisis of the Aristocracy.*

27. Starn and Partridge, *Arts of Power,* 86.

28. Chojnacki, "Social Identity in Renaissance Venice," 348–49. In the reference to Tuscany, Chojnacki is quoting Donati, *L'idea di nobilità in Italia,* 15, 22n24. Chojnacki's essay refines and accentuates a theme already present in his earlier "Kinship Ties and Young Patricians."

29. Kuehn, *Law, Family, and Women;* Jed, *Chaste Thinking,* 74–120.

30. Macpherson, *Political Theory of Possessive Individualism*. For a critique of his insufficiently dialectical approach see Pocock, *Virtue, Commerce, and History*, 59–71. Granted the criticism Pocock and others have made of Macpherson's model, especially as applied to seventeenth-century English political thought, I think it remains useful as a way of describing the major sites of political, social, and economic conflict. Macpherson is discussed further in Chapter 3.

Chapter 2. *Count Ricciardo's Tiny Defect*

1. Erasmo Gemini de Cesis: see della Casa, *Galateo* (Rizzoli ed.), 31–32. *Galateo*, named for this patron, was della Casa's second response to Galeazzo's suggestion and much different in tone from the Ciceronian pedantries of his first effort, a 1546 conduct book written in Latin (*De officiis inter potentiores et tenuiores amicos*) before being translated. The Latin and Italian versions are printed together in della Casa et al., *Prose*, 142–97.

2. English translation from della Casa, *Galateo*, trans. Eisenbichler and R. Bartlett, 7. Future references to this translation will be designated as D (for Dovehouse Editions). Although a revised third edition appeared in 1994, I use the text printed in the second edition. The 1994 revisions consist of a new and much more interesting cover, grammatical alterations in the introductory essay (aimed mainly at clarification), changes of format that include some reparagraphing and—more important—the shifting of notes from the end of the book to the bottom of the page or, in one instance, to the introduction. There are also a few additions to the bibliography. On the basis of an admittedly cursory flip-through I have found only one substantive but unimportant change in the translation (in chap. 25 the Italian name "Chiarissimo," della Casa's translation of the Greek "Polykleitos," is changed to "Clearest"). Irritatingly, the editors don't enumerate, much less explain, the differences between the two editions.

When I quote passages from the editors' introduction, I use the third edition, which I designate as D_3. My frequent departures from or alterations of the Dovehouse translation are noted in the citations. In the very rare cases where there is no reference to D, the translation is my own. On occasion I have silently altered the text in the interest of grammatical clarity (e.g., changing "which" to "that" before restrictive relative clauses).

3. "Era ... già pieno d'anni, molto scienziato e oltre ad ogni credenza piacevole e ben parlante e di grazioso aspetto, e molto avea de' suoi dì usato alle corti de' gran signori." I have departed from D's translation of the first clause—"[he] was ... of advanced age, very learned as well as extremely pleasant, a good conversationalist and handsome, all beyond belief" (8). By moving the idealizing phrase, "oltre ad ogni credenza," to the end, D dissipates its particular force and reference. It is an easy euphemism, a convention of courtly

compliment, so that we understand "beyond every belief" as an exaggeration not to be believed. It doesn't modify "molto scienziato" but leaves it behind to hyperbolize and integrate the trio of more superficial courtly attributes.

The Italian text of the *Galateo* used here and elsewhere in these pages is from Castiglione, della Casa, and Cellini, *Opere*, 368–440. Future references to this work will be designated as *Op.* The passage quoted above is in *Op.*, 373. The numbered *capitoli* are interpolated by editors into Italian editions and treated as chapters by the Dovehouse translators, and I shall follow their practice here.

4. This contention is superficially identical with that of the Dovehouse editors, who claim that the narrator "is not an image of Della Casa" (D₃, 23), but I shall take the claim in a direction very different from theirs.

5. Letter to Cardinal Contarini.

6. Brookes, "Galatezation," 10.

7. The original of the phrase I altered is "tanto più è di mestiero che altri v'affisi l'occhio" (*Op.*, 439), where "mestiero" (trade, business, skill) implies bourgeois busybodies and prepares the way for the economic analogy that follows.

8. This point is belatedly driven home in the first sentence of chap. 5: "Now what do we think the Bishop and his noble circle [brigata] would have said to those we sometimes see who, totally oblivious like pigs with their snouts in the swill, never raise their faces nor their eyes, let alone their hands, from the food in front of them?" (D, 9, altered).

9. I have discussed this entanglement at some length in *Making Trifles of Terrors*, 251–87, especially 253–56 and 261–80. There, following the lead of Marcel Mauss and Pierre Bourdieu, I noted the parallelism between the first two discourses: since honor is always in the gift of another—one can't honor oneself—the person who receives honor is positioned as a donee, while the position of honor-giver obviously equals that of donor and, at some level, has the donor's advantages. I argued further that in both cases to be in the position of a recipient dependent on another's gift renders one vulnerable to symbolic emasculation.

10. "The Love Song of J. Alfred Prufrock," in T. S. Eliot, *Collected Poems*, 16.

11. My translation; for the original, see *Op.*, 369.

12. Miller, "Gluttony," 106.

Chapter 3. Galateo *and the Civilizing Process*

1. Elias, *Civilizing Process*, vol. 1, *History of Manners* (hereafter cited as *Manners*), xvi.

2. Elias, *Civilizing Power*, vol. 2, *Power and Civility* (hereafter cited as *Power*), 229.

3. For some of these critiques, in addition to my own, see my *Fictions of the Pose*, chap. 6.

4. Admittedly, the chapter on banquets is the second longest of the treatise's seven chapters and takes up almost one-third of its total length.

5. See also 83: "Consideration of the behavior of people in the sixteenth century, and of their code of behavior, casts the observer back and forth between the impressions 'That's still utterly medieval' and 'That's exactly the way we feel today.' . . . The people of this time have a double face. They stand on a bridge. Behavior and the code of behavior are in motion, but the movement is quite slow."

6. Bryson, "Rhetoric of Status," 140.

7. Most of the medieval courtesy texts discussed by Elias and Bryson are conveniently collected in *Babees Book*. Pt. 1 contains English texts; the much shorter pt. 2 contains a selection of Latin and French texts. Despite the fact that many of the fragments and treatises collected in this volume were not composed and published until the fifteenth and sixteenth centuries, they reflect conventions of conduct and pedagogy characteristic of noble households since feudal times in England and on the Continent.

8. *Babees Book* contains fragments and sections of treatises in which precepts are directed to nobles in positions of high rank and power. But these are concerned with morality—Christianizing injunctions about the proper way to treat peers and inferiors—and with healthy diet rather than with manners. Most of the material in the volume is specifically devoted to instruction in various aspects of the mensal performance (including food production, serving, carving, the order of seating, the organization of the banquet, etc.) expected of inferiors, juniors, servants, and seneschals.

9. Erasmus, "On Good Manners," 273–74.

10. Erasmus explicitly assigns this tract to a pedagogical hierarchy in which it occupies the lowest rung: "The task of fashioning the young is made up of many parts, the first and consequently the most important of which consists of implanting the seeds of piety in the tender heart; the second in instilling a love for, and thorough knowledge of, the liberal arts; the third in giving instruction in the duties of life; the fourth is training in good manners right from the earliest years." The subject of this fourth task is "the external decorum of the body," which, he concedes apologetically, "is a very crude part of philosophy," but which he justifies in pragmatic terms that gesture toward "a climate of opinion" similar to the one represented by the *Galateo*, a climate in which "external decorum . . . is very conducive to winning good will and to commending those illustrious gifts of the intellect to the eyes of men" (273).

11. The following discussion is a modified version of a discussion in chap. 6 of my *Fictions of the Pose*.

12. Goldberg, *Writing Matter*, 60.

13. The conflict in France between the nobilities of the sword and the robe was anticipated and comically encapsulated in England at the beginning of the sixteenth century by Richard Pace in the prefatory letter to his *De fructu* (Basel, 1517). Pace cites an anecdote in which "one of those so-called gentlemen . . . who always carry some horn hanging at their backs, as though they would hunt during dinner," angrily rebuffs his companions' praise of letters with "I'd rather that my son should hang than study letters. For it becomes the sons of gentlemen to blow the horn nicely . . . , to hunt skillfully, and elegantly carry and train a hawk. But the study of letters should be left to the sons of rustics." Here a member of the nobility of the horn defends against the rise of a nobility of the hornbook. Text and translation (slightly altered) in *Babees Book*, xii–xiii.

14. Chartier, *On the Edge of the Cliff*, 115.

15. For an account of the discursive representations of violence in medieval culture see Bartlett, *Making of Europe*, 85–105.

16. Poggi, *The State*, 6.

17. Duby, *Medieval Marriage*, 113; Powis, *Aristocracy*, 47. On encastellation and the militarization of Europe from the tenth through the thirteenth centuries, see Bartlett, *Making of Europe*, 65–70.

18. Correll, *End of Conduct*, 46. The deep identity reflected in the etymological kinship of "hospitality" and "hostility" expresses a perception of social need and danger that has a long life, going back through Roman culture to the Hellenic institution of *xenia*.

19. The arguments behind this assertion are briefly outlined in Chapter 2 above and discussed at greater length below.

20. For the differentiation of economy from society, see in general the work of Karl Polanyi.

21. On the meaning of "reascription" and its relation to "ascription" see my "From Body to Cosmos." For a compact and suggestive profile of the contradictions producing "feudal entropy" and the development of the reascriptive structures of Christian polity to combat that entropy, see Poggi, *The State*, 37–39. To the factors enumerated by Poggi should be added the development of the reascriptive structures of agnatic lineage along with the corresponding changes in alliance technology so brilliantly analyzed by David Herlihy, Christiane Klapisch-Zuber, F. W. Kent, Diane Owens Hughes, and other historians of family, household, and marriage.

22. *Stans Puer ad Mensam*, ll. 22–25, in *Babees Book*, 28. The other references, by page and line number (where supplied), are as follows: in pt. 1, 14.41, 17.13, 22.84–86, 73.79–80, 246, 252, 271, 309.343, 321, 338.74, 639–66; in pt. 2, 8.55, 9.9–12, 16.1–8, 27.4, 30.11, 34.21, 38–40.64–73.

23. "Social superior" translates Elias's "gesellschaftlich Höherstehenden" (*Über den Prozess der Zivilisation*, 1.106; the sense of permanence is sedimented into "-stehenden" ("standing").

24. Mauss, *The Gift*, 72.

25. Hobbes, *Leviathan*, 1.11, 65.

26. See also *Leviathan*, 1.15, 198: "The value of all things contracted for, is measured by the appetite of the contractors; and therefore the just value, is that which they be contented to give."

27. Macpherson, *Political Theory of Possessive Individualism*, 37.

28. Ibid., 63, and, in general, 46–68. Macpherson's distinction between the simple and possessive market society models is not relevant to this discussion.

29. Pitt-Rivers, *Fate of Shechem*, 2.

30. Burckhardt, *Civilization of the Renaissance*, 98.

31. Kerrigan and Braden, *Idea of the Renaissance*, 26, 42, 44, 45.

32. "For their stated value" is an excellent translation of "per quello che corrono," one that does justice to the connotational richness of a verb that associates currency with circulation, competition, rapid motion, and the flow of force.

33. Arguing that "Macpherson's market model explained only one group of phenomena and did not account for their opposites," and speculating that the ideology of market society might even have been "perfected as an antithesis by those who desired to destroy it," Pocock reminds us that "the classical ideal did not simply die . . . [but] was reborn with the great recovery of the aristocracy which marks the later seventeenth and early eighteenth centuries" (*Virtue, Commerce, and History*, 70).

Kerrigan and Braden note that Burckhardt might have paid more attention to the emergence of "the modern nuclear family" during the Renaissance, and I append the following reflection: the pastiche of old families and new money combines with fluctuating economic fortunes to affect the way alliance strategies bring new blood in from the bottom or expel old blood from the top to produce continuous change of composition within what may appear to be a stable set of aristocratic representations.

Chapter 4. A Perfect Gentleman

1. As Daniel Javitch has noted, Castiglione's courtier differs from his model, the Ciceronian orator, in that "he lives in a milieu remarkable for the prominent role it accords to women," and this is reflected in the dominant role Castiglione assigns the duchess and Emilia Pia in the conversations: Javitch, *Poetry and Courtliness*, 27.

2. Butler, *Gender Trouble*, 136, 140.

3. De Lauretis, *Technologies of Gender*, 3.

4. Jones, *Currency of Eros*, 11. My debt to this splendid study far exceeds the use I make of it.

5. See the groundbreaking discussion in Kelly, "Did Women Have a Renaissance?"

6. On this proto-Lacanian sense of "the gaze" see my *Fictions of the Pose*, chap. 7.

7. Jardine, *Still Harping on Daughters*, 68–102.

8. Jones, "Nets and Bridles," 40–41.

9. Waller, "Usurpation," 160.

10. Jones, *Currency of Eros*, 11–12.

11. For a somewhat more expanded discussion see Jones, "Nets and Bridles," 42–46.

12. Althusser, "Letter on Art," 222–23.

The thesis that Castiglione's is an ironic representation containing a critique of the speakers' "shallow manners" and "trivializing talk" about serious issues is asserted in Kinney, *Continental Humanist Poetics*, 90–92, 104–9. But the assertion is part of a genetic thesis about the composition of the book: the seriousness of bk. 4, written later, redeems the limitations of the speakers emphasized in bks. 1–3.

13. Woodbridge, *Women and the English Renaissance*, 6.

14. I shall use "profeminist" to signify male-authored discourses that promote or defend the status of women but in such a way as to maintain control over the meaning of "woman" and to confirm the male prerogative not only in defining woman but also in defending her and in liberating women from old fantasies only to reenclose them in new ones. Castiglione's Giuliano will be my example of the profeminist position. I distinguish profeminism from the proto-feminism that anticipates the simpler and more whole-cloth latter-day feminisms that provide models for genealogical studies of premodern antecedents. A good definition of profeminism is Constance Jordan's description of treatises that ostensibly defend women but

> are sometimes ambiguous because their intention is in fact two-fold and to a degree contradictory. Thy are designed both to praise and to blame women, to allow them a dignified and honored place in society while at the same time demonstrating that this place is beneath that of men, and to make attractive to women their (new) role as social subordinates by stressing its basis in divine and natural law. In a more general way, this literature is intended to guarantee that the authority of men is unquestioned by anticipating and coming to terms with certain kinds of disaffection among men and women. (Jordan, *Renaissance Feminism*, 18–19)

15. Woodbridge, *Women and the English Renaissance*, 133–35.

16. For a similarly positive view of Giuliano's accomplishment as a profeminist, see Trafton, "Politics and the Praise of Women," 33.

17. Woodbridge's attributions to Castiglione are on 54 and 135.

18. Woodbridge devotes considerable de facto attention to gynephobia in her section on the transvestite controversy, but never clearly distinguishes it from a more diffuse concept of misogyny.

19. There may also be other ways to generate species of the genus gynephobia. Two examples: parthenophobia, the fear of virgin power, that is, the power men invest in women's chastity as patriarchal capital for the preservation of clean lines of inheritance and control of property; matrophobia, fear of the power invested in mothers to control nurture and implicit pedagogy beyond the socially prescribed or customary period.

20. Kelly, "Did Women Have a Renaissance?" 44–46. See also Greene, "*Cortegiano* and the Choice of a Game," 10.

21. Rebhorn, *Courtly Performances*, 42. See also 125–30, especially 130, where Rebhorn briefly describes the general predicament of the courtiers in terms similar to Kelly's.

22. See also Rebhorn's remarks about the battle between the sexes on 146–47. A more measured view of women's power is stated by Javitch in *Poetry and Courtliness*, 26–27.

23. Hanning and Rosand, *Castiglione*.

24. This criticism continues a tradition that goes back to late fifteenth-century French and English critiques of the effeminizing influence of Italianate manners on courtly style and behavior.

25. Martines, "Gentleman in Renaissance Italy," 89–91.

26. Jardine, *Still Harping on Daughters*, 54–56.

27. The phrase in quotation marks is Greene's: "Choice of a Game," 12.

28. Jordan, *Renaissance Feminism*, 78–79.

29. Richard Higgins, undergraduate seminar paper on the *Cortegiano* submitted in Spring 1991. I learned a great deal from this stimulating essay. Incidentally, it isn't entirely clear to me whether one should speak of Gasparo's "fear" or of "Gasparo's" fear—whether the position Gasparo consistently represents is to be taken as his own, his "hangup"—or as a discourse he has more or less agreed—or been assigned—to sponsor. I consider this question more closely in Chapter 6.

30. Rebhorn, *Courtly Performances*, 128. I agree with the overall thesis developed in *Lady Vanishes* by Valeria Finucci, who argues strenuously against the idea that Castiglione's opinions on gender are progressive, and who explores in detail the variety of strategies by which women are disempowered, excluded from discourse, erased as desiring subjects, and reduced to mirrors of masculine desire. As we'll see in the discussion that follows, my view of the *Cortegiano* is

diametrically opposed to Finucci's because I find elements of the critique she levels at Castiglione (the historical author) preemptively developed in Castiglione's text.

31. Jones, *Currency of Eros*, 16.

32. Here I find support in Kelly's account of the real duchess, Elisabetta Gonzaga, whose docility she emphasizes (*Women, History, and Theory*, 33–34).

33. Jones, "Nets and Bridles," 43, 45.

34. Jones, *Currency of Eros*, 16.

35. Jordan, *Renaissance Feminism*, 83.

36. Jardine, *Still Harping on Daughters*, 172–73. Jordan makes a similar observation about the strategic use of the image of the "virile woman . . . to reaffirm patriarchal values" (*Renaissance Feminism*, 137), but since this comment is part of a discussion of symbolic androgyny, she doesn't take into account the ironic devaluation of female sex and sexuality emphasized by Jardine.

37. But it is important to add that this sunlight doesn't make her a dangerous figure, a virago, as the contrast between the duchess and some of Giuliano's stories of heroic women shows (see below).

38. Greene, "Choice of a Game," 10; Javitch, "Constraints of Despotism," 27.

39. In arguing that the duchess and Emilia Pia have some discursive power, albeit limited, I am in disagreement with Finucci's position: see *Lady Vanishes*, chaps. 1–3. Finucci's argument that the limited power of women extends to the duchess and Emilia was first articulated in "Donna di corte," 91–92. I'm grateful to Deanna Shemek for bringing this essay to my attention. The same view is developed at greater length by Guidi in "De l'amour courtois à l'amour sacré."

40. Kinney, *Continental Humanist Poetics*, 97, 94.

41. Compare Ottaviano's reference in 4.47 to Homer's two examples, "the one in deeds (which was Achilles), the other in suffering and enduring (which is Ulysses)" (S, 331).

42. See Finucci, *Lady Vanishes*, 30–37.

43. Jordan, *Renaissance Feminism*, 78. Jordan's final position on the relation of drama to discourse is richer and more complicated than I am giving it credit for being here. See her concluding discussion of the *Cortegiano* (ibid., 84–85).

Chapter 5. A Perfect Lady

1. Rebhorn, *Courtly Performances*, 42, 81, 126.

2. Jones, "Nets and Bridles," 45.

3. See ibid., 44 and 70n9. See also Jones's more expanded discussion of these issues in *Currency of Eros*, 1–35.

I count twenty-seven instances of "donna di palazzo" between 2.98 and 4.3, with an additional four at 4.44–45. The first of the two uses of "cortegiana" is motivated by the speaker's fear of a false version of the "donna di palazzo": Emilia exclaims against the idea of entrusting the task to a "conspirator of signor Gasparo, who should fashion us a *cortegiana* unable to do anything except cook and spin" (2.99)—and also, of course, deceive her husband. The second use occurs precisely when Giuliano begins his account of the Court Lady and complains of a lack of models—after "donna di palazzo" has been introduced by Gasparo for the first time in bk. 3 and before Giuliano has stated his intention to play Pygmalion to the Lady he is about to create.

On the emergence of the courtesan as an instituted gender position, and the distinction between the salon courtesan and the brothel courtesan, see Lawner's chatty but informative *Lives of the Courtesans*. See also Chemello, "Donna di palazzo."

4. See Finucci, *Lady Vanishes*, 42.

5. At 3.10 Giuliano reminds Gasparo that he is "fashioning a Court Lady, not a Queen." Presumably a different set of gender characteristics would be ascribed to the counterpart of the prince.

6. I put "body" in scare quotes because I use it to denote "appearance" as well as physiological structure—"appearance" being the physical and speaking presence court ladies are to learn to represent.

7. I omit the balancing half of this proposition: the man hates "'the woman he first enjoyed'" because he takes "imperfection from the woman" and everyone "naturally . . . hates that which makes him imperfect" (3.15; S, 217). In its pseudo-philosophical rhetoric this proposition betrays the basic tenet of gynephobia, in which the zero-sum battle of sex always ends by transferring power from male to female.

8. This charge was first leveled by Ottaviano in 2.91: Since women are imperfect and of little worth in comparison with men, it was necessary to bridle them with chastity "in order for us to be certain of our offspring."

9. I am expanding Jordan's insight here: she describes the interchange and Emilia's response to it as an example of "the social control of women by men which the conversation makes possible," and an example of the way "men suppress feminist protest, even . . . while acknowledging its fairness" (*Renaissance Feminism*, 80); and even, I add, while articulating the protest—indeed, *by* articulating it.

10. Perhaps I should have followed the text and used the name "Magnifico." Jordan observes, in a passing comment, that in the tradition of Aristotelian physiology and ethics, "the supposedly positive and masculine characteristics of heat" suggest "the quality of magnificence" (*Renaissance Feminism*, 261).

11. Newman, *Fashioning Femininity*, 4–5.

12. Butler, *Gender Trouble*, 139.

13. Jones, "Nets and Bridles," 40–41.

14. Butler, *Gender Trouble*, 136.

15. The account of this episode that follows is lifted from my *Fictions of the Pose*, 192–96.

16. Finucci, *Lady Vanishes*, 51 and 50–54 passim.

17. De Lauretis, *Technologies of Gender*, 25–26.

18. Finucci, *Lady Vanishes*, 52–53.

19. For some helpful comments on Castiglione's interest in and use of the themes dramatized in the Zeuxis and Pygmalion stories, see Hanning, "Castiglione's Verbal Portrait," 133–35.

20. Ovid, *Metamorphoses* 10.238–46, 81–83.

21. For a different and more dramatic interpretation of this interlude in bk. 2 see Rebhorn, *Courtly Performances*, 117–19. See also Finucci, *Lady Vanishes*, 54.

22. Jardine, *Still Harping on Daughters*, 173.

23. Jordan, *Renaissance Feminism*, 135.

24. Kinney, *Continental Humanist Poetics*, 108. Other examples: the shaming of husbands in 3.32, the filicides in 3.33, and the story of Camma in 3.26.

25. Trafton, "Politics and the Praise of Women," 39, 37.

26. Hale, "Castiglione's Military Career," 159–60. See also Pieri, *Rinascimento e la crisi militare*, 599–607, for a survey of the social conflict that contributed to these military failures and the reluctance of the nobility to participate.

27. Bettalli, "Considerazioni," 455. Bettalli also comments on the count's evasion (457).

28. Finucci, *Lady Vanishes*, 61.

29. One sign of homosociality is that Giuliano's "I have said enough" responds in part to Gasparo's amiable jab at his previous hyperbolization of the "donna." "If you think that the Magnifico has not adorned her with enough good qualities, the fault is not with him but with the one who ordained that there should be no more virtues than this in the world, for the Magnifico gave her all there are" (3.52; S, 258). When the duchess replies that he "will find yet others," she forces the polite demurrer that opens the way for Federico to beg him to continue—and to share the blame by helping him find more virtues. The male bonding that follows will be at the expense of women.

30. "Donna di palazzo" reappears in bk. 3 only twice, in the final two chapters, where it is mentioned by Emilia (3.76) and the duchess (3.77), and mentioned defensively in response to the male discussants' desire to return to talk about the ideal courtier.

31. Rebhorn, *Courtly Performances*, 194. Emilia's anticipation of Bembo, understood in Rebhorn's terms, helps explain the—to me—confusing comment by Jordan: Emilia's exchange with Aretino "suggests that if woman is to govern, she is to do so not politically in any direct sense but rather erotically, not in court life but in courtship" (*Renaissance Feminism*, 83). The point is that erotic domination *is* political—as Jordan indicates when she brilliantly argues,

first, that in bks. 1 and 2 the courtier's "concerns and activities, focused on providing their superiors with pleasure and diversion rather than protection or counsel, might be characterized as effeminate"; second, that the situation in bk. 3 "is complicated because they are directed by the duchess, aided by Emilia Pia, whom from time to time she deputizes . . . to act in her place"; and third, that the conversations in bk. 3 "are devoted largely to arguments that serve to console Urbino's male courtiers for the degree to which they are subject to women of the court," women who have a compensatory function, "guaranteeing the effeminate courtier a part of his masculinity by reserving for him at least some power—over women" (78).

32. "Piglia" doesn't actually connote infection until the next clause, but it does connote violence—seizure, or, in the vicinity of battle imagery, despoliation. Singleton's translation ("each takes on the other's qualities") tones it down too much, or at least it one-sidedly stresses the positive or symbiotic aspect of the "dolce intoppo." Perhaps the ideal translation would register the "intoppo" of both aspects at once, symbiosis and disease.

33. I am grateful to Ann Rosalind Jones for this suggestion.

34. See also Cesare's remarks on the same theme in 3.46 and Freccero's reading of the passage in "Politics and Aesthetics," 271–76.

35. They occur in chaps. 52 (S, 258), 56 (S, 261), 58 (S, 264), 64 and 65 (S, 270), 71 (S, 276), 72 (S, 277), the last of which is only apparently nonpolemical, as we shall see.

36. "With his guard lowered by sensuality, it seems, a man is in danger; male companionship involves the sharing of such fantasies of adventure, restoring distance from and control over the passions of the flesh": Pitkin, *Fortune Is a Woman*, 116.

37. Compare Giuliano at the end of 3.67 (C, 64; S, 273) and Gasparo early in 3.72 (C, 260; S, 277).

38. Jardine, *Still Harping on Daughters*, 62.

39. De Lauretis, *Technologies of Gender*, 44.

40. Butler, *Gender Trouble*, 136.

41. Jordan, *Renaissance Feminism*, 21, 309.

42. Pp. 91–115 and passim. See also Rebhorn, "Enduring Word," 81–82.

Chapter 6. Internal Distance

1. Kinney, *Continental Humanist Poetics*, 91. See Ghinassi, *Seconda Redazione*.

2. Kinney, *Continental Humanist Poetics*, 91.

3. Gellius, *Attic Nights*, xxxvi and 2–4. For a discriminating account of Gellius's influence on humanist writing, see Baron, "Aulus Gellius in the Renaissance."

4. Rebhorn, *Courtly Performances*, 95–96.

5. "Thus you, my dear messer Alfonso, by the same reasoning may clearly know how superior the Court of Urbino was to all others in Italy, considering how much these games, which were devised for the relaxation of minds wearied by more arduous endeavors, were superior to those practiced in the other courts of Italy" (S, 201).

6. Though Singleton's "our minds" for "gli animi" is smoother than the more awkward "the minds" or "minds," there is unfortunately no justification for it. I say unfortunately because the author's explicit inclusion of himself among the worthy courtiers at Urbino would strengthen the present interpretation.

7. Rebhorn, *Courtly Performances*, 91–115.

8. Trafton, "Politics and the Praise of Women," 32; Greene, "Choice of a Game," 12.

9. Rebhorn, *Courtly Perormances*, 96.

10. Waith, *Herculean Hero*, 40–41.

11. By Ottaviano at 4.37 and by Bembo at 4.69. The latter is another example of the complication induced by the problematics of gender. Bembo compares "the spiritual fire of love that refines the soul by destroying and consuming what is mortal" to the fire "whereon poets record that Hercules was burned atop Mount Oeta, and by such burning became divine and immortal after death" (S, 355). But this Neoplatonic pyrotechnical troping so conspicuously recalls what it excludes—Deianira's killing Hercules in her attempt to keep Iole from supplanting her in his affections—that even as Bembo uses the trope to preach the transcendence of such entanglements, the diegetic material from which he sublimes the trope brings them back in. Thus the masculine discourse of the poets, the Neoplatonists, and Bembo is undone, unmanned, along with the hero trapped in the trope.

12. That the eyewitnesses are selectively chosen is indicated by his description: "omini degni di fede che vivono ancora, e presenzialmente hanno veduto e conosciuto la vita e i costumi che in quella casa fiorirono un tempo" (C, 205); "men worthy of credence who are still living and who personally saw and knew the life and the customs that once flourished in that court" (S, 202).

13. Gellius, *Attic Nights* 1.1.2.

14. For the significance of the change from Ariosto to Silva see Beer, "Maschere del tempo." Beer comments brilliantly on the shift to an old-age perspective and on the contradictions that involves—contradictions I discuss in the discussion of 2.1–4 in the next section. She also makes the important point that the change of dedicatees is a change of virtual reader perspectives, from the courtly auditor of the turn of the century to the imperial and ecclesiastical viewpoint represented by Silva. What may be registered as nostalgia by the inscription of the former is transformed to a more distanced and pragmatic perspective on a failed ideal by the inscription of the latter.

15. On the linkage between textual and sexual castigation, see Jed, *Chaste Thinking*, especially chaps. 1 and 2. The author of the *Cortegiano* chastises Vittoria della Colonna and castigates his text to undo the effects of her violence to, her rape and laceration of, the text.

16. Langer, *Divine and Poetic Freedom*, 62. I'm indebted to Carla Freccero for directing me to Langer's important study.

The record shows that Ottaviano became a good prince, a respected doge of Genoa, and that he was captured by imperial forces and died from mistreatment at the hands of the marquess of Pescara.

17. Waller, "Usurpation, Seduction," 160.

18. Kahn, *Man's Estate*, 50.

19. Greene, "Choice of a Game," 11.

20. Bk. 4, chap. 3, opens with an unexpected statement: "Parve adunque, secundo che'l signor Gasparo Pallavicino raccontar soleva, che'l seguente giorno ..." (C, 275). From this I infer that Gasparo is the anonymous informant mentioned in 1.1. He is the first whose untimely death the author mourns in 4.1. That the leading antifeminist may also be the author's informant is suggestive. For this and other aspects of Gasparo's unique role, see below.

21. As Rebhorn points out in *Courtly Performances*, 57.

22. See note 15 above.

23. Rebhorn, *Courtly Performances*, 101.

24. Guidi, "Castiglione et le pouvoir politique."

25. Freccero, "Politics and Aesthetics," 267–68.

26. See, for example, my "Origins of Bucolic Representation," *Second World and Green World*, and *Revisionary Play*.

27. Woodhouse, *Baldesar Castiglione*, 183–84; Ghinassi, *Seconda Redazione*, 300. In the final version Bembo still refers to the source in *Asolani*, but less directly than in the *Seconda Redazione*.

28. I put "Platonic" in scare quotes because in my reading of the dialogues the slander of the body is consistently represented as a position Plato's Socrates himself places in scare quotes—the position he citationally attributes to or dialogically elicits from his interlocutors and subjects to critique. See, for example, my "Levels of Discourse in Plato" and "*Phaedrus* and the Politics of Inscription."

29. From this standpoint, Apocalypse, Pandemonium, Armageddon, and Inferno express the paradise principle no less that Arcadia and Elysium.

30. For example, (1) "If Castiglione denounces the old men's nostalgia, isn't he equally vulnerable to the same criticisms?" (2) "To some degree he is. . . ." (3) "Nevertheless, his nostalgia differs from that of the old men. . . ." (Rebhorn, *Courtly Performances*, 100).

31. The effect of reductive caricature is intensified by the citational coun-terplay against Ciceronian texts on old age that Marina Beer has documented and discussed in "Maschere del tempo," 208–11. The conspicuous rejection and reversal of the respected classical opinion helps refocus our attention from the old men to the author's intent on putting them down. Beer goes on to discuss different classical stereotypes of age, including the comic Aristotelian one embodied in Morello, but the most strident echoes in 2.1–3 are, as she demonstrates, counter-Ciceronian.

32. Beer makes this point (ibid., 214, 218) but explains it as one of the inconsistencies remaining from the second redaction—the contradiction, for example, that Castiglione is identical to the old men he criticizes.

33. That such considerations aren't beyond the pale is suggested by the con-versation preceding Bembo's speech in 4.50, in which he insists that though he will describe the kind of love appropriate to old men, he isn't one of them.

34. The point of the analogy is that they don't perceive that the change for the worse is in themselves rather than in the times. But while the nautical figure reflects this point, it encrusts it with rococo details that are distractions. Whether the port (time, pleasure) or the ship of mortality stands still or recedes, the basic dilemma is the same: we grow old and leave the port (time, pleasure) behind in our journey to shipwreck. This formulation confirms and conforms to the pessimism and nostalgia the author shares with the old men, and this is what he deflects and worries about. The explicit point of the analogy is irrelevant and diversionary with respect to this.

35. Beer, "Maschere del tempo," 218.

36. Kristeva, *Powers of Horror*, 8, 7.

37. See my *Fictions of the Pose*, 119–22 and passim.

38. Changes in the selection of speakers and assignment of speeches between *La Seconda Redazione* and the final version make this obvious.

39. Kinney, *Continental Humanist Poetics*, 94–95.

40. Though "gilding the lily" is a misleading figure inasmuch as it presupposes a real lily—and the fear of its festering. Or *is* it misleading?

41. Castiglione, *Book of the Courtier*, trans. Hoby, 186.

42. Ibid., 259.

43. See Rebhorn, *Courtly Performances*, 213n9, which refers to Bettalli, "Considerazioni," 454–57. But Bettalli himself cites no evidence for the claim beyond a brief reference to a neutral comment by Cian and Prezzolini's remark that the example of the Trojan horse was not well chosen because of its negative connotations. He goes on to argue against Prezzolini on the grounds that Castiglione generally dissociated "considerations of moral character" from his representation of the courtiers, and would have been embarrassed by them (454). All this assumes what has to be proved by interpretation.

44. Woodhouse, *Baldesar Castiglione*, 56–57.

45. This concatenation produces an allegory of aristocratic or "horsey" birth from the Urbino womb.

46. Freccero, "Politics and Aesthetics," 272.

47. Javitch, *Poetry and Courtliness*, 45–46. Javitch cites an unpublished paper by Dain Trafton as the source of this argument.

48. Rebhorn, *Courtly Performances*, 96.

49. Rebhorn, in "Enduring Word," notes that the "qualified optimism" of this prediction is "dispelled completely by the letter to de Silva" (77).

50. Rebhorn, *Courtly Performances*, 53–54.

51. Temporal distance is featured from the beginning, of course, with the distanced perspective of the Proem emphasized by the change of dedicatees from the court-culture figure of Alfonso Ariosto to the Portuguese bishop Michel de Silva. As I noted above, the significance of this change has been persuasively characterized by Beer in "Maschere del tempo," 201–3.

52. Rebhorn, "Enduring Word," 82.

53. Frisio, Morello, and Ottaviano are the others.

54. Greene, "Choice of a Game," 9.

55. Woodhouse, *Baldesar Castiglione*, 67.

56. Rebhorn, "Enduring Word," 85–86.

57. At 2.91, Ottaviano argues that because women are imperfect it is necessary to put the curb of chastity on them so that "we may be certain of our offspring." He claims not to be speaking his own mind but to be advancing arguments that Gasparo could use. And Gasparo does use them at 3.37 and 39. Ottaviano's claim of personal disinterest together with his emphasis on citationality indicates that the danger to women comes not from individual animus, personal motives, but from the logic of the discourse of patriarchy. Its power is felt especially in such disclaimers of animus.

58. Guidi, "Castiglione et le pouvoir politique," 267–69.

59. Rebhorn, "Enduring Word," 81.

60. Beer, "Maschere del tempo," 214–16.

61. The ambivalence of Bembo's instructions for sublimating sex is strongly marked in 4.62–64. In chap. 62 he promises the lover that when he has purified his beloved by "seminando virtù nel giardin di quel bell'animo, raccorrà ancora frutti di bellissimi costumi e gustaragli con mirabil diletto; e questo sarà il vero generare ed esprimere la bellezza nella bellezza, il che da alcuni si dice esser il fin d'amore" (C, 324). Morello responds in chap. 63 with the obvious demystification on the kiss, so belaboring the difference between its physical and spiritual aspects that his ingenuity only dramatizes the difficulty of transcending the heterosexual desire materially inscribed in the trope. José Guidi argues that the response represents the erotic practices and subterfuges of aristocratic

gallantry; from this standpoint, Bembo puts a hilarious argument at the disposal of the courtly lover interested in stealing kisses. See Guidi, "De l'amour courtois à l'amour sacré," 76–77.

62. In the *Seconda Redazione* Camillo Paleotti does mention the two Venuses (3.106; Ghinassi, *Seconda Redazione*, 300).

63. Greene, "Choice of a Game," 11.

64. Rebhorn, *Courtly Performances*, 105.

65. Guidi, "Castiglione et le pouvoir politique," 269.

66. At 4.66 Bembo displaces the Phaedrian torments of young eros from the horse's new wings to a comparison with children's teething; now, at 4.67, the wings appear on birds.

67. Greene, "Choice of a Game," 7; my italics.

68. Finucci, "Donna di corte," 96–97.

69. On this portrait, see my *Fictions of the Pose*, 213–15.

70. Castiglione, *Book of the Courtier*, trans. Opdycke, p. 306.

71. Woodbridge, *Women and the English Renaissance*, 134.

72. Rebhorn, "Enduring Word," 85, 87.

73. Lacan, *Four Fundamental Concepts*, 85–90.

74. Copjec, *Read My Desire*, 37.

75. In addition to the editorial premises Ghinassi lays out in the introduction to *Seconda Redazione*, viii–xxiv, see his "L'ultimo revisore del *Cortegiano*" and "Fasi dell' elaborazione del *Cortegiano*."

76. Guidi, "Castiglione et le pouvoir politique."

77. See, for example, Rebhorn, *Courtly Performances*, 55–57.

Chapter 7. Narratorial Sour Grapes

1. *Concise Encyclopedia of the Italian Renaissance*, 72.

2. D, 3–4, slightly altered; *Op.*, 368. See Chapter 2, note 2, for details concerning citation and my use of the second and third editions of the translation I cite, designated as D. Note 3 of that chapter explains the Italian text I have used, designated as *Op.*

3. Though grazia, as we saw in Chapter 1, has several meanings, in this chapter I continue the practice of using it in the ascriptive sense that opposes it to sprezzatura.

4. Whigham, *Ambition and Privilege*, 45.

5. The Dovehouse translators render "fortezza" as "fortitude," which is a little loose but certainly appropriate because of the coupling with justice, and because—as in the Greek term *andreia*—ideas of courage and strength coalesce in the idea of manliness.

6. See Chapter 3 above.

7. See also the advice given in chap. 9: "if there is no danger of harm or shame, one should make other people's desires one's own, and do or say rather what others like to hear than what you yourself like" (D, 15).

8. I have replaced the Dovehouse translation with my own in the final section of this passage. Comparison of the Italian with the Dovehouse version will suggest why: "ma non pertanto a noi non è lecito di mutarla anzi siamo astretti, poiché ella non è peccato nostro ma del secolo, di secondarla: ma vuolsi ciò fare discretamente" (*Op.*, 394); "This does not allow us, however, to change it. On the contrary, we are obliged to abide by it because it is a fault of the times, not of ourselves. Ceremony, however, must be carried out with moderation" (D, 24).

9. Thanks to Deanna Shemek and Patricia Reilly for help with this passage.

10. "Ci proferiamo alle volte a tale per deditissimi servidori, che noi ameremmo di disservire più tosto che servire" (*Op.*, 393).

11. After the narrator begins chap. 17 by frowning on those "cirimoniose persone" who are overprecise in making and observing distinctions among degrees of nobility, he states his belief that these "cirimonie . . . siano state trapportate di Spagna in Italia, ma il nostro terreno le ha male ricevute e poco ci sono allignate" (*Op.*, 400). The direct and indirect references to Spanish intrusion sharpen the ironic resonance of the narrator's express promotion of the "When in Rome . . ." policy in a chapter (16) notable for its attention to violations of the policy. On "cirimonie" as "spagnolerie," see the comments and bibliography in della Casa et al., *Prose*, 227n165.

12. Once again, I thank Deanna Shemek for help in rendering this passage, though she is not responsible for liberties I have taken. It is worth noting that "si pascono di frasche" has decidedly rustic connotations because it can mean browsing on branches, and thus it intensifies the sense of disdain attributed to the noble spirits who identify ceremonial sycophancy with the boors and peasants of the herding class.

13. E.g., "everyone likes victory and hates defeat both in speech and in action," and "most people . . . are so infatuated with themselves that they overlook other people's pleasures" (D, 31).

14. Castiglione, *Libro del Cortegiano*, 2.11; C, 126; S, 103.

15. The phrases in parentheses render "un re, il cui nome fu Edipo," "un buon uomo di quel tempo che ebbe nome Socrate," "un valente uomo, il quale fu nominato Pindaro": *Op.*, 400, 436, 439.

16. D gloss, 63–64. At the end of the treatise, he interjects a final reminder of the contacts and consultations previously mentioned: "molto ho usato con persone scienziate, come tu sai" (*Op.*, 439). For a brief and helpful account of stylistic fluctuations and their effects in the *Galateo*, see Arnaldo di Benedetto's introductory comments in della Casa et al., *Prose*, 9–17.

17. In the dream, as the idiota reports it, Tomarozzo calls the apothecary

Maestro and the latter replies Figliuolo. Whether these forms of address are meant to convey a difference of age or class is unclear. Since Flaminio Tomarozzo was a friend and correspondent of Bembo, his name may have been intended to trigger a thought of the *Cortegiano* and its circle. See the note on Tomarozzo in *Op.*, 387.

18. "Usano tanta solennità nei modi loro, e così vanno contegnosi . . . , ponendosi a sedere pro tribunali e pavoneggiandosi, che egli è una pena mortale pure a vedergli" (*Op.*, 389).

19. "Secondo che racconta una molto antica cronica, egli fu già nelle parti della Morea un buon uomo scultore, il quale per la sua chiara fama, sì come io credo, fu chiamato per soprannome maestro Chiarissimo" (*Op.*, 424). The Dovehouse editors retain the Italian name in their 1st ed. but in D₃ they follow the logic of translation and replace "Chiarissimo" with "Clearest."

For the association of the "chiarissimo liquore" with "Maestro Chiarissimo" I am once again indebted to Kristen Brookes, who makes the connection in her excellent "Galatezation."

20. D, 48, much altered. With thanks to Deanna Shemek for help in rendering the first half of the second quotation. Compare *Op.*, 424–25. "Corrected" translates "dirizzare," which is an interesting if not obvious usage here. It implies that all future sculptures would be better than they would have been had they not been ruled by Chiarissimo's ruler.

21. Galen, *De Placitis Hippocratis*, in Stewart, *Greek Sculpture*, 1.265. See 1.160–63 for a compendious discussion of Polykleitos, his Canon, and the *Doryphoros*, which is assumed to be the statue embodying the Canon. See also the texts and annotations in Pollitt, *Art of Greece*, 88–92.

22. Pliny, *Natural History*, 34.55–56, 264.

23. Stewart, *Greek Sculpture*, 1:160. It is worth noting that although the senses of the Greek term *kanon* range from a measuring rod or ruler through a model or standard to a law, the extension of *regolo* is more strictly limited to the ruler. Thanks once more to Deanna Shemek for pointing this out.

24. *Op.*, 425–26. Since "pulire" and "ammollire" also mean "to flatter" and "to mollify," respectively, and in addition "ammollire" can mean "to enervate," the terms glance at a more devious form of pedagogy, but one that is entirely in keeping with the idiota's Galatean discourse on manners.

25. By me, among others, in "Orpheus, Pan." I present a revised and amplified version of this interpretation in "Second-World Prosthetics."

26. "Galatea" of course appears in Ovid and classical antiquity, but as the name of the nymph beloved by Polyphemus, which doesn't help us too much with Galateo. In my earlier discussions of the Pygmalion myth I made the same mistake, and referred to Pygmalion's statue as Galatea. For this information, and the bibliography that verified it, many thanks to Daniel Selden, Ralph Hexter, Beth Pittenger, Deanna Shemek, and several helpful cyber-

responses to my inquiry from colleagues on the Ficino network. It's worth noting that a painting by Il Bronzino, dated in the 1530s, bears the title *Pygmalion and Galatea*, but I haven't yet been able to ascertain the title's provenance.

27. I discuss the relation of Galeazzo to Galateo in Chapter 2 above.

28. Brookes, "Galatezation," 13–16.

29. This trope excludes the speaker or judge from his sentence on "them" by so conspicuously including him only for emphasis and politeness and the effect of generalization.

30. He mentions the affiliation when he complains of the majority, who, misled by their instincts and deaf to reason, believe they are obeying their natures "quasi la ragione non sia negli uomini natural cosa" (*Op.*, 426).

31. See especially the phrase I have rendered "she cannot make the unmannerly mannerly without custom": "ella non può di scostumato far costumato, senza l'usanza."

32. Two other references to time's power position it as a scapegoat. In the first, which occurs during the discussion of ceremony, the self-excepting "we" lends itself to the mimicry of free indirect discourse. "We" blame hollow and vain customs on the power of time and "our" own powerlessness to resist it. In a word, "we" temporize: "This habit . . . [of bestowing and using titles], so beautiful and becoming on the outside, is totally empty within, and consists in shadows without substance and words without meaning. Nevertheless, it is not permissible for us to change it, on the contrary, we are constrained—since it is not our fault but that of the times [del secolo]—to countenance it; but one should [or would wish to] do this discreetly" (D, 24, seriouly altered; see *Op.*, 394). The second reference appears after the Chiarissimo chapter and has more impact because it is at once laconically matter-of-fact and totalizing: whether customs are good or bad, we have no power to change them as we please, "for it is time that creates them and likewise it is time that destroys them" (D, 55).

33. Examples: "temper and adapt your manners not according to your own choices but according to the pleasure of those with whom you are dealing"— but do so with moderation; "our manners are considered pleasant when we take into consideration other people's pleasures and not our own" (D, 4–5); "if there is no danger of harm or shame, you should make other people's desire your own, and do or say rather what others like to hear than what you yourself like" (D, 15, altered).

34. Leicester, *Disenchanted Self*, 6. Actually, as the translator notes, "the form usually given (*Entia non sunt multiplicanda sine necessitate*) does not seem to have been used by Ockham," who stated it in other forms: William of Ockham, *Philosophical Writings*, xxi.

35. On the related fallacies of simple location and misplaced concreteness, see Whitehead, *Process and Reality*, 208, and *Science and the Modern World*, chap. 3, especially 50–57.

36. If the personal pronoun is itself a fiction of personification, its gender is nevertheless important, as we'll see below. Galatean discourse is male discourse.

37. For a view of della Casa's relations to Machiavelli and Castiglione very different from mine, see D3, 19–20.

38. On this distinction see Pocock, *Machiavellian Moment*, 160–61.

39. Starn and Partridge, *Arts of Power*, 86–88. To revert once again to C. B. Macpherson's models of customary and possessive market societies, features of the possessive market society impose themselves on those who find it in their interest to preserve features of the customary or status society.

40. There are three or four passages in *Galateo* that editors have connected to the *Cortegiano* on the basis of common topics, but in these glosses Castiglione is mentioned as one of several possible sources or analogues.

41. Boccaccio, *Decameron*, sixth day, tenth story.

42. Throughout the treatise, the noun and verb D translates as "desire" are "appetito" and "appetire." The usage is unremarkable, if weighted toward appetite in our sense, but in chap. 25 it receives a more ironic charge because of the idiota's discussion of relations between animals and humans.

43. No doubt because they feed off each other, all the editions I have consulted—Cordié, di Benedetto, Maier, Milanini—gloss "convenevolezza" as "proportion" or "harmony" rather than "propriety" or "decorum," and thus torque the passage more fully toward classical and humanist norms of intelligible beauty, and toward mathematically or geometrically based standards that for more than a century—since the appearance of Alberti's *Della pittura*—had been percolating down into the discourses of perspective and visual art.

44. "E per aventura che quel dipintore, che ebbe ignude dinanzi a sé le fanciulle calabresi, niuna altra cosa fece che riconoscere in molte i membri che elle aveano quasi accattato chi uno e chi un altro da una sola; alla quale fatto restituire da ciascuno il suo, lei si pose a ritrarre, imaginando che tale e così unita dovesse essere la bellezza di Venere" (*Op.*, 429). Many thanks to my colleague Giulia Centineo for help with the translation of this passage and also for observing that in the phrase "spiacevole e sozzi," "sozzi" is a particularly strong word, stronger than "sporco" because of its implications of deformity and sordidness.

45. Pliny, *Natural History*, 35.61; see also Cicero, *De inventione*, 2.1.1.

46. Alberti, *On Painting*, 92–93, slightly altered; Italian text from *Della pittura*, 107–8. In *Idea*, Panofsky oddly quotes this passage as "a sharp attack against those who believe that they can produce something beautiful without any study of nature" (57–58), where "study" takes on euphemistic force to any reader who interprets the Zeuxis passage as a sharp attack on nature.

47. As we saw, when *Cortegiano* glances at the anecdote it is to describe the acquisition of sprezzatura as a skill of robbery: "even as in green meadows the bee flits about among grasses robbing the flowers, so our Courtier must steal

this grace from those who seem to him to have it, taking from each the part that seems most worthy of praise" (C, 1.26; S, 42–43).

48. The italicized phrase replaces the D translation, "you would be disappointed with her inconsistency," which renders "ti dispiacerebbe ella in ciò che ella non si mostrerebbe pure una" (*Op.*, 430). My alteration is even looser than the D version, but it better approximates the sense conveyed by the Italian that the woman is to blame for "your" displeasure, an emphasis consistent with the twist given the Zeuxis story. I have also replaced the D rendering of the first sentence and the last clause of the passage with more literal translations (cf. *Op.*, 429–30). In the former, D reduces "de' visi e delle membra o de' corpi" to "for bodies and faces"; omitting "membra" weakens the link to the most disturbing feature of the Zeuxis story.

49. An appeal missing from the earlier passage referred to in the quotation: "Everyone must dress well according to his status and age, because if he does otherwise it seems that he disdains other people.... A man must try to adapt himself as much as he can to the sartorial style of other citizens and let custom guide him, even though it may seem to him to be less comfortable and attractive than previous fashions," for to do otherwise would make his companions suspect that he has "a low opinion of them" (chap. 7, D, 12–13).

50. The D translation converts the nouns to adjectives and gives the store away in rendering "leggiadria" as "pretty": "those things we call beautiful, pretty, and attractive."

51. And woman idealized as a figure of male desire is also a scapegoat.

52. Jordan, *Renaissance Feminism*, 77.

53. See above, Chapters 2 and 3.

54. Ficino, *Marsilio Ficino's Commentary*, 164, 64.

55. E.g., D, 39–40: "Your words should also be, as far as possible, appropriate to what you want to demonstrate, and as little applicable to other matters as possible. In this manner it will seem that you are bringing forth the things themselves and that they are being described not with words but with your finger." The best words are those "that have only one meaning."

Bibliography

Alberti, Leon Battista. *Della pittura*. Ed. Luigi Mallè. Florence: Sansone, 1950. Published in English as *On Painting*. Trans. John R. Spencer. Rev. ed. New Haven: Yale University Press, 1966.

Althusser, Louis. "A Letter on Art in Reply to André Daspre." In *Lenin and Philosophy*, trans. Ben Brewster. New York: Monthly Review Press, 1971.

The Babees' Book: Medieval Manners for the Young. Ed. F. J. Furnivall. (1868.) New York: Greenwood Press, 1969.

Barish, Jonas. *The Antitheatrical Prejudice*. Berkeley: University of California Press, 1981.

Baron, Hans. "Aulus Gellius in the Renaissance: His Influence and a Manuscript from the School of Guarino." (1951.) In *From Petrarch to Leonardo Bruni: Studies in Humanistic and Political Literature*, 196–215. Chicago: University of Chicago Press, 1968.

Bartlett, Robert. *The Making of Europe: Conquest, Colonization, and Cultural Change, 950–1350*. Princeton: Princeton University Press, 1993.

Beer, Marina. "Le maschere del tempo nel *Cortegiano*." In *La Corte e il "Cortegiano": La scena del testo*, ed. Carlo Ossola, 201–18. Rome: Bulzone, 1980.

Berger, Harry, Jr. *Fictions of the Pose: Rembrandt Against the Italian Renaissance*. Stanford: Stanford University Press, 2000.

———. "From Body to Cosmos: The Dynamics of Representation in Precapitalist Society." *South Atlantic Quarterly* 91 (1992): 557–602.

———. *Imaginary Audition: Shakespeare on Stage and Page*. Berkeley: University of California Press, 1989.

———. "Levels of Discourse in Plato." In *New Directions in Philosophy and Literature*, ed. Anthony Cascardi, 77–100. Baltimore: Johns Hopkins University Press, 1987.

———. *Making Trifles of Terrors: Redistributing Complicities in Shakespeare*. Stanford: Stanford University Press, 1997.

———. "The Origins of Bucolic Representation: Disenchantment and Revision in Theocritus' Seventh Idyll." *Classical Antiquity* 3 (1984): 1–39.

———. "Orpheus, Pan, and the Poetics of Misogyny: Spenser's Critique of Pastoral Love and Art." *English Literary History* 50 (1983): 27–34.

———. "*Phaedrus* and the Politics of Inscription." In *Plato and Postmodernism*, ed. Steven Shankman, 76–114. Glenside, Pa.: Aldine, 1994.

———. "The Prince's Dog: Falstaff and the Perils of Speech-Prefixity." *Shakespeare Quarterly* 49 (1998): 40–73.

———. *Revisionary Play: Studies in the Spenserian Dynamics.* Berkeley: University of California Press, 1988.

———. *Second World and Green World: Studies in Renaissance Fiction-Making.* Ed. John Patrick Lynch. Berkeley: University of California Press, 1988.

———. "Second-World Prosthetics: Supplying Deficiencies of Nature in Renaissance Italy." In *Early Modern Visual Culture*, ed. Peter Erickson and Clark Hulse, 98–147. Philadelphia: University of Pennsylvania Press, 2000.

Berger, Peter L., and Thomas Luckmann. *The Social Construction of Reality: A Treatise in the Sociology of Knowledge.* Garden City, N.Y.: Doubleday/ Anchor, 1967.

Bettalli, Giuseppe. "Considerazioni su di un luogo del *Cortegiano*." *Belfagor* 11 (1956): 454–57.

Boccaccio, Giovanni. *The Decameron*, sixth day, tenth story. Trans. Mark Musa and Peter Bondanella. New York: Mentor Books, 1982.

Bourdieu, Pierre. *Homo Academicus.* Trans. Peter Collier. Stanford: Stanford University Press, 1988.

———. *The Logic of Practice.* Trans. Richard Nice. Stanford: Stanford University Press, 1990.

———. *Outline of a Theory of Practice.* Trans. Richard Nice. Cambridge: Cambridge University Press, 1973.

Brookes, Kristen. "The Galatezation and Reclarification of Man." Unpublished essay, June 1996.

Bryson, Anna. "The Rhetoric of Status: Gesture, Demeanor and the Image of the Gentleman in Sixteenth- and Seventeenth-Century England." In *Renaissance Bodies: The Human Figure in English Culture, c. 1540–1660*, ed. Lucy Gent and Nigel Llewellyn. London: Reaktion Books, 1990.

Burckhardt, Jacob. *The Civilization of the Renaissance in Italy.* Trans. S. G. C. Middlemore. 3d ed. rev. London: Phaidon, 1950.

Butler, Judith. *Gender Trouble: Feminism and the Subversion of Identity.* New York: Routledge, 1990.

Castiglione, Baldassare. *The Book of the Courtier.* (1561.) Trans. Sir Thomas Hoby. London: J. M. Dent, 1928.

————. *The Book of the Courtier.* (1561.) Trans. Leonard Epstein Opdycke. New York: Horace Liveright, 1929.

————. *Il libro del cortegiano.* (1561.) Ed. Giulio Carnazzi [C]. Milan: Rizzoli, 1987. Published in English as *The Book of the Courtier.* Trans. Charles Singleton [S]. New York: Anchor/Doubleday, 1959.

Castiglione, Baldassare, Giovanni della Casa, and Benvenuto Cellini. *Opere di Baldassare Castiglione, Giovanni della Casa, Benvenuto Cellini* [Op.]. Ed. Carlo Cordié. Milan: Ricciardi, 1960.

Cavell, Stanley. *Disowning Knowledge.* New York: Cambridge University Press, 1987.

Chartier, Rogier. *On the Edge of the Cliff: History, Language, and Practices.* Trans. Lydia G. Cochrane. Baltimore: Johns Hopkins University Press, 1997.

Chemello, Adriana. "Donna di palazzo, moglie, cortigiana: Roli e funzioni sociali della donna in alcuni trattati dei Conquecento." In *La corte e il cortegiano*, vol. 2, *Un modello europeo*, 113–32. Rome: Bulzoni, 1980.

Chojnacki, Stanley. "Kinship Ties and Young Patricians in Fifteenth-Century Venice." *Renaissance Quarterly* 38 (1985): 241–70.

————. "Social Identity in Renaissance Venice: The Second Serrata." *Renaissance Studies* 8 (1994): 341–58.

The Concise Encyclopedia of the Italian Renaissance. Ed. J. R. Hale. London: Thames & Hudson, 1981.

Copjec, Joan. *Read My Desire: Lacan Against the Historicists.* Cambridge: MIT Press, 1994.

Correll, Barbara. *The End of Conduct: Grobianus and the Renaissance Text of the Subject.* Ithaca: Cornell University Press, 1996.

de Lauretis, Teresa. *Technologies of Gender: Essays on Theory, Film, and Fiction.* Bloomington: Indiana University Press, 1987.

della Casa, Giovanni. *Galateo.* In Baldassare Castiglione, Giovanni della Casa, and Benvenuto Cellini, *Opere di Baldassare Castiglione, Giovanni della Casa, Benvenuto Cellini*, ed. Carlo Cordié [Op.]. Milan: Ricciardi, 1960.

————. *Galateo.* Trans. Konrad Eisenbichler and Kenneth R. Bartlett. 2d ed. [D]. Ottawa: Dovehouse, 1990; 3d ed. [D3], 1994.

————. *Galateo.* Ed. Claudio Milanini. 3rd ed. Milan: Rizzoli, 1982.

della Casa, Giovanni, et al. *Prose di Giovanni della Casa e altri trattatisti cinquecenteschi del comportamento.* Ed. Arnaldo di Benedetto. (1970.) Turin: U.T.E.T., 1991.

Donati, Claudio. *L'idea di nobiltà in Italia: Secoli XIV–XVIII.* Bari and Rome: Laterza, 1988.

Duby, Georges. *Medieval Marriage: Two Models from Twelfth-Century France.* Trans. Elborg Forster. Baltimore: Johns Hopkins University Press, 1978.

Elias, Norbert. *The Civilizing Process.* Trans. Edmund Jephcott. 2 vols. Vol. 1, *The History of Manners.* Vol. 2, *Power and Civility.* New York: Pantheon, 1982.

——. *Über den Prozess der Zivilisation: Soziogenetische und psychogenetische Untersuchungen.* 2 vols. 2d ed. Bern and Munich: Francke, 1969.

Eliot, T. S. "The Love Song of J. Alfred Prufrock." In Eliot, *Collected Poems, 1909–1935.* New York: Harcourt, Brace, 1936.

Erasmus, Desiderius. "On Good Manners for Boys / *De civilitate morum puerilium.*" Trans. Brian McGregor. In *Collected Works of Erasmus*, vol. 25, ed. J. K. Sowards. Toronto: University of Toronto Press, 1985.

Ficino, Marsilio. *Marsilio Ficino's Commentary on Plato's "Symposium."* Trans. Sears R. Jayne. University of Missouri Studies 19, no. 1. Columbia: University of Missouri Press, 1944.

Finucci, Valeria. "La donna di corte: Discorso istituzionale e realtà ne *Il libro del cortegiano* di B. Castiglione." *Annali d'Italianistica* 7 (1989): 88–103.

——. *The Lady Vanishes: Subjectivity and Representation in Castiglione and Ariosto.* Stanford: Stanford University Press, 1992.

Flynn, Carol Houlihan. "Defoe's Idea of Conduct: Ideological Fictions and Fictional Reality." In *The Ideology of Conduct: Essays in Literature and the History of Sexuality*, ed. Nancy Armstrong and Leonard Tennenhouse. New York: Methuen, 1987.

Freccero, Carla. "Politics and Aesthetics in Castiglione's *Il Cortegiano:* Book III and the Discourse on Women." In *Creative Imitation: New Essays on Renaissance Literature in Honor of Thomas M. Greene*, ed. David Quint, Margaret W. Ferguson, G. W. Pigman III, and Wayne A. Rebhorn, 259–79. Binghamton, N.Y.: Medieval and Renaissance Texts and Studies, 1992.

Galen. *De Placitis Hippocratis et Platonis.* Trans. Andrew Stewart. In Stewart, *Greek Sculpture: An Exploration*, vol. 1. New Haven: Yale University Press, 1990.

Gellius, Aulus. *The Attic Nights of Aulus Gellius.* Trans. John C. Rolfe. Rev. ed. Cambridge: Harvard University Press, 1961.

Ghinassi, Ghino. "Fasi dell'elaborazione del *Cortegiano.*" *Studi di Filologia Italiana* 25 (1976): 155–96.

——. *La Seconda Redazione de "Cortegiano" di Baldassare Castiglione.* Florence: Sansone, 1968.

——. "L'ultimo revisore del *Cortegiano.*" *Studi di Filologia Italiana* 21 (1963): 217–64.

Goldberg, Jonathan. *Writing Matter: From the Hands of the English Renaissance.* Stanford: Stanford University Press, 1990.

Greenblatt, Stephen. *Renaissance Self-Fashioning: From More to Shakespeare.* Chicago: University of Chicago Press, 1980.

Greene, Thomas M. "*Il Cortegiano* and the Choice of a Game." In *Castiglione: The Ideal and the Real in Renaissance Culture*, ed. Robert W. Hanning and David Rosand. New Haven: Yale University Press, 1983.

Grendler, Paul F. *Schooling in Renaissance Italy: Literacy and Learning, 1300–1600*. Baltimore: Johns Hopkins University Press, 1989.

Guidi, José. "Baldassare Castiglione et le pouvoir politique: Du gentilhomme de cour au nonce pontifical." In *Les Ecrivains et le pouvoir en Italie à l'époque de la Renaissance*, 243–78. Centre de recherche sur la Renaissance italienne 2. Paris: Université de la Sorbonne nouvelle, 1973.

———. "De l'amour courtois à l'amour sacré: La Condition de la femme dans l'oeuvre de B. Castiglione." In Guidi et al., *Images de la femme dans la littérature italienne de la Renaissance: Préjuges misogynes et aspirations nouvelles: Castiglione, Piccolomini, Bandello*, 9–80. Centre de recherche sur la Renaissance italienne 8. Paris: Université de la Sorbonne nouvelle, 1980.

Hale, J. R. "Castiglione's Military Career." In *Castiglione: The Ideal and the Real in Renaissance Culture*, ed. Robert Hanning and David Rosand. New Haven: Yale University Press, 1983.

Hanning, Robert. "Castiglione's Verbal Portrait: Structures and Strategies." In *Castiglione: The Ideal and the Real in Renaissance Culture*, ed. Robert Hanning and David Rosand. New Haven: Yale University Press, 1983.

Hanning, Robert, and David Rosand, eds. *Castiglione: The Ideal and the Real in Renaissance Culture*. New Haven: Yale University Press, 1983.

Herlihy, David. *Medieval Households*. Cambridge: Harvard University Press, 1985.

Herlihy, David, and Christiane Klapish-Zuber. *Tuscans and Their Families: A Study of the Florentine Catasto of 1427*. New Haven: Yale University Press, 1985.

Hobbes, Thomas. *Leviathan*. Ed. Michael Oakeshott. Oxford: Basil Blackwell, 1960.

Hughes, Diane Owen. "From Brideprice to Dowry in Mediterranean Europe." *Journal of Family History* 3 (1978): 262–96.

———. "Representing the Family: Portraits and Purposes in Early Modern Italy." *Journal of Interdisciplinary History* 17 (1986): 7–38.

———. "Urban Growth and Family Structure in Medieval Genoa." *Past and Present* 66 (1975): 3–28.

Jardine, Lisa. *Still Harping on Daughters: Women and Drama in the Age of Shakespeare*. 2d ed. New York: Columbia University Press, 1989.

Javitch, Daniel. "*Il Cortegiano* and the Constraints of Despotism." In *Castiglione: The Ideal and the Real in Renaissance Culture*, ed. Robert W. Hanning and David Rosand. New Haven: Yale University Press, 1983.

———. *Poetry and Courtliness in Renaissance England*. Princeton: Princeton University Press, 1978.

Jed, Stephanie H. *Chaste Thinking: The Rape of Lucretia and the Birth of Human-ism.* Bloomington: Indiana University Press, 1989.

Jones, Ann Rosalind. *The Currency of Eros: Women's Love Lyric in Europe, 1540–1620.* Bloomington: Indiana University Press, 1990.

———. "Nets and Bridles: Early Modern Conduct Books and Sixteenth-Century Women's Lyrics." In *The Ideology of Conduct,* ed. Nancy Armstrong and Leonard Tennenhouse. New York: Methuen, 1987.

Jordan, Constance. *Renaissance Feminism: Literary Texts and Political Models.* Ithaca: Cornell University Press, 1990.

Kahn, Coppélia. *Man's Estate: Masculine Identity in Shakespeare.* Berkeley: University of California Press, 1981.

Kelly, Joan. "Did Women Have a Renaissance?" In *Women, History, and Theory.* Chicago: University of Chicago Press, 1986.

Kent, Francis W. *Household and Lineage in Renaissance Florence: The Family Life of the Capponi, Ginori, and Rucellai.* Princeton: Princeton University Press, 1977.

Kerrigan, William, and Gordon Braden. *The Idea of the Renaissance.* Baltimore: Johns Hopkins University Press, 1989.

Kinney, Arthur. *Continental Humanist Poetics: Studies in Erasmus, Castiglione, Marguerite de Navarre, Rabelais, and Cervantes.* Amherst: University of Massachusetts Press, 1989.

Klapisch-Zuber, Christiane. *Women, Family, and Ritual in Renaissance Italy.* Trans. Lydia Cochrane. Chicago: University of Chicago Press, 1985.

Kristeva, Julia. *Powers of Horror: An Essay on Abjection.* Trans. Leon S. Roudiez. New York: Columbia University Press, 1982.

Kuehn, Thomas. *Law, Family, and Women: Toward a Legal Anthropology of Renais-sance Italy.* Chicago: University of Chicago Press, 1991.

Lacan, Jacques. *The Four Fundamental Concepts of Psycho-Analysis.* Trans. Alan Sheridan. New York: Norton, 1978.

Langer, Ullrich. *Divine and Poetic Freedom in the Renaissance: Nominalist Theology and Literature in France and Italy.* Princeton: Princeton University Press, 1990.

Lawner, Lynne. *Lives of the Courtesans: Portraits of the Renaissance.* New York: Rizzoli, 1987.

Leicester, H. Marshall, Jr. *The Disenchanted Self: Representing the Subject in the "Canterbury Tales."* Berkeley: University of California Press, 1990.

Linton, Ralph. *The Study of Man.* New York: Appleton-Century, 1936.

Macpherson, C. B. *The Political Theory of Possessive Individualism: Hobbes to Locke.* Oxford: Oxford University Press, 1962.

Martines, Lauro. "The Gentleman in Renaissance Italy: Strains of Isolation in the Body Politic." In *The Darker Vision of the Renaissance,* ed. Robert S.

Kinsman. UCLA Center for Medieval and Renaissance Studies 4.
Berkeley: University of California Press, 1974.

Maus, Katharine Eisaman. *Inwardness and Theater in the English Renaissance.*
Chicago: University of Chicago Press, 1995.

Mauss, Marcel. *The Gift: Forms and Functions of Exchange in Archaic Societies.*
Trans. Ian Cunnison. New York: Norton, 1967.

McEachern, Claire. *The Poetics of English Nationhood, 1590–1612.* Cambridge:
Cambridge University Press, 1996.

Miller, William Ian. "Gluttony." *Representations* 60 (Fall 1997): 92–112.

Newman, Karen. *Fashioning Femininity and English Renaissance Drama.* Chicago:
University of Chicago Press, 1991.

Ovid. *Metamorphoses.* Trans. Frank Justus Miller. (1916.) Vol. 2. Cambridge:
Harvard University Press, 1946.

Panofksy, Erwin. *Idea: A Concept in Art Theory.* Trans. J. J. S. Peake. Columbia:
University of South Carolina Press, 1968.

Pieri, Piero. *Il Rinascimento e la crisi militare italiana.* Turin: G. Einaudi, 1952.

Pitkin, Hannah Fenichel. *Fortune Is a Woman: Gender and Politics in the Thought
of Niccolò Machiavelli.* Berkeley: University of California Press, 1984.

Pitt-Rivers, Julian. *The Fate of Shechem, or The Politics of Sex: Essays in the
Anthropology of the Mediterranean.* Cambridge: Cambridge University
Press, 1977.

Pliny. *Natural History.* Trans. Andrew Stewart. In Stewart, *Greek Sculpture: An
Exploration,* vol. 1. New Haven: Yale University Press, 1990.

Pocock, J. G. A. *The Machiavellian Moment: Florentine Political Thought and the
Atlantic Republican Tradition.* Princeton: Princeton University Press, 1975.

———. *Virtue, Commerce, and History.* Cambridge: Cambridge University
Press, 1985.

Poggi, Gianfranco. *The State: Its Nature, Development, and Prospects.* Stanford:
Stanford University Press, 1990.

Pollitt, J. J. *The Art of Greece, 1400–1431 B.C.* Englewood Cliffs, N.J.: Prentice-
Hall, 1965.

Powis, Jonathan. *Aristocracy.* Oxford: Basil Blackwell, 1984.

Puttenham, George. *The Arte of English Poesie.* (1589.) Ed. Gladys Doidge
Willcock and Alice Walker. (1936.) Cambridge: Cambridge University
Press, 1970.

Rebhorn, Wayne. *Courtly Performances: Masking and Festivity in Castiglione's
"Book of the Courtier."* Detroit: Wayne State University Press, 1978.

———. "The Enduring Word: Language, Time, and History in *Il Libro del
Cortegiano.*" In *Castiglione: The Ideal and the Real in Renaissance Culture,*
ed. Robert W. Hanning and David Rosand, 69–90. New Haven: Yale
University Press, 1983.

Saccone, Eduardo. "*Grazia, Sprezzatura, Affettazione* in the *Courtier*." In
    Castiglione: The Ideal and the Real in Renaissance Culture, ed. Robert W.
    Hanning and David Rosand, 59–64. New Haven: Yale University
    Press, 1983.
Shearman, John. *Mannerism.* Harmondsworth: Penguin, 1967.
Starn, Randolph, and Loren Partridge. *Arts of Power: Three Halls of State in Italy,*
    1300–1600. Berkeley: University of California Press, 1992.
Stewart, Andrew. *Greek Sculpture: An Exploration.* 2 vols. New Haven: Yale
    University Press, 1990.
Stone, Lawrence. *The Crisis of the Aristocracy, 1588–1641.* Oxford: Clarendon,
    1965.
Trafton, Dain A. "Politics and the Praise of Women: Political Doctrine in the
    Courtier's Third Book." In *Castiglione: The Ideal and the Real in Renais-*
    sance Culture, ed. Robert W. Hanning and David Rosand. New
    Haven: Yale University Press, 1983.
Waith, Eugene M. *The Herculean Hero.* New York: Columbia University Press,
    1962.
Waller, Marguerite. "Usurpation, Seduction, and the Problematics of the
    Proper: A 'Deconstructive,' 'Feminist' Rereading of the Seductions
    of Richard and Anne in Shakespeare's *Richard III*." In *Rewriting the*
    Renaissance: The Discourses of Sexual Difference in Early Modern Europe,
    ed. Margaret W. Ferguson, Maureen Quilligan, and Nancy J. Vickers.
    Chicago: University of Chicago Press, 1986.
Whigham, Frank. *Ambition and Privilege: The Social Tropes of Elizabethan Courtesy*
    Theory. Berkeley: University of California Press, 1984.
Whitehead, Alfred North. *Process and Reality: An Essay on Cosmology.* New York:
    Social Science Bookstore, 1929.
————. *Science and the Modern World.* (1925.) New York: Mentor Books, 1956.
William of Ockham. *Philosophical Writings: A Selection.* Trans. Philotheus
    Boehner. Library of Liberal Arts. Indianapolis: Bobbs-Merrill, 1964.
Woodbridge, Linda. *Women and the English Renaissance: Literature and the Nature*
    of Womankind, 1540–1620. Urbana: University of Illinois Press, 1986.
Woodhouse, J. R. *Baldesar Castiglione: A Reassessment of "The Courtier."*
    Edinburgh: Edinburgh University Press, 1978.

Index

abjection, 148–50, 157
aemulatio, 128, 134–35. *See also* conspicuous allusion; *imitatio*
affettazione, 94, 197, 214. See also *grazia; sprezzatura*
Agrippa, Cornelius, 70
Alberti, 218–19, 253n. 43
Alexander, 163, 195
Althusser, Louis, 69
androgyny, 89, 98, 241n. 36. *See also* effeminacy
antifeminism, 70–71, 73, 79–80, 83–84, 90–92, 95, 97, 99, 104, 106, 108–9, 113–14, 128, 142, 167, 175–76, 246n. 20. *See also* gynephobia; misogyny
Aretino, Unico, 105, 243n. 31
Ariosto, Alfonso, 23, 120–21, 129, 133, 245n. 14
Aristotle, 17, 23, 88–89, 97, 134, 156, 181, 195
ascription, 17, 21, 23–24, 156, 180, 213, 231n. 2 (Pref.), 249n. 3; and reascription, 43

Bari, Roberto da, 105
Beer, Marina, 148, 169, 245n. 14, 247nn. 31–32
Bembo, Pietro, 106, 126, 140, 157, 161, 165–66, 168–74, 176, 195, 243n. 31, 245n. 11, 247n. 33, 249n. 66, 251n. 17

Betalli, Giuseppe, 247n. 43
Bibbiena, Bernardo, 17, 95–96, 106, 108–10, 113, 165
Boccaccio, 197, 213–14
Bourdieu, Pierre, 22, 233n. 23, 235n. 9
Braden, Gordon, 55–57, 238n. 33
Brookes, Kristen, 27, 205, 251n. 19
Bryson, Anna, 37, 39, 42, 44–45, 47–48, 235n. 7
Burckhardt, Jacob, 44, 46, 55, 213
Butler, Judith, 63–64, 91

Calmeta, Vincenzo, 172
Castiglione, Baldassare, 35, 58, 238n. 1, 239n. 12, 239n. 14, 240n. 30; *Il libro del Cortegiano*, 1, 3–5, 9–25, 33, 55, 59–60, 63–115, 119–80, 201, 210–15, 226–27; parerga, 114–15, 129, 135, 144, 153–55, 162, 165
castration, 93, 177, 226
Cavell, Stanley, 175
ceremony, 184, 186–87, 191–93
Chartier, Roger, 40
Chiarissimo, 200–205, 217–18, 251n. 20, 252n. 32
Christine di Pizan, 67
Cicero, 23, 135, 138–39, 142, 160, 218, 238n. 1
citationality, 120, 135–36, 138, 140–42, 166–67, 247n. 31, 248n. 57. *See also* conspicuous allusion

civilizing process (Elias), 33–34, 36,
39–40, 44, 60
ClementVII, 160
conduct books. *See* courtesy books
conspicuous allusion, 139, 168
conspicuous exclusion, 10, 18, 27, 82,
88, 100–102, 107, 113, 128, 139,
164–65, 168, 172, 175, 178
Contarini, Cardinal, 27
convenevolezza, 196, 222, 224, 253n. 43
Correll, Barbara, 42–43, 45–48
courtesans, 88
courtesy books, 1, 25, 36–38, 59, 68–69,
236nn. 7–8; conduct books, 18, 34,
42, 44, 60, 66–67, 91, 179, 227
courtier: absolute, 17–19, 81, 155, 201,
212; ideal (or perfect), 9, 12–13,
17–19, 31, 59, 73, 79, 81–82, 87,
92–93, 95–96, 101, 151, 155, 164, 172,
201, 203–4, 212, 226, 243n. 30

Dante, 195
decorum, 32, 196, 219–24, 236n. 10,
253n. 43
de Lauretis, Teresa, 64, 94, 113
della Casa, Giovanni, 38, 234n. 1;
Galateo, 1, 3–5, 25–36, 39, 43, 46–52,
55–60, 179–228
della Rovere, Francesco Maria, 173–74
Desainliens, Claudius, 40
despotism, 10, 167, 171, 175, 181,
187–89, 191
disempowerment, 11, 81, 101, 103, 106,
112, 114, 128, 148, 155–57, 162, 167,
170, 223
disinvoltura, 9, 11
Divine, 63
Domeneddio, 198, 200–201
donation, 51–59, 81, 235n. 9; discourse
of the gift, 31
donna di palazzo, 87–88, 95, 97, 102–6,
109–10, 113, 241n. 3, 243n. 30
Duby, Georges, 41

early modern discourse networks, 3, 66,
85
effeminacy, 11, 53, 71–75, 83, 101–2, 106,
156, 167, 183–84, 223–24, 226, 244n.
31
Elias, Norbert, 1, 33–37, 39–40, 42,
44–45, 47–49, 57–60, 236n. 7
Eliot, T. S., 31
Elizabeth I of England, 79
Emilia Pia, 72–73, 75–77, 79–80, 89–90,
105–6, 166, 170–71, 173–76, 238n. 1,
241n. 39, 242n. 3, 242n. 9, 243nn.
30–31
Erasmo Gemini de Cesis, 26–28
Erasmus, 33, 35–36, 38, 60, 236n. 10
Erikson, Erik, 82
Este, Ippolito da, cardinal of Ferrara, 15
Euclid, 23

famigliari, 26, 28, 31, 46, 51
Federico, 11, 13–14, 80, 102, 131–32,
173, 232n. 6, 243n. 29
Ficino, 140, 169, 225–26
Finucci,Valeria, 83, 93–95, 103, 172,
240n. 30, 241n. 39
Florimonte, Galeazzo, bishop of Sessa,
26–32, 51, 58–59, 203–4, 225, 234n. 1
Flynn, Carol Houlihan, 18
fortezza, 54, 58, 181, 212, 249n. 5
Freccero, Carla, 139, 160
Fregoso, Federico, 103, 165
Fregoso, Ottaviano, 72, 79–80, 89, 95,
101–3, 111, 126, 130–31, 156, 161,
163–68, 175–76, 195, 212, 242n. 8,
245n. 11, 246n. 15, 248n. 57
Freud, Sigmund, 34, 82
Frisio, 80
Frost, Robert, 4

Galatean code, 31–32, 184, 202–4,
207–16, 221–26, 251n. 24, 253n. 36
Galateo. See under della Casa, Giovanni
Galen, 97

Gellius, Aulus, 120–21, 128
genetic interpretation, 119, 129, 146,
    154, 177
gerontology, 145, 149
Ghinassi, Ghino, 119, 129, 177
Giberti, bishop of Verona, 26, 28–32,
    49–52, 57–59, 203
gifts. *See* donation
Goldberg, Jonathan, 40
Gonzaga, Cesare, 17, 19, 73, 77–78, 80,
    90, 92, 103, 106, 109, 111, 165, 173,
    232n. 6, 233n. 14
Gonzaga, Elisabetta, duchess, 72–73,
    75–80, 83, 96, 241n. 32, 241n. 39,
    243nn. 29–30
grazia, 13, 15–19, 31, 54, 58–59, 81, 92,
    155–57, 172, 181, 198–99, 201, 207,
    212, 215, 223–24, 227, 231n. 2 (Pref.),
    233nn. 14–15, 249n. 3; grace, absence
    of, 25, 207, 211–12, 227, 233n. 15. See
    also *sprezzatura*
Greenblatt, Stephen, 19–20
Greene, Thomas, 125, 131–32, 166,
    171–72
Guidi, José, 137, 168, 178, 248n. 61
Guidobaldo, Duke, 80–83, 130–32, 144,
    164–65, 173–74, 177
gynephobia, 71–77, 90, 92, 98, 101,
    103–6, 111–14, 126, 131, 167, 169,
    174–76, 240nn. 18–19, 242n. 7

Hale, John R., 101, 179
Hanning, Robert, 74, 232n. 10
Henry of Burgundy, 38
Herculean ratios, 120–30
Hercules, 101–2, 119–21, 125–26, 128,
    156, 163, 165, 178, 245n. 11
Higgins, Richard, 76, 240n. 29
Hobbes, Thomas, 51–53, 55–56, 59, 204
Hoby, Sir Thomas, 159, 175
Holbein, Hans, 177
homo clausus (Elias), 227
homosociality, 71, 89, 104, 109–14, 141,
    243n. 29

idiota, 189, 196–228, 250n. 17, 251n. 24
imitatio, 135, 138–39
inability topos, 123–24, 127, 132, 140,
    154, 156, 162, 197, 208
inwardness, 1–4, 45, 59, 226–27, 231n. 3
    (Intro.)
Isocrates, 160

Jardine, Lisa, 65–66, 75, 79, 97, 112,
    241n. 36
Javitch, Daniel, 10, 74, 79, 161, 238n. 1,
    240n. 22
Jed, Stephanie, 24
Jephcott, Edmund, 49
Jones, Ann Rosalind, 64, 66, 68–69,
    77–79, 87, 112
Jordan, Constance, 73–75, 79, 83–85,
    91, 98, 101, 112–14, 223, 239n. 14,
    241n. 36, 241n. 43, 242nn. 9–10,
    243n. 31

Kahn, Coppélia, 131
Kelly, Joan, 64, 73, 75, 112, 184, 240n. 21,
    241n. 32
Kerrigan, William, 55–57, 238n. 33
Kinney, Arthur, 80–81, 98–101, 119, 155,
    239n. 12
Kristeva, Julia, 148, 150
Kuehn, Thomas, 24

Lacan, Jacques, 177
Langer, Ullrich, 130
lectorial enhancement, 124, 127–28
Leicester, H. Marshall, 208
Libro del Cortegiano, Il. See under
    Castiglione, Baldassare
Ludovico di Canossa, Count, 9, 14–18,
    92–93, 165
Ludovico Pio, 102

Machiavelli, 97, 99–100, 211–13, 223
Macpherson, C. B., 24, 53, 234n. 30,
    238n. 33, 253n. 39
Magnifico, 73, 84, 87, 90, 101, 109

male fantasy, 66, 69, 79, 83, 85, 93, 98,
    112–13; ophthalmological fantasy,
    106–8; Venerean fantasy, 172, 218,
    222, 224
Mannerism, 20–22
manners, courtly, 25–26, 28, 31, 33,
    57–58
manners, table, 29–32, 35–39, 42, 46–48,
    50, 55, 59
Marin, Louis, 40
market societies, customary and posses-
    sive (Macpherson), 24, 53, 238n. 33,
    253n. 39
Marvell, Andrew, 139
Maus, Katherine, 1–4, 231n. 3 (Intro.)
Mauss, Marcel, 51, 235n. 9
McEachern, Claire, 231n. 1
Medici, Giuliano de', 70–71, 88–92,
    95–101, 103–11, 113, 125, 127,
    165–67, 170, 174–76, 195, 239n. 14,
    241n. 37, 241n. 3, 242n. 5, 243n. 29
Medici, Lorenzo de', 211
metapastoral. *See* pastoral
Michelangelo, 21, 159
Miller, William Ian, 32
mimesis, 22, 152–55, 176–77, 219
mimetic idealism, 152–53, 155, 176
misanthropy, 140, 142, 149, 179, 193–94,
    198–99, 204–5, 207, 209, 215–16,
    218, 227–28. *See also* misogyny;
    misophysis
misogyny, 70–73, 87, 89–90, 96, 98–99,
    103–5, 109, 120, 141, 166, 170, 175,
    183, 203–4, 218–23, 227, 240n. 18
misophysis, 204, 218
More, Sir Thomas, 20

narrator, reliable and unreliable, 27–28,
    210–11, 215
Newman, Karen, 91–92
nostalgia, 18, 127, 133, 136, 138–39, 142,
    144–49, 157, 161–68, 172, 176, 178,
    245n. 14, 246n. 30, 247n. 34

old aristocrat, 194, 199, 212, 215–17, 221–
    22, 226–27; and new aristocrat, 210
Opdycke, Leonard, 175
Orpheus, 96–97, 111
Ortona, Morello da, 169, 248n. 61
Ovid, 96, 104, 110–11, 113, 169, 202–3,
    251n. 26

Pace, Richard, 237n. 13
Pallavicino, Gasparo, 16, 72, 76–77,
    79–80, 88–90, 92, 95–97, 99, 102–4,
    106, 109–11, 127, 158, 164–67,
    169–70, 173–76, 240n. 29, 242n. 3,
    242n. 5, 243n. 29, 248n. 57
Panofsky, Erwin, 253n. 46
paradise principle, 140–43, 146, 148–50,
    168, 171, 178, 246n. 29
paranoia, 25, 57, 166, 179, 199, 216, 223,
    227–28
Partridge, Loren, 24
pastoral, 83, 98, 103, 136, 139–55, 158,
    161–68, 171, 176, 178; metapastoral,
    139–55, 161–68, 171–72, 176, 178
pedagogy, explicit and implicit, 22–23,
    42, 59, 68, 82, 91
performance anxiety, 1, 4, 18, 149. *See
    also* representation anxiety
Petrarch, 195, 197
Petrarchism, 79, 105, 108
physiognomic idealism, 16–17, 22, 88,
    91, 93; and pathognomy, 90, 112. *See
    also* mimetic idealism
Pindar, 197
Pitt-Rivers, Julian, 54
Plato, 14, 135, 140, 156, 163, 169–70, 197,
    233n. 23, 246n. 28
Pliny, 218
Plotinus, 170
Plutarch, 121, 128
Pocock, J. G. A., 234n. 30, 238n. 33
Poggi, Gianfranco, 41, 43–44
Polykleitos, 200–201
Powis, Jonathan, 41

profeminism, 70–76, 79–80, 83–84, 90–114, 120, 128–29, 142, 166–67, 174, 176, 239n. 14. *See also* antifeminism
Proust, Marcel, 136
psychogenesis (Elias), 34–35. *See also* sociogenesis
Puttenham, George, 10–11, 232n. 5
Pygmalion, 93–98, 103–4, 109–13, 169, 202–4, 218, 223, 242n. 3, 251n. 26
Pythagoras, 120, 122, 124–25, 128, 201

Raphael, 21, 95, 152, 178
reascription. *See* ascription
Rebhorn, Wayne, 9–10, 12, 72–75, 77, 83, 87–88, 106, 112, 115, 121, 124, 136–40, 142–45, 148–55, 161–63, 165–66, 168, 171, 178, 240n. 21, 243n. 31
representation anxiety, 4, 12, 24, 31, 113–14, 128, 162. *See also* performance anxiety
Ricciardo, Count, 28–32, 48–52, 57, 184, 203, 225–26
Rosand, David, 74
Rousseau, Jean Jacques, 203

Saccone, Eduardo, 10, 14–17, 233n. 15
self-representation, 1, 4, 14, 21–24, 38, 45, 48, 64, 69, 92–95, 113–15, 122, 126, 129, 134–35, 138, 162, 169, 181–84, 193–98, 206, 213, 227; objective, 3, 12; reflexive, 12
sex-gender system, 63–64, 67–73, 77–80, 83, 87–92, 95–99, 103, 106, 112–14
Shakespeare, William, 3
Shaw, T. E., 160
Shearman, John, 20–21
Silva, Michel de, 129–30, 143, 245n. 14
Singleton, Charles, 16, 110, 124, 146, 159, 244n. 32, 245n. 6
socialization, primary and secondary, 22–23, 42

sociogenesis (Elias), 34–36, 39. *See also* psychogenesis
Socrates, 27, 163, 170, 197, 215–16, 246n. 28
sprezzatura, 1, 4, 5, 9–19, 22–23, 31, 45, 54, 58–59, 63, 68–69, 75, 79, 81–82, 92–94, 108, 111, 121–24, 128, 152, 155–57, 165–66, 181, 197–98, 207, 211–12, 214–16, 223–24, 226–28, 231n. 2 (Pref.), 232nn. 5–6, 232n. 8, 232n. 10, 249n. 3, 253n. 47. See also *affettazione; grazia*
Starn, Randolph, 24
Stewart, Andrew, 201
Stone, Lawrence, 23
surveillance, 12–13, 25, 29, 48, 59, 67, 184, 196, 211, 223, 226–27
suspicion, culture of, 4, 12–13, 25, 48, 64, 66, 85, 92, 207, 227–28

thanatography, 165–66, 177
Themistocles, 155
Theocritus, 139
Titian, 173
Tomarozzo, Flamineo, 198–200, 250n. 17
Trafton, Dain, 74, 99–102, 125
Trojan horse, 158–62, 247n. 43

virago, 98, 101, 131, 164, 169
Virgil, 160–61
Vives, Juan Luis, 40

Waller, Marguerite, 67, 131
Waters, John, 63
Whigham, Frank, 9–12, 181, 232n. 8
William of Occam, 208
Woodbridge, Linda, 70–71, 73, 176, 240n. 18
Woodhouse, J. R., 112, 141, 160, 166, 169
Wyatt, Sir Thomas, 20

Zeuxis, 13, 95–96, 218–19, 222, 253n. 46, 254n. 48